IN SEARCH OF
CIVIL
SOCIETY

IN SEARCH OF CIVIL SOCIETY

INDEPENDENT PEACE MOVEMENTS
IN THE SOVIET BLOC

EDITED BY VLADIMIR TISMANEANU

Routledge
Taylor & Francis Group
New York   London

Published in 1990 by
Routledge
711 Third Avenue,
New York, NY 10017
Published in Great Britain by
Routledge
2 Park Square, Milton Park,
Abingdon, Oxfordshire OX14 4RN
First issued in paperback 2014

Routledge is an imprint of the Taylor and Francis Group, an informa business

Library of Congress Cataloging in Publication Data

Tismaneanu, Vladimir.
 In search of civil society : independent peace movements in the
Soviet bloc / by Vladimir Tismaneanu ; with contributions by Miklós
Haraszti . . . [et al.].
  p. cm.
 Includes bibliographical references.

 ISBN 978-0-415-90248-9 (hbk)
 ISBN 978-0-415-86672-9 (pbk)

 1. Peace movements—Soviet Union. 2. Peace movements—Europe,
Eastern. I. Title.
JX1961.S75T57 1990
327.1'72'0947—dc20   89-70107

British Library Cataloguing in Publication Data also available

Table of Contents

Preface

For a long time communist studies focused on the ruling elites and tended to consider political opposition as a marginal rather than a fundamental feature of Soviet-type systems. In recent years, however, events in the Soviet Union and East-Central Europe have challenged this traditional and initially justified approach. The rise of independent movements in societies once perceived as almost immutable has shown that totalitarian rule is not perfect. In spite of the huge police mobilization and incessant ideological campaigns, citizens can and indeed do organize themselves in grass-roots voluntary associations that undermine the status quo. The proclamation of the martial law in Poland in December 1981 could not inhibit those who identified their best hopes with the independent union Solidarity. Similarly, the continuous anti-dissident campaigns launched by the Hungarian, Czechoslovak, and East German regimes could not deter unofficial groups from pursuing their agendas. Gorbachev's perestroika from above has been paralleled by an unprecedented intensification of autonomous activism with tens of thousands of independent groups defying the Communist party's hegemonist ambitions.

What is now happening in the communist world amounts to the awakening of long-dormant social aspirations and the coalescence of a genuine alternative to the one-party system. Indeed, when the Hungarian Communists renounced their claim to the monopoly of power and dissolved their party in October 1989, they implicitly recognized the bankruptcy of the Stalinist model of socialism. Not only oppositional activists, but also reform-minded communists admit nowadays that the record of the command-administrative system, as developed since Lenin's times, is blatantly negative. The time has come, therefore, for a general overhaul of the economic and political communist institutions. Pluralism, without limitations and restrictive qualifications, is now the first point on the independent movements' agenda. The rhythm of change has become so hectic that any effort to offer conclusive generalizations is practically futile. Instead, we should keep pace with the events and recognize that in the Soviet Union and East-Central Europe politics is so fluid that no time-honored scheme can do it justice. With immense courage and unfettered inventiveness, independent groups and movements in those countries have striven to reinvent the very notion of politics. They have rediscovered the basic principles that make people associate and commonly aim at the improvement of the social order. Their notion of change represents the opposite of the logic of acquiescence: They speak up against injustice, defend the values of honesty, decency, and openness, and try to purify the political realm of the corruptive relics of totalitarianism. Radical de-Stalinization culminates in the reinstatement of politics in its own right.

This book represents an effort to examine some of the most significant moments in this historical adventure. It is not my intention to write a new study in comparative sociology. The theory of social movements is certainly a most respectable scholarly field, but this book does not claim to belong to it. Its principal purpose is to highlight the origins, strategy, ideology, and dynamics of a new form of political activism in the Soviet Union and Eastern Europe: the grass-roots, unofficial, nongovernmental peace movements. A focus on empirical information is thus absolutely necessary to provide the reader with an accurate and convincing picture of these new movements. While I am absolutely aware that to present independent peace activism as symbolizing the most important social development in the area is quite preposterous, I am, however, convinced that these movements represent a significant fragment of the far-reaching phenomenon described as the rebirth of civil society in post-totalitarian (post-Stalinist) regimes. Documenting this fascinating world-historical process, noting its inner dialectics, its ups and downs, its inevitable zigzags, appeared to me to be a daunting but a uniquely urgent task. With this idea in mind, I deliberately espoused the chronological/analytical instead of the conceptual/synthetical approach. Before we engage in speculations on the nature of civil society we must identify the phenomenon's reality. To the best of my knowledge this is the first attempt to offer a comparative survey of one of the major components of civil society, i.e., the unofficial peace movements. The only book-length study dealing with this topic was published as a Helsinki Watch report in October 1987. Elaborated by an activist human-rights organization, this splendid documentation, however, did not provide a scholarly analysis and interpretation of these movements. Being aware of the pressing need for a comprehensive investigation of the new social movements and their impact on communist societies, I decided to write a book addressed not only to students of communist politics but to all those for whom peace and human rights represent sacred values. I also see my undertaking as a response to the growing demand for informative analyses of the current changes in the communist world as well as in East-West relations. Independent peace activism in communist societies does not challenge only the regimes' self-serving rhetoric, but also the whole structure of a world divided on the basis of ideological conflicts. These programmatically anti-ideological movements have long anticipated Gorbachev's "new thinking" about the supremacy of universal human values in the nuclear age. But before the advent of glasnost, such statements were considered subversive and their proponents ruthlessly persecuted. Until very recently, in Czechoslovakia and the German Democratic Republic, activists are harassed for daring to say that no class interests could or should prevail over the rights of human beings to live in a world free of statal violence.

Since my approach has been inspired by an interest in the political philosophy and practical behavior of the new movements, I think that the reader will discover in this book sufficient material to better understand the nature of contemporary radicalism in its anti-totalitarian variant. We deal, to be sure, with a strand of radicalism very different from those who advocate an outright break with the powers-that-be. It is a radicalism rooted in the consciousness of the limits of human nature and the refusal to embrace any millennial dreams of collective salvation. It is the radicalism of lucidity as opposed to that of revolutionary eschatology. Although it is not a theoretical treatise, this book necessarily touches on such aspects of the reemergence of the civil society as the typology of dissent and opposition, the relation between intra- and anti-systemic opposition, the role and value of nonviolence, the stages of de-totalitarianization, the moral and political implications of the right to conscientious objection and the link between peace and human rights. All these notions are discussed within a historical-political framework: The reader can thus follow the development of the new movements, grasp their visions, expectations, anguishes, and dilemmas.

Some words on the structure of the book. To strengthen the informative component of the book I have considered it necessary to include a number of case studies written by personalities who are scholars and oppositional activists at the same time. The relevance of these chapters is that they offer microanalyses of the situations in each country. Some of them try to go beyond the descriptive pattern and put forward thought-provoking theoretical generalizations. Because the peace movement in the German Democratic Republic is by far the most developed in East-Central Europe, the section dealing with that country is much larger than the other ones. The book does not cover Yugoslavia because that country does not belong to the Warsaw Pact—and therefore the implications of autonomous pacifism are different from those discussed here. The long introduction represents my effort to insert the experience of independent peace activism in the broader picture of the struggle for social and political renewal in the Soviet Union and East-Central Europe. As the principal author of this book I assume, of course, full responsibility for its flaws. Its merits, however many they may be, belong to all those who believed in and supported this project. Among these, I owe special thanks to the contributors who covered the case studies in a manner I could have hardly carried out in such systematic and illuminating ways. They are critical intellectuals whose knowledge "from within" allows them to engage in innovative and insightful interpretations of these movements. I am also grateful to Ferenc Fehér as well as to an anonymous reviewer who gave me precious suggestions to make this book more readable and more articulate.

The idea of writing this book originated in discussions with my colleague and friend Adam Garfinkle. Written at the Foreign Policy Research Institute, this book could not have been successfully completed without the continuous help provided by Daniel Pipes, the Institute's director, as well as my colleagues Alan Luxenberg and Michael S. Radu. Judith Shapiro offered excellent editorial suggestions. The thankless task of supervising my dubious computer skills devolved upon Gina Minda-Grecescu. My research assistants, Joydeep Bhattacharya, Marco Bianchini, and Mary Sladek loyally ensured the everyday logistics of this project and were infected with my passion for Central Europe. Let them all be assured of my gratitude. I also thank Barbara Donovan of Radio Free Europe Research who shared with me her wonderful data base on the independent peace movement in the German Democratic Republic. The United States Institute of Peace generously supported research for this project. None of the above, of course, bears responsibility for the opinions and interpretations offered here.

Vladimir Tismaneanu
Philadelphia
December 1989

1

Unofficial Peace Activism in the Soviet Union and East-Central Europe

Vladimir Tismaneanu

> "Peace is not threatened only where new offensive weapons are being manufactured. Peace is threatened everywhere, where the voice of the critically thinking citizen has been silenced. . . . Real peace does not mean only the removal of despotism from relations among states, but also from relations between state power and a human being."
>
> Charter 77, October 1986

The dramatic changes in the once-unified Soviet bloc during the last four years may have come as a surprise even to those who have carefully followed the Western media's coverage of that area. More important, the depth of change has challenged long-held assumptions about the nature of totalitarian societies and their resistance to transformation. But this process has been catalyzed by the rise of important and increasingly vocal political movements from below and the heightening of the conflict between state and society in those countries. Political dissent has thus become a salient feature of contemporary communist systems. The times of the monolithic control by the party over society are definitely a thing of the past. Instead, new and polymorphous experiments in opposition to bureaucratic authoritarianism have contributed to the gradual erosion of the prevailing ideological myths and to the coalescence of loosely structured, grass-roots groups, associations, organizations, and movements.

These alternative social activities do not aim at overthrowing the existing political system. Though they disapprove of it, they do not programatically question the party's monopoly on power. Their goal is to restore society's gravely damaged self-confidence, help citizens internalize democratic values, and initiate a dialogue with the power elite that could lead to a new "social contract."

The philosophy of the "new evolutionism" formulated by Polish dissident thinker and activist Adam Michnik suggests the role of the democratic opposition

1

as a catalyst for societal self-organization. Such opposition, he believes, would take the form of autonomous, nonviolent associations of critically-minded citizens. Indeed, this strategy guaranteed the rise of Solidarity and the development of pluralistic trends within Polish society.[1]

The "new evolutionism" breaks with the Marxist revisionist faith in the reformability of the Communist party. Rejecting conspiratorial methods and sectarian mentalities, it values openness as a means to overcome fanaticism and exclusiveness: ". . . the democratic opposition must be constantly and incessantly visible in public life, must create political facts by organizing mass actions, must formulate alternative programs. Everything else is an illusion."[2] The development of alternative structures, or even of a "parallel polis,"[3] has been favored by political trends within the post-totalitarian order, including the palpable erosion of the system's ideological underpinnings and the need to discover areas of social activism uncontaminated by official corruption and duplicity. This strategy has entailed attempts to rehabilitate political symbols emptied of meaning by propaganda abuses. In other words, new forms of joint action, communication, and even self-organization have been devised that do not follow state-prescribed rules and taboos.

Speaking one's own mind and opposing the hypocrisy of the system—living in truth, in Václav Havel's (the Czechoslovak playwright and human-rights activist and then Czechoslovakia's President) formulation—become major forms of political socialization. Creative forms of social organization cannot emerge without this search for reinstating the sovereignty of truth. Concepts and ideas long compromised by state manipulation must be semantically purified. After decades of totalitarian rule, the unofficial groups and movement have shown that the system is not totally integrated and that its "weak spots" can be exploited by the opposition to advance its goals.

The Renaissance of Civil Society

The new social movements play the game of taking the rulers "at their own word": If the government preaches peace, let the independents define peace in such a way as to make it a politically relevant notion. The same is true for human rights, environmental issues, and so forth. As Havel put it: ". . . the original and most important sphere of activity, one that predetermines all the others, is simply an attempt to create and support the 'independent life of society' as an articulated expression of 'living within the truth.' "[4] But the authorities cannot accept this. The leaders know that without social activism the body politic will further decay, yet social self-organization and the redistribution of power that it would entail would eventually undermine their claim to political hegemony. The power elite is thus caught between the Scylla of self-destructive bureaucratic inertia and the Charybdis of sweeping political reforms and genuine democratization. A remarkably candid avowal by journalist Daniel Passent published in the official Polish magazine *Polytika* expresses this inescapable dilemma of post-totalitarian communist states: "Without civic activism, which finds expression in . . . the creation . . . of various associations, the renovation of the republic is impossible. But in a situation in which political activity is limited, a natural pressure exists that gives a political character to every organization and association, regardless of whether its declared cause is the inculcation of love for literature, self-governing schools, or the battle at Grunwald."[5]

Single issues of broad social significance—human rights, peace, conscientious objection, ecology, preservation of historical monuments, and so on—are embraced and promoted by independent activists in the attempt to further their agenda for change without granting the government a rationale for overall repression. Unofficial peace movements have thus rapidly developed in the USSR and East-Central Europe since the late 1970s. They represent a new stage in the reconstitution of the civil society in countries where the conflict between government and opposition has often turned into direct confrontation.[6] Their coagulation is an effect of the ripening of the political opposition and indicates a new stage in the struggle for the pluralization of Soviet-type regimes. At the same time, as the rapid changes in Poland and Hungary indicate, the reconstruction of the civil society is not the ultimate goal of the new movements. It is a premise for the full-fledged de-totalitarianization and the restoration of a constitutional state based on pluralism and universal observance of laws. Gorbachev's tolerance of political experimentation in East-Central Europe has contributed to the broadening of the opposition's agenda. In 1987, it seemed that civil society—both as a strategy and a methodology—was the alpha and omega of the opposition's political imagination. After the legalization of Solidarity in the summer of 1989 and formation of a Solidarity-run government, the limits of the possible have substantially expanded. The same can be said about Hungary, where only in March 1988 dissidents were beaten up by the police and where the Communist party decided to dissolve in September 1989. This extraordinary fluidity of the political dynamics in East-Central Europe has made it possible to envision and even schedule the transition to a multi-party system in Poland and Hungary. But this sea-change transformation did not occur only because of Gorbachev's benign approach to the bloc's problems or as a result of a sudden and hard-to-explain desire of the ruling elites to renounce their power and privileges. The most profound cause is to be looked for in the inner dynamics of the Polish and Hungarian societies. The same can be said of the Soviet Union where, for decades, the unofficial groups and movements have paved the ground for the current opening.

Independent peace movements in the USSR and East-Central Europe are an unprecedented, original, innovative extension of the civil-rights movement of the 1960s and 1970s. Their commitment to the restoration of the public space necessarily brings them into conflict with the authoritarian-bureaucratic institutions of the mono-organizational systems.[7] Their agenda is not limited to pacifist stances; they do indeed belong to a general movement toward social self-regeneration whose main outcome could be the invention of a new form of polity where citizens would escape the ideological and political constraints imposed by the system. Refusing the prevailing matrix of domination, these communities practice a new approach to political matters, which Hungarian writer George Konrád aptly described as *antipolitics*.[8] Independent peace groups in the Soviet bloc are thus a component of the broader orientation toward social autonomy from the institutional framework characterized by the Communist party's monopoly of power.[9] However, because they have a specific agenda, specific methods, and a specific constituency, independent peace groups represent a new oppositional direction within Soviet-style regimes. More than any other independent movements, they address the major problems of international relations and criticize the governments' double-talk. They repudiate the militaristic logic and demand a democratic discussion of the defense issues. Advocating the right to conscientious objection, they stir responsive chords among the youth who resent forced draft into armies they do not identify with. More than any other unofficial initiatives, the independent peace movements challenged the very legitimacy of the status quo: They deny the official peaceful rhetoric by pointing to the truly bellicose nature of the communist governments in dealing with their own subjects. At the same time, because they embrace a universal concept of peace, these movements could establish close links with Western anti-nuclear groups and thereby have a strong impact on Western public opinion.

In Eastern bloc countries civil society has long been repressed through political uniformization and atomization, all-pervading controls, and ideological manipulation.[10] Limited to fractious rivalries at the top, politics as such appears to the ruled as a sterile exercise in conformity. For a long time, because of police repression and widespread skepticism, autonomous political activities seemed to be inconceivable in the Soviet Union and East-Central Europe. For many citizens, the only way to repudiate the ubiquitous mendacity propagated by the system was the complete avoidance of politics—the de-politicization of human discourse and the emancipation of social communication from the ideological burden imposed by the ruling power. Regaining autonomy has long been regarded as a struggle against the frozen figure of *Realpolitik*. The universalization of politics, professed by Leninists, discouraged many citizens from weighing the possibility of devising a counter-politics rooted in a renewed sense of community, noninstitutional forms of communication, and the refusal of the alienated symbols of power, including the language of domination.

The emergence and consolidation of these informal structures, which are indeed society *in embryo*, have transformed the political landscape in Central Europe. But, among other obstacles, independent civic initiatives must confront a widespread distrust of politics as such. After all, when the official rhetoric constantly exalts political values like peace, freedom, and equality, it is extremely difficult to articulate a political counter-discourse without facing the problem of credibility and, even more difficult to overcome, *apathy*. Restoring the civil society entails, therefore, a moral rebuilding: the reconstruction of the sense of solidarity which has been undermined by the system; the reassertion of the dignity of politics, the rehabilitation of the individual against the officially sanctioned cult of the collectivity; and the identification of niches where autonomous actions and initiatives could develop. This is a long-term process, with both exhilarating achievements and disappointing setbacks. Nevertheless, it represents the *only* chance to make society politically dynamic within the existing authoritarian order.

The search for the civil society is, therefore, one of the most important social and political developments nowadays in the Soviet Union and East-Central Europe. It is society's response to the accumulation of chronic difficulties and the blatant ineptitude of the leaders to articulate convincing solutions for political renewal.[11] The emergence of a myriad of autonomous spontaneous groups and initiatives whose basic aims consist of enlivening the public space would turn society into a real partner to the government in the exercise of power. At the moment when the most reform minded of the party leaders are ready to engage in liberalization, partisans of genuine change call for thoroughgoing democratization. For example, in a speech delivered in March 1988, Soviet playwright Aleksandr Gelman, one of the most outspoken advocates of glasnost, pointed precisely to this need to allow society to express its basic needs and concerns: "The most intelligent and farsighted opponents of perestroyka . . . try to replace democraticization with liberalization. What is the difference? Democratization provides for the redistribution of power, rights and freedoms, the creation of a number of independent structures of management and information. And liberalization is the conservation of the foundations of the administrative system but in a milder form. Liberalization is an unclenched fist, but the hand is the same and at any moment it could be clenched again into a fist. Only outwardly is liberalization sometimes reminiscent of democratization, but in actual fact it is a fundamental and intolerable usurpation."[12] This is indeed the major fear of the radical reformists in East-Central Europe: the confiscation by the ruling elites of precisely those symbols that define the break with the *ancien régime*.

In order to become real, reforms should go beyond the paternalistic model favored by enlightened apparatchiks. In other words, the higher-ups should admit as a legitimate actor the long-repressed social forces from below. Reflecting on the current changes in the Soviet Union, French social philosopher Cornelius Castoriadis has poignantly shown the limits of party-induced "reforms from above": "The Gorbachev illusion is the idea (predominant today in the West, possibly shared by Gorbachev himself) that substantive reforms, in a country like today's Russia, can be introduced strictly from above, that you can order people to be self-active while restraining themselves within some vague (therefore, more threatening) limits, that you can retain the absolutist power of bureaucracy while dismantling the social and economic bases of this power—in brief that, like

Descartes's God, you can send society moving with a fillip and that you can change the system without changing it."[13] The duality of Gorbachev's strategy is engendered by this simultaneous desire to emancipate social initiatives, on the one hand, and the reluctance to permit the free competition of political forces, on the other. The reconstruction of civil society certainly transcends the restrictive agenda of intrasystemic changes. It represents a natural process of political and cultural awakening which restores the individual as a true citizen, i.e., a free person endowed with a sense of personal dignity and civic responsibility. It is the creation of "a space where independent discussion and criticism can grow, where an alternative to the state's monopoly on information and education can thrive, where an effort can be made to restrain the state's arbitrary or arrogant use of power against its own citizens or other countries and, finally, where the rigidity and isolation of the bloc mentality can be challenged."[14]

The reaction of the authorities to independent initiatives has shown the widening gulf between *power* and *society*. Far from engaging in a dialogue with these autonomous groups and associations, the party-state apparatuses have undertaken systematic campaigns to suppress them. The degree of repression and the success of these offensives have differed from country to country. But the rise of the independent peace and ecological movements indicates new elbow room for oppositional activities in post-totalitarian regimes. The search for an alternative society includes the need to redefine basic human values and imagine methods to pursue them in everyday life.

Dynamics of Independent Peace Activism

What have been the premises for launching these types of unofficial initiatives? First and foremost, their emergence has been catalyzed by local traditions of political dissent in each state. It is thus clear that independent pacifism has developed more forcefully in countries where autonomous actions had previously been undertaken on other socially significant issues (cultural freedoms, civic rights). Without completely overlapping with dissident movements and groups, autonomous peace movements necessarily question the official structures, institutions, and values. They put forward alternative views on the nature of the war danger and promote both peace and human rights. This means a significant extension of traditional dissident goals, in that the system is confronted on the ground of undisputable universal values: "To fight under the banner of peace and the quality of life is to struggle for values that the Party itself cannot gainsay. Those values are universal, and their adoption by East European dissidents really means that dissent has been 'universalized,' and thereby strengthened."[15]

The evolution of independent pacifism has been linked to the growing awareness of the militarization of Soviet-type regimes, especially during the 1970s. The widely documented Soviet military buildup under Brezhnev and the Soviet direct or indirect military adventures in the Third World have also generated anguish among independent activists. Several events and processes have accelerated the coagulation of these movements. First, there was the impact of the Helsinki Final Act on Security and Cooperation in Europe on the struggle for human rights in the Soviet Union and East-Central Europe.[16] At the moment when their rulers claimed to abide by the international human rights covenants and norms, many Soviet and East European politically concerned people realized that a new space for activism had been opened. By signing the Helsinki Agreement and publicizing it through the official media, Communist leaders unwillingly raised the threshold of expectations among their subjects. At the same time, they admitted that human rights are a matter of international concern and that national sovereignty does not amount to immunity to international monitoring of the states' compliance with the Helsinki Agreements. Naturally, Warsaw Pact regimes have continued to violate human rights, but the very existence of the Helsinki process legitimates and strengthens human-rights initiatives in the Eastern bloc. It is thus symptomatic that a new wave of public protest against the Czechoslovak regime's repressive policy immediately coincided with the conclusion of the Vienna meeting of the Conference on Security and Cooperation in Europe and the signing of a promising accord on the protection of human rights.[17]

Another factor that has contributed to the formation of unofficial peace groups was the experience of the independent, self-governing union Solidarity in Poland. More than anything else, Solidarity has demonstrated that grass-roots political initiatives can result in a nonviolent revolutionary breakthrough.[18] With its new strategic outlook, flexible political tactics, and ability to maintain large popular support in spite of official harassment, Solidarity has fundamentally modified the variables of the political equation in East-Central Europe. With Solidarity, the Leninist elites (not only in Poland, but in the whole bloc) were for the first time confronted with a radical challenge from precisely the social group they claimed to represent, i.e., the industrial working class. What Solidarity was heralding was not another attempt at tinkering with the system, but the need to admit its failure and embark on fundamental systemic change. As Adam Michnik wrote, Gorbachev's "reforms from above" can be interpreted as an effort of the bureaucratic elites to preclude the infectious consequences of Solidarity as the genuine reformist movement within the boundaries of the communist world: "A counter-reformation is . . . not a restoration of the pre-reformist order, but rather an attempt to transform the institutions from within. It is a self-critical show of strength with the aim of incorporating those values created· against the will of and outside the social institutions in order to stop them becoming antagonistic and subversive."[19] In January 1989 the Jaruzelski regime decided to engage in negotiations with the Solidarity leadership regarding the union's re-legalization. This recognition of the government's failure to quell the independent union was both a consequence of social pressure exerted on the ruling group and of the new Soviet approach to the concept of socialism. As

General Jaruzelski admitted himself: "There is in this a certain logic in the historical process. This logic is, after all, connected closely with all those phenomena which are taking place in the socialist community, which has reached a certain threshold beyond which certain changes are necessary in order to cross it and to cause a deepening and acceleration of those processes and aims which socialism has, after all, engraved on its banners."[20] To sum up: Underground or aboveground, Solidarity has catalyzed the emergence of unofficial, alternative groups. As the elections in the summer of 1989 showed, the Polish United Workers' Party (the Communist party) has no popular mandate to govern. Solidarity candidates won in a landslide, and the formation of a non-Communist government sanctioned this situation. From an independent workers' movement, Solidarity has become a political party, or, better said, a conglomerate of emerging political parties. But genuine political parties can exist only where the society is able to rationally articulate its objectives and interests, i.e., where a civil society can function normally.

Other elements that explain the development of independent pacifism are: the militarization of the public life within the Warsaw Pact countries (primarily the Soviet Union, Poland, and the GDR); the intensification of the military competition with the West in the early 1980s through the escalation in the deployment of intermediate-range nuclear missiles in Europe; and the contagious effect of campaigns organized by the Western anti-nuclear movement.

With regard to the relation between Eastern and Western pacifism, some qualifications are necessary. There is a major difference between the status of pacifists in democratic regimes and that of independent activists in the USSR and East-Central Europe, where dissenting views on war and peace are automatically discarded as seditious. Being anti-militaristic and anti-nuclear in such a country implies the obligation to assess not only Western, but also Soviet international behavior. In other words, one runs the risk of being labeled and prosecuted as an enemy of the state.

Václav Havel wrote a thoughtful analysis of the communication gap between Western peace activists and East European dissidents.[21] The issues formulated by Havel suggest the approach to peace characteristic of independent groups active in the Warsaw Pact countries. Several themes are particularly striking:

(a)   the dangerous nature of independent peace initiatives in Soviet-type regimes: "The peace movement in the West has a real impact on the dealings of parliaments and governments, without risking jail. Here the risk of prison and at least at this point the impact on the government's decision-making is zero."[22] The situation described by Havel is somewhat different in the GDR, where the government has been compelled to accept a dialogue of sorts with the exponents of the independent peace movement because of the support they have enjoyed from the Evangelical Church.

(b)   the interpretation of Soviet international behavior as expansionist. Independent peace activists in Eastern Europe emphasize issues that Western peace groups have tended to play down, such as the Soviet occupation of Afghanistan: "What are we to think of a peace movement, a European peace movement, which is virtually unaware of the only war being conducted today by a European state?"[23]

(c)   despite their sympathy for the anti-nuclear ethos of peace activists in the West, East European independent groups point out that the real cause of war "is not weapons as such but political realities . . . in a divided Europe and a divided world."[24]

(d)   autonomous peace activities in Eastern Europe require a general reconsideration of the political course of Warsaw Pact regimes both in domestic and foreign policy. In this respect, East European independents underline the inextricable link between internal external peace. For them, no promise of benign international behavior should be trusted from governments who hold their citizens as permanent hostages. Only free, self-respecting, and autonomous citizens can ensure the existence of free and independent nations: "Without internal peace, that is peace among the citizens and between the citizens and the state, there can be no guarantee of external peace . . . A state that refuses its citizens their right to public supervision of the exercise of power will not be susceptible to international supervision."[25] In other words, respect for human rights is "the fundamental condition and the sole, genuine guarantee of peace."[26]

The contrast between Eastern and Western peace groups is primarily related to their dissimilar motivations, interests, and values. They have had different existential experiences and modalities of political radicalization; their general approach to the systems they live in ranges from qualified opposition (in communist countries) to qualified identification (in the West). However, especially in recent years, the East-West independent pacifist dialogue has developed to an unprecedented extent. Soviet and East European groups have thus benefited from the unequivocal solidarity manifested by many of their Western peers.[27]

Other East European critical intellectuals go even further in suggesting that peace cannot be postulated as a unique, self-contained goal separate from broader political and social objectives. In a controversial essay on pacifism in communist societies, Hungarian dissident philosophers Ferenc Fehér and Agnes Heller advance the following negative prediction: " . . . of all the possible autonomous social movements, the anti-nuclear movement is the one the least likely to become of any consequence and least likely to exert an impact on the future course of Soviet societies. . . . Should anti-nuclear movements emerge in Soviet societies on a wide scale, they will either immediately become bearers of other, broader and more complex, social issues, or will degenerate into state-sponsored peace carnivals."[28] One could argue that this skeptical view tends to draw general conclusions from the aborted experience of the Hungarian autonomous peace movement. It is certainly true that the ephemeral Hungarian independent group Dialogue did not try to overstep the boundaries charted by the authorities, and that it eventually became irrelevant.[29] But the situation is totally different in Poland where the Freedom and Peace initiative has generated a powerful and dynamic social movement without turning into a substitute for or merging with the oppositional groups and organizations.

The Chernobyl catastrophe in April 1986 has further increased the widespread anxieties about the risks of a nuclear showdown in the heart of Europe.[30] Since then, independent ecological activist groups have mushroomed in most East European countries. On many occasions, these environmentalists cooperate with independent pacifists in their criticism of the official militaristic orientation. Moreover, as the Moscow Trust Group put it, the nuclear accident has shown the absurdity of the bloc's logic: "Chernobyl became the tragedy that united East and West. In spreading throughout the whole world, radiation lifted the 'iron curtain,' because international efforts were required to eliminate the effects of the disaster."[31]

To pursue their goals, the independent peace movements have emerged as autonomous associations of like-minded individuals which are unique in their avoidance of hierarchical organization and institutionalization. Previous experiences in dealing with a repressive state apparatus and a monopolistic ideology have certainly helped to imagine new forms of independent activism. It is precisely this informal, loose structure that permits unofficial eco-pacifism to withstand countless attempts to disband the newly constituted groups. The term "movement," therefore, should be understood as a relatively structured, collective effort based on shared values and aimed at furthering an original set of objectives that would influence the established patterns of thought and behavior.

The rise of independent pacifism in communist countries has created new opportunities not only for grass-roots East-West dialogue, but also for unprecedented East-East contacts and cooperation. Peace efforts can aid the formulation of a common platform for Central European dissident and oppositional groups. Václav Havel rightly points to the paramount significance of these contacts for the internationalization of political opposition in Eastern Europe: "First and foremost, it is highly likely that any self-liberation movement in the Soviet bloc countries will only succeed if it goes beyond the borders of any single country. So far, most independent activities have been rather self-centered. . . . I really do see the citizens of the other Central and East European countries as my brothers, subjected to a similar predicament, facing it in a similar manner. It seems to me that we might be able to better withstand pressure from the ruling structures the stronger our mutual contacts are."[32] To be sure, peace will not be interpreted as the sole basis for such a joint program, but there are indications that it can be the core value unifying and integrating other interests, goals, and aspirations. It is increasingly obvious that not only Central European, but also Soviet dissidents are tending to work for the establishment of an international peace and human-rights movement.[33]

Shaping the New Peace Activism

Several moments have decisively marked the evolution of independent peace movements in the Soviet Union and East-Central Europe. In January 1977 a group of Czechoslovak human-rights activists established the Charter 77 initiative. Over the years, the movement has elaborated original answers to important problems of both domestic and international policy.[34]

On March 6, 1978, a concordat was signed between the GDR Evangelical Church (*Kirchenbund*) and the ruling Socialist Union Party (SED). But the high hopes for a relaxation of the East German regime's militaristic course were soon dispelled. In June 1978, the government announced a plan to introduce mandatory military instruction into secondary education. The leadership of the Evangelical Church—the Conference of Governing Bodies—engaged in open criticism of this measure. In 1980 the church decided to sponsor the first "peace decade" from November 10–19. The slogan of that gathering was "Make Peace Without Weapons" (*Frieden Schaffen ohne Waffen*). In May 1981, an appeal was released by an initiative-group called Social Service for Peace calling for the establishment of an alternative civilian service. On January 25, 1982, the protestant pastor Reiner Eppelmann published the Berlin Appeal, which spelled out the basic claims of the unofficial peace movement in the GDR. The moral thrust of East German religious pacifism was summed up in its major slogan: "Turn Swords into Plowshares."[35]

In June 1982, a group of eleven Moscow intellectuals founded the Group to Establish Trust Between East and West. In May 1983, the "Trust Group" sent an open letter to the Second Conference for Nuclear Disarmament in Europe, which took place in West Berlin. At that critical juncture in international relations, when détente seemed doomed and a new arms race inevitable, the Soviet pacifists called for a new approach to global conflicts. In their view, not only governments but also citizens should engage in an uninhibited dialogue: "It is time for the West and East to learn to exchange opinions not only at the diplomatic round table and behind closed doors. . . . Détente can be viable when it is not reduced to the context of formal protocols at meetings and bilateral conferences, but rather when international cooperation and contacts become part of the day-to-day existence of the average citizen."[36]

In November 1981, Charter 77 issued statements emphasizing the intrinsic link between peace and freedom. In March 1982, the Czechoslovak human-rights group addressed an open letter to Western peace movements calling for unofficial cooperation among ordinary citizens. In April 1983, in an open letter to Edward P. Thompson of the European Nuclear Disarmament (END), former Charter spokesman Jaroslav Sabata elaborated the thesis of *democratic peace.* According to him, "to propose a Pact on the non-use of armed force and the maintenance of peaceful relations while refusing peaceful relations and a dialogue with one's own people (and indeed sending them to prison for holding contrary views) means proposing a signature on a worthless piece of paper."[37] In June 1983, representatives of Charter 77 were denied participation in the government-sponsored World Assembly for Peace and Life Against Nuclear War, held in Prague. In February 1984, members of the Polish democratic opposition signed an appeal on behalf of a group of imprisoned Czechoslovak human-rights activists. In

July 1984, the Chartists signed a joint statement with Hungarian independent peace activists. In November 1984, they signed a declaration with East German activists protesting against the stationing of Soviet missiles in their countries and expressing solidarity with the Western peace movements.[38] In the meantime, alternative cultural groups have espoused pacifist ideals. The Lennonists—named after the late John Lennon—are young people concerned with music, ecological and peace issues.

In the spring of 1985, a group of Polish independent pacifists formed the group Freedom and Peace (*Wolnosc i Pokoj—WiP*). This was a response to the trial in December of Marek Adamkiewicz, a young draftee sentenced to a prison term of two and a half years for refusing to take the military oath. As mentioned, the Chernobyl disaster in the spring of 1986 provoked widespread pacifist actions in Poland, East Germany, and the USSR.

The philosophy of independent pacifism reached a higher degree of maturity with the release, also in the spring of 1985, of the Prague Appeal, which had been drafted by a group of Charter 77 activists representing a cross section of opinions within this organization. The appeal offered suggestions and proposals for the transformation of Europe into a united, democratic, and sovereign continent of free citizens and nations. Drawing from previous Charter documents, the Prague Appeal insisted that international dialogue should involve not only government representatives and agencies but also committed individuals and groups of concerned citizens. Dwelling upon the issue of European unification, the Chartists called for a reconsideration of the division of Germany. Such an approach would not mean in any way a further revision of European frontiers but rather the discovery of a new sense of collective responsibility: "In the process of European rapprochement, frontiers should gradually lose much of their significance, but even this should not be regarded as an opportunity for the revival of nationalistic backsliding."[39] Foreign troops should be withdrawn within national boundaries. NATO and the Warsaw Pact should enter into negotiations on the dissolution of their military organizations. The humanist ideal of mutual rapprochement should be opposed to the irrational prospect of mutually assured destruction. A decent, i.e., democratic and prosperous, European future was said to depend on abandoning the strategy of bipolarism in favor of a post-bloc, or better said, trans-bloc mentality: "We do not seek to turn Europe into a third superpower, but instead, to overcome the superpower bloc structure by way of an alliance of free and independent nations within a democratic and self-governing all-European community living in friendship with nations of the entire world." But, the Chartists acknowledged, this is a utopian objective as long as certain governments continue to deprive their citizens of the possibility of exercising basic human rights: "The freedom and dignity of individual citizens are the key to the freedom and self-determination of nations. And only sovereign nations can transform Europe into a community of equal partners which would not pose the threat of a global nuclear war, but instead, serve as an example of real peaceful coexistence."[40] The Chartists were aware that the ideal of a democratic peace might sound like a pipe dream, but they were right in assuming that their appeal would stir responsive chords in both East and West.

Indeed, in November 1986 independent activists from Czechoslovakia, Hungary, Poland, the GDR, the USSR, and Yugoslavia joined Western peace and ecological groups in signing a memorandum entitled "Giving Real Life to the Helsinki Accords." The appeal was addressed to citizens, groups, and governments of all countries participating in the Conference on Security and Cooperation in Europe. The initial version of this document was drafted at the end of 1985 by a coalition of West European peace groups known as the European Network for East-West Dialogue, in response to the Prague Appeal. A manifesto for genuine détente, the memorandum shows that the East Europeans' conception of a democratic peace had influenced Western groups. It is thus of major importance that the document regards peace as a comprehensive objective, including freedoms, rights, and social justice—not just as the renunciation of weapons and the elimination of force from international relations. The signatories of the memorandum emphasized the interdependence of the three "baskets" of the Helsinki Final Act. They bluntly rejected any tendency to play peace against freedom or vice versa.

A new concept of détente was said to be needed in order to root this process in the very structure of society. According to the signatories, direct, informal contacts among citizens from all countries should complement inter-state negotiations. Without "détente from below"—the document stated—official pledges of peaceful intentions cannot be trusted. In accordance with the philosophy of comprehensive peace elaborated by Eastern activists, the memorandum stated: "Stability in international relations also rests on the independent and democratic development of societies. Peace on our continent can only be secure if it is a really democratic peace, based on civil liberties and social justice . . . "[41] For the signatories, the implementation of fundamental human rights—such as freedom of thought and of conscience, freedom of assembly and of association, and freedom of information—is a precondition for societies to exert democratic control over their own governments and to guarantee a democratic peace in Europe. A full set of demands was formulated, including: the right to form independent trade unions; freedom of travel abroad and freedom of mobility within one's own country; right of emigration; civil rights of ethnic and national minorities; recognition of the existence of an independent editing and publishing sector; consideration of the proposal to acknowledge the status of political prisoners for people convicted for exercising their civil rights and political beliefs, etc. At the same time, the memorandum expressed the deep disaffection of peace activists from communist countries with the artificial division of Europe.

For the independent activists, it was vitally urgent to regenerate the very notion of a unique and common European identity. The term "Eastern Europe" was held to be discriminatory when applied to countries and cultures once associated with the Central European space. But, the memorandum maintained, this semantic fraud was not fortuitous: "Forty years of separation and living in very different social realities have created a deep mutual alienation between Europeans on both sides of the rift. Even geographic terms seem to have changed their meaning. People in the West often speak of 'Europe' when, in fact, they mean the member countries of the EEC. On the other hand, terms like 'East' and 'West' are used in a rather loose political sense. Thus countries that by geography as well as political and cultural traditions belong to Central rather than to Eastern Europe find that they are considered as part of the 'East.' "[42] The document depicted the dismal state of human rights in the Eastern half of Europe where governments were not held accountable by freely elected parliamentary bodies. According to the peace activists, this situation has continuously nourished social discontent and has adversely affected East-West relations. The document concluded that a really stable, lasting, and democratic peace could not be safeguarded without ceaseless working for civil liberties and social rights. In the long run, the memorandum stated, a new, pluralistic Europe would emerge, one that would have shredded the bipolar straitjacket of power blocs and whose strength would stem from its internal democracy.[43]

It seems obvious that the Soviet bloc has entered an era of deep changes and instability. The specter of a Soviet military intervention against internal liberalization in Eastern Europe has lost much of its deterrent force as a result of Gorbachev's pledges to allow more experimentation and searching for "socialist pluralism."[44] Members of democratic oppositional forces in East-Central European countries commemorated the thirtieth anniversary of the Hungarian Revolution with a joint statement published simultaneously in Prague, East Berlin, Budapest, and Warsaw on October 23, 1986. The declaration indicates a belief that the region is not paralyzed, that things can change and that citizens should rebel against injustice. The significance of this appeal can hardly be exaggerated. This was the first time that dissidents from East-Central Europe had issued a joint statement pointing to their common values and objectives. The legacy of 1956 was invoked to justify the ongoing fight for a decent and free society: "We proclaim our common determination to struggle for political democracy in our countries, for their independence, for pluralism founded on the principles of self-government, for the peaceful unification of a divided Europe and for its democratic integration, as well as for the rights of all national minorities. We emphasize our mutual reliance on the efforts of all of us to achieve, in our countries and the whole world, a better life that is free and decent. The traditions and the experiences of the Hungarian revolution of 1956 remain our common heritage and our inspiration."[45]

Between May 7 and 9, 1987, an international seminar titled International Peace and Helsinki Agreements took place in Warsaw in a small parish church. At this point, it is important to emphasize that support from the church is of immense importance for the success of independent pacifism in countries like

Poland and the GDR. As activist Jacek Szymanderski stated, the Catholic Church is supportive of independent human-rights and peace initiatives: "It is important to understand that in Poland, the Church and 'Freedom and Peace' are not at opposite poles because on issues like support for human rights there is agreement. You could say that the difference is only one of language. The Church expresses this support for human rights by saying that Christ incarnated himself in a human being and not in the Party, State or Trade Unions so the human being is paramount. . . . If I were to use a nonreligious language I could say that the twentieth century history shows us that wherever Politics, supported by myths of scientific rationalism or the logic of class conflict overcomes the special dignity of human beings, the outcome has been a tragedy for mankind. It's the same message, but couched in different language. In this sense, we feel we can have frank and close relations with the Church."[46]

The seminar was organized by the Polish group Freedom and Peace, and was attended by 250 activists from East and West. To emphasize the continuity of collective independent peace efforts, the seminar discussions focused on the memorandum "Giving Real Life to the Helsinki Accords." The gathering was exceptional because it was the first time that representatives of various East and West European peace and human-rights groups and initiatives had gathered in an East European country. Western and Eastern participants have not always agreed on the best ways to create a just, democratic, and peaceful world, but the fact that this dialogue has continued can be seen as a positive development.

In order to prevent a large international attendance, the Polish authorities denied visas to many foreign activists. Jerzy Urban, the government's spokesman, declared that Freedom and Peace (WiP) was an illegal movement and therefore any event organized by its members contravened the law. Members of the Freedom and Peace movement were harassed in the days immediately preceding the gathering. Jacek Szymanderski, a forty-year-old WiP leader from Warsaw, referred to his group's relations with the authorities as a continual "game." A former delegate at the first assembly of Solidarity in Gdansk and a prominent member of the Solidarity board in Warsaw, Szymanderski depicted the hardships experienced by independent peace activists in a communist regime: "[WiP membership] is not only a political decision but it involves one's entire philosophy of life because it entails such risk. I decide to become a member and I have made a decision which greatly affects my wife, which greatly affects my daughter."[47]

In addition to the 65 representatives from 14 Western countries, the conference was attended by about 100 WiP members, a number of Solidarity leaders, a representative of Charter 77 from Czechoslovakia, and a delegate of a peace and human-rights group from Ljubljana, Yugoslavia. Activists in the USSR, GDR, and Hungary were denied permission by their governments to travel to Poland. The seminar received a greeting message from the Moscow Trust Group.

Hungarian dissident philosopher János Kis, an editor of *Beszélö*, the main publication of the Democratic Opposition in that country, sent a message symbolically titled: "Can We Have a Joint Programme?" According to Kis, current trends in Eastern Europe favor the development of a broader approach than the agenda of the Human Rights Movement of the 1970s. Taking advantage of the ongoing Moscow "thaw," new aims should be formulated, including the dissolution of the bloc system and the cultural and political unification of a democratic Europe. According to Kis, it is necessary to develop a joint strategy based on the following demands: a definition of the constellation of human rights which every state and every international organization in the area must respect as well as the establishment of regional institutions for the enforcement of this code of rights; the constitution of the rights of the population at the regional level; the formulation of a code to bring about the ending of transnational environmental damage; bold economic reforms and the transformation of the CMEA into an East European common market; and guarantees for the collective rights of national minorities both within the state where they live and at the regional level. With regard to the most sensitive issue—the military occupation of the dependent countries—the Hungarian philosopher wrote: ". . . we can make the demand independently of the disarmament negotiations in Europe that neither the Warsaw Treaty nor the bilateral mutual assistance treaties of the member states may be cited to justify aggression within the region. . . . they must not be interpreted in such a way as to provide the right forcibly to block the internal political processes of member states."[48]

The main topics discussed during the seminar were: the relationship between peace and human rights; ways and methods to pursue détente from below; the struggle for the recognition of conscientious objection as a basic human right; forms of nonviolent struggle in East and West; post-Chernobyl environmental issues; and disarmament proposals.

Such grass-roots initiatives can only contribute to the development of détente from below. Commenting on the results of the Warsaw conference, Freedom and Peace leader Jacek Czaputowicz noticed: "Détente cannot be an issue exclusively between governments. Breaking this monopoly is our goal. One can only ensure that peace exists when societies can contact one another. The major goal of the Eastern peace movement at this point is to pressure the governments into allowing some contacts between societies."[49] A new type of solidarity has to be considered, one that would allow concerned citizens from East and West to pursue the cause of peace and democracy together. International gatherings such as this one can dispel persistent misunderstandings between Eastern and Western peace activists. They also provide opportunities to expand grass-roots dialogue across frontiers. Support from Western activists and organizations is thus needed to continue the struggle for peace and freedom in the East: "Without the presence of Western peace movement representatives, our meeting would have surely been dispersed by the police. By supporting the seminar, they have helped us to take another step. And by their very participation, they have become involved in our situation, now knowing as they do that our very existence depends on their support. If they were to abandon us now and deal only with officials on matters of peace, this would not be merely neglectful but an action against us, because the officials would certainly note this abandonment."[50]

The participants in the Warsaw Seminar agreed that the basis of all human rights is human dignity: "This principle means that we in peace movements are obliged to struggle for human dignity wherever it is violated or not respected." In accordance with this principle, the final document of the conference emphasized the inseparability of the struggles for human rights and for peace and disarmament: "Strong and independent societies with control over their own destinies are essential for the implementation and observance of human rights, and for the preservation and strengthening of peace."[51]

On November 20–21, 1987, a seminar was held in Budapest on the initiative of the European Network for East-West Dialogue and of members of Hungary's Democratic Opposition. The gathering was attended by Western participants, as well as representatives of independent groups from Yugoslavia, Poland, the GDR, and Czechoslovakia. The discussions reflected the widespread interest among independent activists generated by Mikhail Gorbachev's domestic and foreign-policy initiatives. In his written contribution to the Budapest Seminar, Charter 77 member Jaroslav Sabata focused on the implications of Gorbachev's reformism for the future of Eastern Europe. Gorbachev's politics of glasnost should be welcomed by all those committed to the struggle for peace and freedom. For Sabata, a showdown between the advocates of the new course and the conservative, bureaucratic forces within the Warsaw Pact is inevitable. In his view, the task of the democratic opposition, including independent human rights, pacifist, and ecological groups, is to speed up the process of coordination and cooperation beyond state frontiers: "Independent activists must understand they are part and parcel of a pan-European democratic movement which fights for the transformation of Europe into a continent of united nations. This does not mean that the movement for a united, democratic Europe should identify itself uncritically with Soviet policies. The movement should, however, put its weight behind the democratic wing of the official reform movement, help the reforms along and enhance their revolutionary aspects."[52]

Between December 10 and 15, 1987, the unofficial Moscow group Press Club Glasnost organized an international independent seminar on human rights. Because of the official opposition to the very idea of such a seminar, only Jan Urban, a Charter 77 activist, could get to Moscow. His presence allowed Soviet independent activists to become familiar with the Charter's views on peace and human rights: "The greatest achievement is that we carried it off. The fact that Charter 77 was represented in Moscow greatly enhanced the importance of the seminar—as its organizers themselves acknowledged. . . . The prestige of Charter 77 and its moral influence is immense, even though very little information about Charter 77 is available (in the Soviet Union). Most people aren't even familiar with the Charter's founding declaration, its fundamental ideas, its structure or its *modus operandi*."[53] The Charter's letter to the Moscow seminar summed up the philosophy of détente from below: "We want something quite simple from our governments: we want them to implement what they have declared; we want them to fulfill the obligations which they voluntarily accepted when they signed the two Covenants on Human Rights and the Final Helsinki Act. . . . We are convinced that respect for human rights and freedoms is one of the basic preconditions of the policy of peace and cooperation between nations and states. If today, during the negotiations on arms control and disarmament the decisive implementation of mutual trust between states is acknowledged, then one of the expressions of each state's trustworthiness should be the relationship between government, citizens and society—the recognition by those in power of civic and human rights."[54]

According to Lev Timofeyev, the seminar's organizer, the gathering had more than symbolic meaning. In addition to permitting activists to develop informal links, it was a signal to the authorities that independent groups have become a major political force: "The hunger for free expression and independent public opinion in our country is so great, that of course, none of the Moscow apartments could possibly hold all the people who wanted to attend the seminar. We demonstrated that we cannot yield the responsibility for the country's events to the authorities. Our independent public has announced definitely that it has a claim to participate in the solution of political, economic, legal, and moral destiny of our country."[55] In Moscow alone there are now between one and two thousand independent clubs and associations. Many of them have articulated daring proposals for the relaxation of international tensions and the democratic development of the USSR. Without disputing the existing political structure, most of them advocate its radical democratization. Their thriving under Gorbachev is an unprecedented evolution in the dynamics of Soviet society.

International coordination of dissident actions in Eastern Europe and the USSR intensified in 1988. It appears that, despite police obstacles, independent groups have acquired a high degree of sophistication in communicating and consulting with one another. On February 1, 1988, following a Charter 77 appeal for solidarity with the Romanian people, East European independent groups organized demonstrations in front of the Romanian embassies in Budapest, Prague, and Warsaw. In February, peace and human-rights activists from Poland, Czechoslovakia, Hungary, Yugoslavia, and the Soviet Union protested the new crackdown on dissenters in the GDR. They condemned the East German authorities' practice of considering peace and human-rights activism as treason. Raising their voices in support of the imprisoned East Germans, the signatories declared: "They are not guilty of anything other than asserting their right to think differently and express their views without the consent of the authorities. They are in prison because they could not reconcile themselves with the suppression of democratic freedoms and with police violence."[56]

The Right to Conscientious Objection

Serving in the army is compulsory in the Soviet Union and Eastern Europe. The Polish constitution refers to military service as the "holiest duty." The East German regime defines it as "a right and an honorable duty." Refusing to take the military oath on grounds of conscience is considered illegal in those countries.[57] For years, human-rights and pacifist groups have sought to sensitize world public opinion to the plight of East European conscientious objectors. There is no real alternative for those who do not want to serve in the army. Conscientious objection is regarded by communist regimes as a legally punishable offense. In February 1987, for example, the Hungarian police arrested Zsolt Keszethelyi, a human-rights activist who refused to serve in what he described as an army "that is not placed under the control of a government elected by universal suffrage."

Similar statements and situations have occurred in Poland where young people have refused to take a military oath that consecrates the "fraternal alliance with the Soviet Union." It was indeed the refusal to take the military oath that led to Marek Adamkiewicz's imprisonment in 1985 and the subsequent formation of the Freedom and Peace group. Only East Germany and Hungary permit unarmed military service on religious grounds: In Hungary, since 1977, members of some small religious sects have been allowed to serve in unarmed units, whereas in the GDR there is the possibility of serving in construction units. Both the East German Evangelical Church and the independent peace groups have advocated the institution of an alternative social service for peace that would not force the draftees to work on military sites and take the regular military oath.

In the Soviet Union and Eastern Europe, conscientious objection is a politically charged issue. As Miklós Haraszti, the Hungarian writer and human rights activist, put it: "The only armed conflicts in Europe in the last forty years have occurred when the Soviet Union used Warsaw Pact armies to repress democratic ferment. Thus, objection to military service in the bloc is not only a matter of religious principle but also an indication of popular nonviolent resistance and solidarity."[58] For East European activists, the refusal of communist regimes to grant their subjects the right to conscientious objection is a flagrant violation of the Helsinki spirit: "The absence of this right in the East represents a threat to Western security. Can the Warsaw Pact's aims be truly seen as nonaggressive while it punishes its citizens for not wanting to look at other nations as enemies?"[59]

The right to conscientious objection has thus become a new integrative issue for international campaigns organized by civil-rights and peace activists from the Soviet bloc. This development is closely linked to the growing tendency of East Europeans to claim conscientious-objector status not only on religious but also on political grounds. Like peace and the environment, the issue of conscientious objection has thus become a major political issue. Independent activists oppose not only the general militarization of their societies but also the transformation of the military service into an emblem of patriotism. To the official militaristic creed they oppose the belief that conscientious objection is a basic human right. According to international covenants, they are not mistaken. The January and March 1987 resolution of the Council of Europe and the United Nations Human Rights Commission acknowledged conscientious objection as a universal human right and called upon governments that have not yet done so to release detained objectors and establish alternative service for them.

These resolutions have encouraged independent activists in Eastern Europe to intensify their efforts for the legalization of conscientious objection. In March 1988, 438 democratically-minded citizens from six countries (the Soviet Union, Poland, Czechoslovakia, East Germany, Hungary, and Yugoslavia) signed a joint appeal to the Vienna follow-up meeting of the Conference on Security and Cooperation in Europe. Significantly, the East Europeans were joined by an impressive number of Soviet citizens like Andrei Sakharov and members of the Moscow Trust Group, the Leningrad Trust Group, the Lvov Trust Group, the Perestroyka 88 group, the Dialogue Group, and the Hare Krishna Group in Moscow.

The appeal was initiated by members of the Hungarian Democratic Opposition associated with the samizdat journal *Beszélö* and coordinated by the London-based East European Cultural Foundation. The appeal expressed the common concern about the harassment and persecution of conscientious objectors by Communist regimes. In its basic points, the document reflected the philosophy of democratic peace, based on the idea that true détente cannot be reached without recognition of the right to conscientious objection by all European states: "As long as people who refuse to consider other nations as enemies are prosecuted, détente cannot be firmly established in a divided Europe. Governments that demand that other governments renounce violence publicly, while they themselves imprison those who reject it, cannot be trusted."[60] Among the Hungarian signatories were seventy-nine members of the Bokor (Bush) Roman Catholic base communities. When signing the Appeal, they added the following sentence: "I support the above Appeal in the spirit of Jesus Christ's teaching: Love your enemies!"

The peace and human-rights groups have become a major pressure group in post-totalitarian societies. It is therefore difficult for Communist governments to ignore them. In January 1988, the Polish government announced that it will soon propose the establishment of an alternative to military service, whereby conscientious objectors could choose to work for a period twice as long as the regular service—which is two to three years— doing nonmilitary jobs. According to the Polish government's press spokesman Jerzy Urban, the text of the military oath should be rewritten "in a more contemporary style" and pacifists will be free to join an alternative service instead of being imprisoned for refusing the draft.

At the same time, Urban ruled out the legalization of the Freedom and Peace group, maintaining that "this is a political organization hitting out at Poland's defenses."[61] The pacifist campaigns bore fruit: In July 1988 a law was adopted by the Polish parliament which regulates the civilian alternative service.[62] Poland has thus become the first East European country to have instituted a genuine alternative service.

A precedent has thus been created that might become infectious in the region and further erode the official image of the Warsaw Pact armies as carriers of national interests. At any rate, the very idea of legalizing conscientious objection indicates a radically different approach to a subject long taboo to communist regimes.

Patterns of Evolution

Freedom and Peace in Poland is an example of the transformation of an independent group into a social movement. In Czechoslovakia, peace issues are integrated in the broader platform of Charter 77, a group initially dedicated to monitoring human-rights abuses. A most interesting case is East Germany, where independent peace groups have benefited from their association with the Evangelical Church. The short-lived Hungarian independent peace movement averted a radical divorce from the government-sponsored peace council and decided to remain a semi-official association.

The rise of the independent peace movements in East-Central Europe cannot be understood without reference to the international situation. Being anti-militaristic and anti-nuclear in that region involves a realistic assessment of Soviet international behavior. In the view of East European independent peace activists, no promise of benign international conduct should be trusted from governments who hold their citizens as permanent hostages. The precondition for international peace is internal peace. Without respect for human rights, official pacifist pledges remain perfunctory and unconvincing. Most East European dissident authors suggest that peace cannot be postulated as a goal dissociated from broader and more comprehensive political objectives. Self-limitation to a solely peace-focused agenda is widely regarded as inappropriate and, in the long run, counterproductive.

Czechoslovakia

More than any other independent East European group, Charter 77 has masterfully articulated the relationship between peace and human rights. What started as an initiative in defense of human rights has evolved into a social movement interested in discussing all political and social issues, including those related to foreign policy and international cooperation. The Charter has remained loyal to its founding declaration and shunned its transformation into a political organization. The group's basic goal is to promote the general public interest: "It does not aim, then, to set out its own programs for political and social reforms or changes, but within its own sphere of activity it wishes to conduct a constructive dialogue with the political and state authorities, particularly by drawing attention to various individual cases where human and civil rights are violated, by preparing documentation and suggesting solutions, by submitting other proposals of a more general character aimed at reinforcing such rights and their guarantees, and by acting as a mediator in various conflict situations which may lead to injustice and so forth."[63] But the group's agenda has gradually expanded, and the Charter has become the thinking nucleus of what might emerge as a Czechoslovak independent peace movement. The reflexive, rather than active, nature of the Charter's peace activities has been determined by the increased level of anti-oppositional repression in Czechoslovakia.

In its statements, Charter 77 has addressed a large range of issues, and taking into account its conception of peace and human rights as a unified field, it has necessarily approached thorny topics dealing with East-West relations. In this respect, some Chartists have expressed criticism of Western European wishful thinking about Soviet ambitions and goals. For Charter 77 it is important "to maintain an unbreakable commitment to the basic demands of human rights to which, in this sense, and only in this sense, does the right to peace, and by extension the fight for peace, belong."[64] The Chartists advocate an uninhibited approach to independent initiatives by ordinary citizens. The purpose would be to continuously question the legitimacy of the repressive institutions and compel the rulers to take social grievances into account. As Václav Havel recently put it: "Applying permanent pressure from below is, in my view, the most important thing to do, and also the only thing that ordinary people can do. To wait for those in power to make a gesture of good will is not, again in my view, a viable alternative. We must constantly be making demands on those in power. We must demand what we think is right and we must apply pressure in order to gain these things. We simply have to rely on ourselves."[65] The "Prague Appeal," issued by a group of Chartists in March 1985, has unleashed peace discussions within the movement. Not fearing official besmirching campaigns, the group criticized manifestations initiated by the Soviet-dominated World Peace Council as shallow and stripped of credibility.[66] On various occasions, Charter 77 has strongly advocated the gradual withdrawal of Soviet troops from Czechoslovakia and the dismantling of nuclear missiles there. In letters addressed to Czechoslovak leaders and to Mikhail Gorbachev in March 1987, on the eve of the Soviet general secretary's official visit to Prague, a group of Chartists described the reestablishment of Czechoslovakia's national and state sovereignty as a contribution to peaceful development of the European continent.

In the aftermath of the Chernobyl accident, the Chartists issued a document criticizing the official scarcity of information. In a statement published in May 1987, the Charter exposed the scope of the ecological crisis in Czechoslovakia and the government's irresponsible attitude to it: "We all know how catastrophic the ecological situation is in our country. Why do we talk about it only in private? Why do we talk in public about only one-tenth of these problems? . . . We should open, in various settings and on all levels, a basic discussion about the ecological situation here."[68]

Heated controversies have developed within Charter 77 between those who favor continuous development of relations with Western peace groups and those who see their main priority as an unwavering commitment to the defense of human rights. Whether Charter 77 has become surreptitiously politicized by its own espousal values of Western pacifist radicalism has become a source of concern for many members. However, in interpreting controversies within dissident groups from communist countries one should not underestimate the impact of the unpropitious environment in which they operate. Hence, for Western activists, one of the major errors in dealing with East European and Soviet independent movements is to project the divisions and animosities characteristic of a pluralistic order onto a totally different social context. For example, Western antinuclear campaigners often utilize ideological terms such as "right" and "left," yet these words to not effectively describe political options in a Soviet-type society. In Havel's view, Charter 77 acts beyond the limits of the traditional right-left dichotomy, and this is precisely the source of its fresh and insightful approach: "Purely and simply, the Charter does not bow to anyone; it is not a covert offshoot of Husák's regime (as some very militant warriors for democracy—most of whom are nicely ensconced away from the battlefield—suspect it to be); nor is it, however, a covert Czechoslovak offshoot of Reagan's Administration (as some very militant warriors for socialism suspect it to be)." According to Havel, Charter 77 is solely preoccupied with seeking the truth. It recognizes only one authority, that of "truth and conscience." As a civic initiative on behalf of human rights, Charter 77 is not ideological.[69]

Havel's viewpoint was formulated during a debate with fellow Chartists Petr Uhl, Ladislav Hejdánek (a philosopher with Protestant inclinations), Václav Benda (a philosopher and mathematician with Catholic leanings) and Jiří Hajek (Alexander Dubček's foreign minister). More than other participants, Hajek assigned great value to the growing dialogue between Chapter 77 and Western peace groups. He described these movements as "a reflection of the attempt to defend man against being manipulated by military-political machines." He also emphasized the Charter's role in sensitizing Western pacifists to the importance of the struggle for human rights in the Soviet Union and East-Central Europe. A different view was advanced by Václav Benda, who rejected the negative view of the West as a political system based on universal manipulation by the authorities. For Benda, the true danger lies in the appearance of "alternative, vicarious forms of authority" and the proliferation of "ultra-ideological movements that bring to the world much harm and contribute to the disintegrative tendency."[70] These polemics show that Chapter 77 has remained the principal

repository of the pacifist impulse in Czechoslovakia. All the other groups—
the Jazz Section, the Lennonists—have drawn from the political philosophy
elaborated by the Chartists. The Charter has succeeded in capturing the civil
society's views on vital political, social, cultural, and moral issues. Its intellectual
diversity has also enhanced the Charter's perception by the public as a genuine
carrier of pluralistic values. An outstanding illustration of the Charter's impact
was the foundation in April 1988 of an Independent Peace Association calling
on the authorities to "demilitarize society, promote overall glasnost, and make
efforts to strengthen peace and confidence among nations."[71] According to its
five-point programmatic statement, the group is an "open gathering of people
who are not indifferent to the future of mankind and the nation and who
understand the positive shift in world history (détente, demilitarization, disarmament) as a challenge for and commitment to civic and personal engagement."[72]

In terms of international contacts, the Charter has developed intensive contacts and cooperation with groups from other Central European countries. Its
main partner in the GDR has been the Initiative for Peace and Human Rights
group whose members have frequently visited Czechoslovakia. Links have been
established in Hungary with the editors of the samizdat journal *Beszélö* and
with the Danube Circle, an ecological group that has criticized the negative
consequences of a Czechoslovak-Hungarian dam on the Danube. In 1987, the
Charter published a collection of documents on human-rights abuses against
members of the Hungarian minority in Slovakia. Close contacts have been
developed with the Committee for the Defense of the Rights of the Hungarian
Minority in Czechoslovakia, led by Miklos Duray. The Charter has good relations
with Yugoslav independent peace and human-rights initiatives like the Ljubljana
group People for Peace Culture. But the closest cooperation has developed
between Charter 77 and Polish oppositionists. The first formal contacts took
place in August 1978, when representatives of Charter 77 and KOR (Workers'
Defense Committee) met on the Polish-Czechoslovak border, exchanged information about their activities, and analyzed forms of cooperation. They adopted
a statement on the anniversary of the Warsaw Pact suppression of the Prague
Spring emphasizing their willingness to continue their struggle for human rights
and democracy: "In these days of the tenth anniversary of the events of 1968,
united in the defense of truth, human and civil rights, democracy, social justice
and national independence, we declare our common will to maintain these ideals
and to act in their spirit. That inalienable human dignity which, as a value,
gives meaning to the lives of the individuals and nations is the source of all our
desires and actions."[73]

As a result of continuous consultations between activists from the two countries, a Polish-Czechoslovak Solidarity initiative was launched in 1981. This
group published interviews with Solidarity leaders in the Charter's bulletin,
organized a Wroclaw demonstration on behalf of the Czech human-rights activist
Petr Pospichal and Hungarian conscientious objector Zsolt Keszthelyi, and ex-

panded its base by founding in July 1987 a new group called "Circle of Friends of Polish-Czechoslovak Solidarity."[74]

In the summer of 1987, independent activists met again at the Polish-Czecho-slovak border. The statement they issued on the occasion of the nineteenth anniversary of the Warsaw Pact intervention in Czechoslovakia highlighted the major values of the developing international civil-rights and anti-militaristic movement in East-Central Europe. The signatories made a positive assessment of Gorbachev's reforms for the future of Eastern Europe. They also warned the Soviet leaders that reforms cannot be successfully implemented without a new approach to human rights and a much deeper respect for the traditions and aspirations of other countries. The participants agreed that independent groups in East-Central Europe should further continue their cross-frontier cooperation. The main assumption of this document was that in spite of national differences among the countries of the region, "the basic ideals of all those engaged in independent civic activities are on the whole identical." They all seek to restore the dignity of the individual and consolidate the role of civil society as the base for a self-governing republic. Their ideals consist of: " . . . a deeper respect for human rights and a consequent reconstitution of the legal system and the legal code; a deeper respect for social rights including the right to found independent trade-unions; the ideal of political pluralism and self-government; spiritual, cultural and religious freedom and tolerance; respect for national individuality and the rights of national minorities; the freedom to search for and create a better-functioning economic system which would provide space for people's creativity and also for real responsibility of all workers for the results of their labor and their share of economic decision-making; the ideal of a peaceful, democratic and environmentally conscious Europe, as a friendly association of independent states and nations.[75] The participants also tackled the issue of fostering the cooperation of independently engaged individuals and groups in the European countries of the Soviet bloc. They agreed on several aims they should pursue together, including "the demand for a reduction in the length of military service and thereby a reduction of the absurdly high level of strength of conventional armies in this part of Europe . . . and the creation of possibilities for citizens whose convictions or religious faith do not allow them to carry arms to do some form of alternative to military service."[76]

The government opposed the intensification of pacifist stances and activities by independent groups in Czechoslovakia. In June 1988, the Czechoslovak police broke up an international peace seminar initiated by Charter 77 and the Independent Peace Association in Prague and expelled thirty-two foreign participants in the gathering.[77] In a preliminary document, Charter 77 formulated as the main objective of the seminar "to conduct a dialogue about human rights and the securing of peace democratically between civil movements and groups within nations in the East as well as in the West."[78] The chief organizers of the seminar—well-known Chartists like Peter Uhl and Jan Urban—were detained and interrogated by the police. On June 19, 1988, the official Czechoslovak news agency Ceteka stigmatized the seminar as an "antisocialist provocation" formented by the "so-called Charter 77" in order "to take advantage of Czechoslovakia's active struggle for peace."[79]

The official propaganda accuses the pacifist movement of having been infiltrated by "openly anti-Communist organizations and individuals." The authorities maintain that a NATO plan exists to encourage selected pacifist organizations in the West "to intensify contacts with some individuals and groups in the socialist countries with the objective of creating 'independent peace movements.' Thus they are to trade the noble aim of the struggle for peace for anti-communist activity under the mantle of anti-war forces." In Czechoslovak President Gustav Husák's own words: "We will not permit anyone to violate laws, to undermine our political system, our socialist order, no matter what insidious phrases about freedom, democracy, and the so-called struggle for human rights he hides behind."[80]

Instead of emulating Gorbachev's "new thinking" in foreign policy, the Czechoslovak leaders seem to retain an increasingly anachronistic philosophy of East-West relations. This rigid attitude can only widen the gap between political elite and civil society in that country. The January 1989 demonstrations in Prague showed that the state of widespread political lethargy is over. The youth who took to Wenceslas Square belonged to a generation who had not experienced the uplifting ideals of the Prague Spring and the cruel disappointments of "normalization." They share with the Chartists the belief that in spite of all obstacles "Truth Will Prevail!" The advent of this new political radicalism had been prefigured in one of Charter's most elaborate theoretical statements released in January 1987: "Let us stop waiting for what others will do; let us do something ourselves. Let us wake up from a state of apathy; let us not surrender to the sense of futility; let us overcome our fears."[81] With liberalization progressing at full steam in the Soviet Union, independent activities (peace and human-rights initiatives, avant-garde cultural groups, samizdat, flying universities) will certainly play a greater role in all the countries of the Soviet bloc. As Charter 77 activist Peter Uhl put it: "These independent activities can, under normal circumstances, influence the democratization process if they manage to involve a large number of people. However in a crisis situation, the impact of such movements is greater than their numbers would normally warrant. The future depends on a link-up between the development of independent structures and the process of reform 'from below' of the existing institutions."[82]

Precisely because of its nonpartisan nature, Charter 77 is bound to remain in the foreseeable future a uniting force for different political orientations involved in the democratization of Czechoslovakia. It will also continue to broaden its human-rights agenda and further elaborate a strategy for the de-militarization of Central Europe.

East Germany

In the fall of 1989 major unrest troubled the long-planned ceremonies orga-
nized to celebrate the fortieth anniversary of the German Democratic Republic.
Tens of thousands of East German tourists crossed Hungary's border with Austria
and went to the Federal Republic. "Trains of freedom" were formed to transport
East Germans from Czechoslovakia, through East Germany, to West Germany.
But not all East Germans want to leave their country. During the first week of
October, exhilarated by Gorbachev's presence in East Berlin, tens of thousands
of East Germans took to the streets and called for reforms and democratization.
Critical intellectuals, disenchanted party members, and human-rights activists
formed the New Forum, the first opposition party in East Germany. The backbone
of this nascent organized opposition has been East Germany's growing unofficial
peace movement, the most developed in Eastern Europe. Symptomatically, one
of New Forum's founders was Bärbel Bohley, a prominent participant in previous
human-rights and pacifist activities.[83]

Several characteristics of the East German political culture should be mentioned here in order to understand the development of independent peace
activities in that country. First, the SED (Socialist Unity Party of Germany) is
the only East European Communist party governing a part of a divided nation.
The presence of the Soviet military forces in the GDR has profoundly influenced
the political configuration in that country. To ensure its authority, the SED has
long tried to insert itself into the German national tradition. Values and symbols
linked to the Prussian military and political tradition have been incorporated in
the official ideology. The SED has also tried to appropriate for its own propagan-
distic interests the memory of Martin Luther, the founder of one of the country's
leading Protestant denominations.[84] In order to consolidate its power and institute a national consensus, the party has engaged in a dialogue with the Evangelical Church, especially after 1978. On the other hand, successive cycles of
repression have aimed to weaken the domestic opposition to the SED's rule. The
basic deal imposed by the East German leaders on their subjects consists of
economic security in return for abstention from independent civic initiatives.

Second, because of the country's location, the East German population has
direct access to Western TV and radio broadcasts. In the early 1980s, East
Germans could watch the development of the West European peace movement.
Many young people came to the conclusion that independent pacifism was as
much needed in the East as in the West.

Third, the Evangelical Church has encouraged the formation of nongovernmental peace groups under the aegis of local religious communities. Church
leaders have long opposed the regime's militaristic course and demanded the
introduction of an alternative to mandatory military service. The emergence of
the independent peace movement in the GDR expressed the growing concern

of East German citizens with the danger of a nuclear confrontation in Central Europe. Independent activists have rejected the official attempt to identify peace and socialism. Because of its rejection of the party's monopoly on power, the movement has become increasingly oppositional. This political radicalization has led to clashes not only with the security forces, but also with some of the church's prominent figures. The Evangelical Church is committed to the defense of human rights, but it does not want to be drawn into political conflicts with the regime. One should, however, underline the role of the church as an umbrella institution for peace activities that run counter to the government's militaristic policy.

The unofficial peace movement has recruited members primarily among young workers who resist military conscription, but also among university students and dissident intellectuals. Indeed, the latter have profoundly influenced the radicalization of religious pacifism and the formulation of an articulate peace and human-rights agenda by the newly formed groups.[85] Noted cultural figures like Jürgen Fuchs, Christa Wolf, Stefan Hermlin, Stephan Heym, Reiner Kunze, and others, had long criticized the regime's militaristic course. On various occasions, they manifested their discontent with "barracks socialism," and their ideas greatly contributed to the coalescence of an anti-war conscience in East Germany. For the peace activists, radical humanism as conceived by intellectuals like Robert Havemann, Rudolf Bahro or Wolf Biermann has been a powerful stimulus in their own thinking. As a result of this permanent dialogue with the critical intelligentsia, the independent peace movement has extended its agenda from strictly delineated peace issues to a deeper commitment to the defense of civic and human rights.

A major event in the development of the East German pacifist movement was the publication on January 25, 1982, of the Berlin Appeal, drafted by the young Protestant pastor Reiner Eppelmann and the dissident Marxist Robert Havemann. Because of widespread concern among East Germans about the deployment of new Soviet medium-range missiles on their territory, the statement aroused considerable support in various strata of the population.

The Appeal proposed a large public debate on the question of peace, in an atmosphere of tolerance and recognition of the right of free speech. The signatories' call for the right to free expression of independent views parallels the major theme of the organic link between peace and human rights. The division of Germany was described as a historical anomaly perpetuated by the failure of the victors of the Second World War to conclude peace treaties with the two German states. In order to secure peace, all countries should get rid of their weapons, and the first step would be to remove nuclear weapons from Germany. The whole European continent must become a nuclear-free zone. The survival of the species required all governments to act quickly to put an end to the race toward mutual annihilation. The East German regime must assess the possibility of allowing social work for peace instead of the present alternative service for conscientious objectors, which forces them to contribute to military-linked activities. Lastly, the Appeal opposed military instruction in schools as well as civil-defense exercises, as they amount to psychological preparation for war.

The Berlin Appeal expressed the need to rethink the whole philosophy of war and peace in our age: "Make peace without weapons—this does not just mean ensuring our own survival. It also means stopping senselessly wasting our people's labor and wealth on producing the engines of war and equipping enormous armies of young men, who are thereby taken out of productive work." Quoting the Sermon on the Mount—"Blessed are the meek: For they shall inherit the earth"—the document called for an unencumbered discussion of the most urgent question: what is conducive to peace, what is conducive to war?[86]

Following the Berlin Appeal independent peace groups formed in many East German cities. Contacts intensified with critical intellectuals, and many peace activists found sources of inspiration in novels and essays by unorthodox writers.[87]

Peace has been increasingly approached as a complex and delicate issue, in relation to the palpable realities of the GDR. In an appeal addressed to Western pacifists, a group of East German independent activists described the current militarization of their country. They criticized the secretive psychology created by the communist regime and asked their peers in the West to protest against the anti-pacifist repression by East German authorities. They informed their Western peers about the imprisonment of three activists in Halle only for having written a paper on peace issues: "The three from Halle were offering advice on how to become a *Bausoldat* (a soldier who works on construction projects) or a conscientious objector—entirely within the law. But giving advice on how to make use of the laws is regarded as punishable. It is called 'prevention of state-controlled measures.' . . . In the interest of peace we object to such measures and demand the demilitarization of the public life. This is an area where the GDR could carry out unilateral disarmament without suddenly being defenseless." East German activists voiced their hope that Western peace groups will realize how important their solidarity is for the continuation of anti-militaristic efforts in countries where such activities are seen as seditious.

Young pacifists adopted the "Swords into Plowshares" (*Schwerter zu Pflugscharren*) slogan as the main symbol of their movement. This was another way of conveying the idea that securing peace means a break with the militaristic practices and mentalities epitomized by official slogans like "I want to be a professional soldier" or "Peace must be defended."[88]

In 1982, the Conference of the Governing Bodies of the Evangelical Churches in the GDR issued a statement in support of the young pacifists. The document described the Biblical "swords into plowshares" phrase as "a signpost pointing the direction in which those who seek disarmament must go." Deeply aware of their moral responsibility, the bishops expressed their solidarity with the young people seeking an answer to whether they should serve in the army or opt for service in the construction units, or whether they should refuse to undertake military service altogether: "It remains our view that even in our present era, and despite the greater danger, Christians may risk serving in the army. We would stress that the young Christians in the construction units, indeed even the conscientious objectors in prison, are not trying to make a point against the state, but in favor of disarmament. We support these young Christians who are demonstrating by their words or their deeds that even the efforts for peace being made by our state do not make striving for disarmament superfluous."[89]

Despite its often critical pronouncements, the church does not intend to become a disguised opposition party in the GDR. Its denunciation of the ongoing militarization of public life is based on the general concept of loyal cooperation between religious and state institutions. The concept of "church within social-ism" (Kirche im Sozialismus) defines precisely this dynamic relationship where the church enjoys spiritual autonomy without being totally subjected to party control. On various occasions church figures have insisted on the need for dialogue between the unofficial peace groups and the government. Acting as a moderator with regard to the most radical claims of the independent activists, the church has also offered strategic guidelines and institutional support for autonomous initiatives, becoming "the programmatic center of the peace movement."[90] With-out the church's active support, these groups could have been easily dismantled by the well-trained East German security police apparatus. The church's willing-ness to offer shelter and spiritual guidance to anti-militaristic initiatives from below has thus been fundamental for the rise of the unofficial peace movement. Despite occasional tensions between radical activists and church personalities, the pacifist-religious symbiosis has decisively helped the independent movement to reduce isolation and become an active social force.[91]

Although the church deplores militarism, it does not wish to antagonize the authorities unnecessarily. Many church leaders are therefore irritated by the growing politicization of the peace movement. In November 1986 the church organized a seminar called Human Rights—the Individual and Society to channel independent pacifism in a less controversial direction. In the view of radical activists, the association with the church narrows the movement's agenda and prevents a thoroughgoing discussion of human-rights issues.[92] These tensions mounted during the "church day" (Kirchentag) in June 1987, when radical activ-ists voiced frustration with what they perceived as a lack of vigor on the part of the Evangelical hierarchy. Following this conflict, some independents challenged the religious and political officialdom with calls for "glasnost in the church, glasnost in the state."[93] They even created their own "Kirchentag from below." This is an unequivocal signal that the East German youth are attracted to more active forms of protest than those tested so far.

Incessant conflicts with the authorities convinced the East German pacifists that peace and human rights cannot be divorced. In January 1985, a group of young East Germans sent an open letter to Erich Honecker on the occasion of the United Nations Youth Year. In addition to familiar calls for the demilitarization of public life and the introduction of an alternative civilian service for conscientious objectors, the letter condemned travel restrictions and demanded freedom of assembly and the suppression of censorship.[94] In 1985, the Initiative for Peace and Human Rights group was founded by well-known activists like Reiner Eppelmann, Ralf Hirsch, and Wolfgang Templin. In an appeal issued in July 1985, the group called for observance of basic human rights, including freedom of speech and association. The language of independent pacifism in the GDR has become strikingly similar to that of related groups in other East European countries: "Peaceful assembly and the founding of initiatives, organizations, associations, clubs and political parties should not be dependent on official permission. The unrestricted work of independent groups would protect the society from petrification in an inflexible administrative order that inhibits creativity among its citizens."[95]

In January 1986, a group of East German peace activists addressed an appeal to the government of the GDR with the following demands: an end to restrictions on the freedom to travel; an end to the practice of juridical persecution for political activity; nomination of independent candidates for municipal and parliamentary elections; revision of the laws that restrict freedom of assembly, public meeting, and association; the legalization of conscientious objection through the creation of an alternative civilian service independent of all military structures. The appeal marked a turning point in the evolution of the unofficial peace movement in the GDR. The leading activists have come to the conclusion that the self-limited peace agenda has been exhausted and that an innovative approach to the issue of political change is vitally needed. International peace remains a utopian dream as long as internal peace is not established and critically minded citizens are treated as potential enemies by authoritarian governments. Communist leaders should surrender their methods of bureaucratic control and embark on a dialogue with people of different opinions.[96]

In recent years, as civic activism has gathered momentum in East Germany, the authorities have resorted to harsh punitive measures against those they describe as "troublemakers." In November 1987, raids were organized against the East Berlin Church of Zion were samizdat publications were printed. In January and February a new repressive wave was triggered and many leading figures of the independent peace and human-rights movement were first arrested and then deported to West Germany.[97] Among those expelled were Stefan Krawczyk, a political balladeer, and his wife Freya Klier, as well as Wolfgang Templin and Ralf Hirsch, prominent members of the Initiative for Peace and Human Rights.[98] The crackdown on peace and human-rights activists—arrested and/or expelled— has generated deep worries among young East Germans about the prospects for liberal reforms in their country. Mass demonstrations took place in October 1989, when tens of thousands marched on the streets of East Berlin, Leipzig, and Dresden calling for reforms and freedom. The regime's first reaction was to send the police and use police dogs, truncheons, and tear gas. Later, however,

Honecker and his colleagues realized that repressive measures could not curb the mounting discontent. Dialogue between the government and the pro-reform groups was therefore vital for avoiding the escalation of civil disobedience and bloody clashes.[99]

Following the 1988 repression, many activists were forced into emigration, and the mass basis of the movement shrank because of the increased dangers associated with participation in unofficial activities. Few university students dared show themselves at church services for fear of being blacklisted. East German workers seemed contemptuous of the young activists who fought for peace and human rights, referring to them as "peacies."[100] But as events in the fall of 1989 have shown, repression has not worked. The regime is increasingly worried about the prospects for an alliance between intellectuals and workers. The government has managed to handle industrial conflicts and offers sufficient economic incentives to the workers in order to prevent open discontent. On the other hand, critical intellectuals have been so far too preoccupied with their own demands and neglected the need for a major economic restructuring. In the words of a young civil-rights supporter, "only if workers realize that mere grumbling no longer helps and intellectuals realize that we can't achieve anything without re-forming the economy, is there a chance to create a bond between them."[101] But, as the East German economic situation seems to deteriorate and sweeping reforms develop in the USSR, the political radicalization of the independent peace and human-rights movement in the GDR has become inevitable.

Hungary

The Hungarian regime is more tolerant of dissent and criticism than the East German and Czechoslovak ones. But even under the apparently enlightened despotism symbolized by János Kádár's rule, nongovernmental peace initiatives were not able to develop freely. Its liberal facade notwithstanding, Kádárism was inimical to the emergence of any alternative political force. To be sure, after Kádár's resignation at the May 1988 party conference, the whole political equation in that country has undergone tremendous modifications. Social initiatives long considered seditious are now officially endorsed. As Miklós Haraszti emphasizes in his contribution to this volume, this is a consequence of the gradual disintegration of the post-Stalinist authoritarianism under the influence of both domestic and global factors. But, under Kádár, the regime resorted to a wide range of methods to deter independent activists from organizing their own groups distinct from official peace institutions. Nowadays peace issues are primarily dealt with in major samizdat publications of the Democratic Opposition like *Beszélö*, *Demokráta*, and *Hirmondo*.

An attempt to set up a Hungarian autonomous peace movement was undertaken in the early 1980s, when Hungary was experiencing its own period of "stagnation." The Peace Group for Dialogue (*Dialogus*) was established in Sep-

tember 1982 and recruited primarily among university students and recent graduates. During its troubled existence, it organized an officially sponsored peace
march, public meetings, and a lecture by Western historian and peace activist
E.P. Thompson, who later gave the following description of the group's goals:
" 'Dialogue' existed to further not only direct Hungary/West communication on
questions of peace, but also internal dialogue within the country: they sought to
bring around the same round-table people from the official (peace) Council
and the constructive opposition."[102] But this was precisely the main illusion
entertained by the founders of Dialogue: their belief that the government would
cling to its commitment to "civilized repression" and would tolerate the emergence of a semi-autonomous peace organization. Dialogue did not identify itself
with the opposition and preferred to appear as the embodiment of a "third way"
equally distant from the official structures and the oppositional ones.

The whole program of Dialogue was thus based on the hope for a compromise
with the government. Their ideology was inspired by the desire to preserve the
group's autonomy without antagonizing the authorities: "The pressures put on
the new peace movement were two-fold: on the one hand it had to be independent. But in order to survive, it had to be endorsed by the State. There is of
course nothing new in this compromise. In another form it has long been a
recurring dream of the Kadar-era intelligentsia. But so far everyone has had to
choose between official recognition or the independence of the outlaw. The new
peace movement assumed that a realistic compromise was attainable in its case,
despite discouraging precedents."[103] In order to convince the government of their
good faith, the leaders of Dialogue made consistent efforts to distinguish peace
from human-rights issues. In this respect, the Hungarian experiment represented
the opposite of the path adopted by independent peace movements in other
communist countries. Far from espousing the aims of the dissident community,
Dialogue leader Ferenc Koszegi did not conceal his hostility to seeing the independent peace group involved in oppositional activities. He rejected attempts on the
part of the human-rights campaigners to join the autonomous peace movement.

According to Koszegi there are three important forces that would want to
coopt and manipulate the new peace movement. The first one is the official
Peace Council, whose goals are not totally different from those of the new
movement. The distinction would thus be primarily one of methods: "The
Council is a bit clumsy and bureaucratic, and this turns off the young. It also
does not comprehend the deep anti-militarist sentiments of the youth."[104] In the
light of this premise, there was room for cooperation between the official peace
institution and the new movement. Moreover, Dialogue leaders thought that
the goal of the new group could be accomplished through the revitalization of
the government-controlled Peace Council.

Koszegi was more concerned with the possibility of seeing the new movement
penetrated by members of the dissident counterculture. Mentioning that his
remark applied only to the Hungarian situation, Koszegi went so far as to describe

the dissidents as a "manipulating force": "The attempts of the opposition elements to gain prominent places in the emerging movement could be of great danger to the movement itself. If the movement gets itself identified as being primarily or even secondarily a movement of political opposition, this would surely mean a decline in support for it among the large population."[105] Interesting enough, he offers an original—and obviously reductionist— interpretation of the "Peace and Freedom" slogan which eliminates the connection between peace and human rights: "The slogan *Peace and Freedom* is a valid one, but not in the sense of political opposition. What is meant in this context is the freedom to choose our fate with regard to the nuclear destruction. The one link that unites the new peace movement is the desire for an enduring peace. The new movement has developed into a force which cannot be identified with either the Peace Council or with political opposition. It is and must remain an open and public movement, resisting all attempts at cooptation and manipulation."[106]

Finally, the third manipulating force would be the state itself and its constitutional regulations preventing the formation of unofficial organizations: "It is for this reason, among others, that we hesitate to speak of a peace 'movement' as such, but continue to speak only of small and loosely organized groups and/or individuals who feel themselves responsible for the cause of peace."[107]

Because Dialogue made it a matter of principle to define itself as both nongovernmental and nonoppositional, the group was extremely prudent in the formulation of its aims. Most of its demands consisted of abstract and quite innocuous calls for gradual nuclear disarmament and the abolition of military blocs. The group members did, however, join the campaign for the introduction of a civilian alternative to military service. But the really controversial issues linked to the establishment of détente from below were skillfully shunned: ". . . Dialogue did not demand the withdrawal of troops, nor did they demand public discussion of the arms budget. Their political demands were simply aimed at securing the right for everyone to express a desire for peace, and the right to be in unrestricted contact with any other peace group in Europe."[108]

The Hungarian group rejected all oppositional stances, methods, and techniques from the very outset, but it also refused to endorse the status quo. Not surprisingly, therefore, Dialogue was marked by the ambiguity of its commitment: The members' self-image was romantic, but in practice the group valued self-restraint and moderation. On the one hand, they aspired to transcend the systemic constraints on independent activism, but on the other, they refused to assume the risks associated with unofficial undertakings. Members of the group publicized their interest in a "policy of alliance" with the government-sponsored peace organizations. It can be argued that because of its inherent inconsistency, Dialogue was doomed to failure. There were of course numerous attempts on the part of the Hungarian Peace Council to coopt Dialogue. But the hard-liners in the party leadership did not see any reason to allow this group to be active, even as a loyal partner to the Peace Council. In their view, there was no need for a parallel peace organization.

In the end, the Communist party itself decided to suppress independent peace activities. A Politburo resolution adopted on March 29, 1983, discarded Dialogue's endeavors to distance itself from the opposition and announced the Communist party's intention to disband all independent initiatives. Even semi-legal associations would not be tolerated. The resolution stipulated that the Hungarian peace movement must be united and adhere to the guidance of the National Peace Council. Subsequently, movements outside this framework would not be legalized. The party could not accept the proliferation of independent peace activism: "The [Dialogue] group does not have any significant mass support, but its influence is growing. At the present moment, Dialogue groups are operating in Budapest, Szeged, Debrecen, and Pecs. Their ideas are in equal measure mixed, immature, and self-contradictory, even giving rise to controversy within their own circles. . . . Pacifist efforts making their appearance in church and religious circles are also on the increase."[109] This resolution dispelled the "accomodationist" fallacy which takes for granted the readiness of the authorities to cooperate with independent associations. Miklós Haraszti's diagnosis is thus justified: "The government got over the fact of having flirted for a while with a new type of political formula, to return to the safe and traditional theory of a Communist structure of society: society must equal the state, and if society does not think so, then the police will help change its mind."[110] Despite its failure, Dialogue's experience contributed to a discovery by many young people of the possibility of being politically active without being totally incorporated within the system. It created a taste among many of its members for genuine political participation and thus prepared them for joining more radical formations: ". . . Dialogue was not just *another* movement, but a movement that had never existed before in any form. Dialogue's members were undoubtedly prone to see ghosts even where there were none, and it is obviously due to the legacy of the Kadar era that many useful initiatives were strangled and watered down. And yet: Dialogue was the very first group to offer a movement to young people who craved independence and a spiritual way of life."[111]

Following the forced dissolution of the group, Dialogue split into two wings: Koszegi and his partisans, who formed a Youth Club directly linked to the official Peace Council; and those who have become increasingly involved in the activities of the Hungarian Democratic Opposition.[112]

Commenting on the avatars of Dialogue and similar groups in the GDR, E.P. Thompson rightly concluded: ". . . while there have been great difficulties in maintaining autonomous organizational structures, the general *peace culture* (especially among young people) continues to grow. It is inevitable that new forms of expression will be found. And the search for these new forms must be carried out by the citizens of these nations alone. It is no business of Western activists to interfere in any way in these internal affairs, or to seek to import their own prescriptions. Any such attempts will, anyway, be counter-productive."[113] One should add, however, that these new peace initiatives have increasingly emphasized the intimate link between peace and freedom in a much more comprehensive sense than that recognized by the founders of Dialogue. In other words, the independent peace culture should be seen as a branch of the larger movement for democracy and human rights.

Peace issues have been extensively discussed by members of the Hungarian Democratic Opposition. One of their major concerns is the legal persecution of conscientious objectors. There are at present 150 innocent men being held in Hungarian prisons for refusing to serve in the army. Among those imprisoned are followers of Father György Bulányi, a Piarist in his late sixties who spent eight years in prison during the Stalinist years.[114] His 5,000 or so disciples organized in unofficial "basic groups" form the *Bokor* (Bush) movement. It includes a number of pacifists, some of whom are in prison for refusing to serve in the army. The Catholic bishops have accused Bulányi of undermining their authority and have denounced him to the Vatican for presumed doctrinal faults.[115]

Instead of opposing compulsory draft, the Catholic bishops unanimously noted in a statement that the obligation of military service may not be refused by the citizen and cannot be condemned from the Christian point of view. Károly Kiszely, considered to be the spokesman of the Hungarian conscientious objectors, was expelled from the country in 1987.[116] Also in 1987, Zsolt Keszthelyi, twenty-three years old and an editor of a samizdat magazine, was sentenced to a prison term of two and a half years because he refused to serve in the Hungarian army. Keszthelyi's conscientious objection was motivated by political reasons, as he explained in his statement sent to the recruitment center: ". . . I wish to refuse military service because of political motives. I am not inclined to put my trust in a 'people's democratic' army which is not placed under the control of a government elected by universal suffrage involving competing political programs. I think that by this action, just like by my struggle for a free press, I can contribute to the creation of a society which is free of fear and in which the management of social affairs is determined by the responsibility and conscience of individuals and not by unquestioning faith and fear."[117] In January 1989, seven months before the expiration of his term, Keszthelyi was released. This was more than mere symbolism on the part of Károly Grosz's regime—only one day after Keszthelyi's release, the Hungarian parliament passed a bill introducing a civilian service for conscientious objectors.[118]

Another major concern of the Hungarian independents is the catastrophic destruction of the environment. Ecological groups have emerged that openly question the government's industrial policy. The Hungarian "Greens" have established links with Austrian counterparts and cooperate in opposing the implementation of a dam project on the Danube. In an advertisement published by the Austrian newspaper *Die Presse*, thirty prominent Hungarian intellectuals criticized the project and deplored Austrian participation in it: "A democratic society—and we regard Austria as such—must not allow itself to exploit the lack of democracy in another country for its own material advantage."[119]

It is thus clear that in as much as it is an independent initiative the environmentalist movement must become increasingly involved in political issues. This inevitable civic radicalization was emphasized by Judith Vásárhelyi, a leading member of the Danube Circle: "The Danube movement is becoming a protest for democratization. It's being done by people who a few years ago wouldn't have thought of taking such a stance. And it's showing that civic courage is increasing."[120]

This is the reverse of the universalization of politics imposed by the communist system. Whatever issue is selected for independent activity, be it peace, environment, rock or jazz music, the movement spontaneously becomes politically oriented. The same would happen to movements for the purity of language, for decent public transportation, or for a better quality of TV broadcasts. They will either evolve into political movements or become absolutely irrelevant.

Poland

Freedom and Peace, the main independent peace movement in that country, was founded in 1985. Its chief objective is to oppose the regime's militaristic rhetoric and practices. The group's philosophy was inspired by the experience of Solidarity as a nonviolent, autonomous form of social self-organization.[121] There were, to be sure, references to the relation between peace and human rights in statements by influential advisors to the Solidarity leadership. Adam Michnik, for instance, wrote that "the struggle for peace is conceivable only as a struggle against totalitarian enslavement."[122] But Solidarity did not specifically approach peace issues.[123]

Freedom and Peace came into being at a moment when other independent groups and associations, and primarily Solidarity, had been forced to act clandestinely. The movement's aim is the reappropriation by society of the notion of peace, semantically distorted by the official propaganda. Following the Solidarity model, the movement is programatically nonviolent. Its worldview and strategy are rooted in the ethos of Solidarity: respect for the individual, an evolutionary approach to social change, commitment to pluralism. To disseminate its views, the group stages peaceful demonstrations which are widely publicized by independent media.

Freedom and Peace emerged as a protest against the hegemony of the military in Polish society. In an interview given to *Robotnik* (Worker), a publication of Solidarity, one of the group's leaders, Piotr Niemczyk, said: "This state needs soldiers, not because it fears for the permanence of its boundaries but because the army in this country is part of the police force. History made this very clear in December 1970 and December 1981. The authorities use the army to maintain their privileges, and this is probably why they refuse to admit precedents showing that some people refuse to serve. They are afraid of that! They are afraid that the time may come when they will lose one of the bases on which this system rests—lose the army that can be deployed at any time against the internal enemy."[124]

For many young people, the army has ceased to inspire respect. A booklet published by the Alternative Society Movement offers a grim picture of today's Polish army: "They'll teach you to obey—so that you'll have no scruples. They'll beguile you with propaganda—so that you'll believe that your father, your brother, and your friend are 'class enemies' . . . this army is there not to defend Polish independence but to maintain dependence on the USSR. Under these circumstances, opposing the army in Poland takes on an additional aspect: It is part of the struggle for independence."[125]

The immediate impulse for the creation of a Polish independent peace movement was the trial in December 1984 of Marek Adamkiewicz, a young draftee who was sentenced to a prison term of two and a half years for refusing to take the military oath. Many Poles resent the reference in the oath to the "fraternal alliance with the army of the Soviet Union and other allied armies." Expressing their support for Adamkiewicz, a dozen signatories to one of the protest letters sent to the State Council wrote: "Forcing anyone to swear an oath to something that contravenes his convictions is a violation of that person's conscience. On the other hand, an oath sworn under duress is not binding and no one has to keep it."[126]

The first Freedom and Peace group was formed in Cracow in April 1985, soon followed by other ones in Warsaw, Wroclaw, Szczecin, and Gdansk. The example of East German independent pacifism turned out to be contagious in Poland, as it appears from this statement by a contributor to the independent paper *Tu Teraz* (Here Now): "I believe that we must follow with great care and respect the development of the East German opposition, especially since even the introduction of martial law in Poland failed to cause any far-reaching rethinking let alone any new initiative, about military service or the possibility of the public's refusing to serve."[127] Tomas Wacko, one of the founders of the Freedom and Peace movement in Wroclaw, gave the following explanation for his refusal to take the military oath in February 1986: "Despite the pompous slogans about 'a new kind of army,' an antifeudal and democratic army, one that is devoid of orderlies, it is in fact an army of servants and footmen. It is a part of a system set up to destroy human character and conscience. My refusal to take the military oath is a form of protest against the entire system of enslavement."[128]

The founding declaration of the first Cracow group defined the basic goals and assumptions of the new peace movement:

1. To propagate the true and unfalsified idea of peace among the Polish public. Opposing what they called the demagogic manipulation of this sacred notion, the group announced its intention to restore the moral and political worth of peace.

2. For the independent activists, the struggle for peace cannot be separated from the defense of personal freedoms and human rights: "There is no peace wherever there exists a system of state aggression, of ideological coercion; wherever individuals

have been deprived of their rights to independent decisions, to initiative; where traditional political freedoms have been eliminated . . ."[129]

3.   Their strivings are to be inspired by the conviction that international peace is inseparable from internal peace: "We shall . . . condemn the expressions of disdain for freedom—so frequent in the world today—particularly when they are justified by ideologies that have turned violence into a successful instrument."[130]

Freedom and Peace is structured as a loose federation of groups from major Polish cities. They print bulletins to disseminate their views on issues bearing on domestic and international affairs. Being a public, above-ground movement, based on personal associations and friendships, Freedom and Peace does not require formal membership. Its informal structure is the only way to prevent systematic reprisal on the part of the authorities. There are now 100 to 200 Freedom and Peace activists, but the movement's appeal is much broader. Its success stems from an ability to promote a warm sense of community among activists and sympathizers. Thousands of supporters often join demonstrations organized by Freedom and Peace and sign their petitions.

Before the formation of a Solidarity-run government in 1989, the official reaction to independent pacifism combined campaigns of slander, high fines, trials, and prison sentences. Pressure from below forced the Communist government to release conscientious objectors from jail and to promise the introduction of an alternative service.

The Communist government did not, however, surrender to the movement's demand for a total overhaul of the military oath. That would have amounted to a change in the professed goals of the regime. Freedom and Peace asks for the deletion from the oath of the reference to ideological obligations and the promise of allegiance to the Soviet ally, a highly sensitive issue that touches upon the international obligations of any Polish government. Therefore, it is to be expected that even a Solidarity-dominated government will be reluctant to accept all the movement's demands.

Despite police harassment from the Communist government, independent pacifism spread. A letter sent to the State Council by Tomas Kulczewski, a twenty-year-old math teacher in a school near Warsaw, bears out the intimate link between peace activism and political opposition. Following his refusal to serve in the army, Kulczewski was fired from his job, arrested, and sentenced to two years in prison. The sentence was suspended for three years: "I have learned within a few months that it is impossible to be a pacifist in Poland. I was treated like a common criminal. I was forced to act like a common criminal, since pacifism for me is not simply a means to avoid military service. I found myself in jail because I am a citizen of People's Poland. A citizen of a country whose ideology I cannot comprehend, incidentally. . . . I consider myself in no way to be a full-fledged citizen of this country. This is why I request to be deprived of the citizenship of the Polish People's Republic."[131]

The Communist government's decision to introduce an alternative service represented a major success for Freedom and Peace. The movement's methods were summed up in one of the Polish underground publications: ". . . this is a tactical skill: to fight for a definite aim that is possible to achieve, to create for the authorities a threat graver than the demanded concession. Moreover, to wage the struggle for an aim that is generally accepted as right and just, using methods that awaken no revulsion and risk only one's own skin, no one else's."[132]

In their contacts with Western peace groups, Polish activists have contributed to a better understanding of the relation between anti-nuclear campaigns and the struggle for human rights. In an appeal addressed to the European Nuclear Disarmament Amsterdam Conference in July 1985, Freedom and Peace emphasized the indivisibility of the struggles for peace and human rights. They asked for a comprehensive and politically focused interpretation of peace issues. In their opinion, justice and civic freedoms should be included in the interpretation of peace, and "the struggle against totalitarian systems (should) be treated on an equal plane with disarmament undertakings."[133] Freedom and Peace has thus assimilated and developed themes initially introduced by Charter 77 into the international nongovernmental peace discussions. Together with the Czechoslovak, East German, and Soviet unofficial peace movements, Freedom and Peace activists have put forward a new set of guidelines for the development of international peace activism. They have revitalized the discussion on the fate of the Helsinki agreements and the need to go beyond the détente from above. Together with other East European independents, they played a pivotal role in the formulation of the Vienna Memorandum, "Giving Real Life to the Helsinki Accords." In an article published in a samizdat journal, Freedom and Peace activist Jacek Czaputowicz wrote: "One cannot dismiss the fact that our East European viewpoint has been accepted by the peace movements in the West. This will also make it harder on East European governments to continue to exploit the actions of West European pacifists for their own propaganda purposes."[134]

During the pre-Solidarity-run government period, Freedom and Peace activists operated under extremely difficult circumstances. They were continuously exposed to police persecution, arrests, interrogations, and smears. In an open letter to Joanne Landy of the New York–based Campaign for Democracy/East and West, prominent Freedom and Peace member Piotr Niemczyk wrote: "In Poland, the Freedom and Peace (WiP) movement members are constantly harassed by the Security Service, and there is a propaganda campaign against them. Its most striking example is a report on a press conference at the National Defense Ministry where a spokesman journalist described WiP as 'a small group with no substantial influence on the present and future situation in Poland. In this anarcho-pacifist movement, controlled by the inheritors of KOR [Committee of Workers' Defense] and sponsored by the West, not a single member is of worker or peasant origin. The program of this small but noisy group, pretending to be a peace movement, makes no genuine appeals against war, nuclear weapons or the policy of aggression. What they want is just and only to abolish compulsory

military service, and that in Poland of all countries.' "[135] Understandably therefore, Polish independents have often expressed irritation with the Western
pacifists' failure to see the totalitarian threat to peace. Criticizing the unilateral
concern with disarmament, Jacek Szymanderski, the spokesman for Freedom and
Peace said: [Western pacifists] are disarmament freaks. We are not necessarily
armament supporters, but it is people who shoot, not guns. Totalitarianism is
more dangerous than missiles. It is not enough to supply a man with a uniform
and a gun to make him shoot. He must also be supplied with a false idea, deprived
of a part of his (personal) freedom—and this is what totalitarianism does. Those
who only add up megatons prefer not to see this. . . . The attitude toward
homegrown pacifists gives lie to the statement that the imperialist policy of the
USSR and the whole bloc is a policy of peace. Yet the world has been buying
this for years and years."[136]

The cooperation of independents from both sides of the Iron Curtain in the
elaboration of the Vienna Memorandum indicates that many Western peace
groups have reconsidered their initial distrust of messages sent from Eastern
Europe. According to Niemczyk this tendency should be consolidated, in order to
avoid the resurgence of past misunderstandings stemming from Western euphoria
with the new Soviet foreign-policy initiatives: "From the point of view of independent peace activities in Poland, nothing is more alarming than a recurrence
of the situation where the Western peace movement's activities become, undoubtedly with no intention, a tool of Soviet policy and propaganda."[137]

The international seminar International Peace and the Helsinki Agreements,
organized by Freedom and Peace in May 1987, represented a major success for
independent pacifists in Poland and in the whole Soviet bloc. Freedom and
Peace has asserted itself as a significant component of the Polish opposition, with
a broad agenda encompassing peace, human rights, and ecological issues. For
the independents, human rights, peace, and environmental protection are inter-
related. According to them, freedom requires also the right to live in unpolluted,
nondangerous areas. It might be expected that the ecological agenda will become
increasingly attractive in the future. This might be the beginning of a new stage
in the evolution of anti-totalitarian struggles in the region: the "greening" of the
East European opposition. Far from representing its de-politicization, this process
will involve the formulation of alternative development programs critical of the
current abusive treatment of both nature and society.

To conclude, Freedom and Peace has articulated widespread anti-militaristic
feelings and legitimate human-rights concerns. The movement has convincingly
advanced a philosophy of democratic peace based on the assumption that society
has the right to oppose the state's claim to unlimited exercise of power: "Only
a sovereign society can guarantee real disarmament and peaceful policy. No
individual, even one bestowed with complete power as the Soviet General
Secretary is, can issue such a guarantee. Independent trade unions limit war
industry, independent parliaments control official foreign policy, and a free press

informs on abuses in international relations and brings pressure to bear on politicians."[138]

USSR

No theme is more frequently present in Soviet official language than peace. Nothing is more praised in Soviet pedagogy than commitment to peace. Unlike similar institutions in Eastern Europe, the Soviet Peace Council has managed to attract wide support from various strata of the Soviet population. Many Soviet citizens are convinced that their country has always been the victim of external aggression and that, when it had to wage wars abroad, it was for defensive purposes. The Soviet Peace Fund is a popular institution, and members of the liberal intelligentsia do not significantly differ from the average Soviet citizen in endorsing this operation.

The Peace Council is, however, an official agency. Its goals are party defined, formulated, and assigned. Peace campaigns are scheduled in accordance with the party's priorities. The mass character of peace campaigns in the Soviet Union should not be taken as an indication of spontaneous activity.

The relation between authorities and society has gong through different stages in the post-Stalin era. After Khrushchev's aborted attempt at liberalization, a new freeze was imposed by the Brezhnev leadership. The civil-rights movement was suppressed, Andrei Sakharov was harassed, and independent initiatives looked quixotic in the petrified Soviet system. Lately, under Mikhail Gorbachev, the politics of glasnost has allowed the emergence of thousands of independent groups and associations. Sakharov was permitted to return home to Moscow, where he has resumed his scientific and political activities. Many political prisoners—though not all of them—have been released.

Peace has become the central value, the major point of reference for all these emerging unofficial groups. They all appear to feel entitled to air views on peace and national-security issues. But there have been a number of citizens who have long advocated a new approach to peace issues, even at a time when such independent stances could and sometimes did lead to interrogations and imprisonment.

The Moscow Trust Group (MTG) is one of the very few unofficial groups that has managed to survive during the last six years despite unpropitious political circumstances.

The MTG was founded in June 1982 by eleven Moscow intellectuals. Its initial name was the Group to Establish Trust Between the Soviet Union and the USA, but in 1985, broadening its agenda, it changed its name to Group to Establish Trust Between East and West. The initial nucleus consisted of intellectuals from Moscow and the suburb of Dolgoprudny, many of whom were Jewish refuseniks.[139] Later they were joined by young artists and writers from the alternative subcultures as well as religious activists, high-school and university students. A major role in the founding and activities of the group was played by Sergei Batovrin, son of a Soviet UN diplomat, who was forced into psychiatric detention. He emigrated to the United States in 1983.

The Founding Appeal was signed by several hundred Soviet citizens. The Appeal called for actions to implement genuine détente: the abolition of nuclear weapons in East and West; the establishment of a "four-sided dialogue" (not only between superpower leaders, but also between Soviet and American societies); measures to increase mutual trust and eliminate fear and suspicion. The group founders assigned a major role to independent citizens from both the USSR and the USA in the promotion of genuine peace: "We call upon the citizens of both countries to create combined international public groups, based on the principles of independence."[140] During the difficult times that preceded Gorbachev's reforms, the Trust Group fulfilled a very important task: it provided Soviet and foreign citizens with a place to discuss important issues in an independent way and thereby advanced "an alternative to one-sided official propaganda that blames only the West for the threat of war."[141]

The Trust Group does not conceive of itself as a political organization. Accordingly, it has refrained from assessing various Soviet or American disarmament proposals. Its basic aim is to create "a space where an exchange of views can take place between ordinary citizens of the Soviet Union and the West outside their political systems."[142]

Like the East European independents, the Trust Group emphasizes the inseparability of peace and human-rights issues. This is not because they underestimate the need to focus on specific peace issues, but rather because they realize that genuine peace cannot be achieved without abandoning totalitarian habits and mentalities. The Trust Group has opposed ideological straitjackets and advocated a renunciation of Cold War clichés.

Because of the nature of the Soviet system, wherein independent views on military issues can be stigmatized as subversive, the Trust Group has avoided unequivocal criticism of the Soviet nuclear program and the military buildup. But the government has not tolerated even this self-limited form of autonomous pacifism. Independent activists have been arrested, deported, and besmirched. Since the struggle for peace cannot be considered a crime, the authorities harassed the pacifists on trumped-up charges.[143]

In May 1986, the Trust Group organized the first public demonstration against the use of nuclear energy in the USSR. In September 1986, four of the group's spokespersons emigrated to the West. In December 1986, a splinter group was formed which tried to put an end to the activities of the Trust Group. The majority counterreacted and confirmed their willingness to continue their struggle. The group counts now 15 to 30 members, with 75 to 100 who regularly attend seminars. It recruits primarily among Jewish refuseniks, scientists and professionals, Pentecostal and religious activists, and young people from alternative rock and "hippie" movements.[144]

In May 1987, the Trust Group fully resumed its activities and published a Declaration of Principles. In consensus with East European independent movements, the declaration insisted that peace and human rights are inseparably linked. The group espoused the strategy of détente from below, which, in their view, can be attained "through the growth of a worldwide revolution of grass-roots peace initiatives." Starting from the premise that "peace in the world and peace within society depend on one another in the most intimate fashion," the document formulated the following demands to the Soviet government:

- irreproachable adherence to the constitutional rights and freedoms of citizens;

- an amnesty for all prisoners of conscience, that is, persons deprived of their freedom because of their convictions, if they did not use or advocate violence;

- changes in the legislative and judicial-executive practices in the USSR with the objective of preventing opportunities for the persecution of people for their convictions;

- complete abolition of the death penalty;

- guarantee of the "right to pacifism," which includes establishment of alternative civilian service for persons who are unable, for reasons of conscience, to serve in the army;

- exercise to the fullest extent of the right to freedom of movement and choice of residence both outside one's country (unimpeded departure and return) and within one's country (the dismantling of the system of obligatory residence permits).[145]

The activities of the Trust Group have contributed to the emergence of an embryonic civil society in the Soviet Union. The independent peace activists have defined their undertaking as a form of participation in the discussion of major problems concerning not only the government and the party, but the whole society as well. The Trust Group understands the difficulties of creating alternative political organizations in a nondemocratic climate like the Soviet one. The informality, with its commitment to maintaining a loose structure, have long been basic requirements for avoiding direct clashes with the security police. According to their Declaration of Principles, the Trust Group is an informal association of citizens who share the above-mentioned principles: "It is not an organization and does not presuppose 'party discipline,' strict membership, or the presence of a leader. It does not have an obligatory program of action. The degree of activity of each person is determined by himself or herself, both concerning actions in the framework of the Group as well as actions taken individually, on one's own volition. By the same token, the degree of responsibility the Group takes for each of its activists is determined separately in each concrete instance."[146]

Groups with similar pacifist platforms are now mushrooming in the Soviet Union. Their estimated membership is between 1,000 and 2,000 persons. Under

Soviet circumstances, this is remarkable. The groups have to deal with very complex issues, including the repressive measures adopted by the authorities and internal factionalism. For instance, the group Friendship and Dialogue was created in 1983 by scientists who disagreed with the tactical orientation of the Trust Group. More recently, members of Friendship and Dialogue have become directly involved in the increasingly dynamic human-rights movement. Together with the Press Club Glasnost, the Trust Group activists and other independents participated in the organization of the December 1987 Moscow seminar on human rights.

Independent peace activism criticizes all the forms of militarization of public life. Opposition to militarism means, therefore, protesting against ideological manipulation, including the so-called "military patriotic education" of the Soviet youth. According to Nikolay Khramov, a samizdat publisher and journalist and a leading member of the Trust Group, this is "the most disturbing trend in the inner life of our country. This trend has reached its most alarming proportions under Gorbachev."[147]

In May 1988, members of the Trust Group were among the founders of the Democratic Union, an association that proclaimed itself an opposition political party. Aptly described as an "audacious venture," the Democratic Union is an alliance of different independent groups whose demands include: the dissolution of the Soviet system; the withdrawal of Soviet troops from Eastern Europe; and the establishment of a Western-type democracy. The police interfered, some activists were arrested, and the meeting was dispersed.[148]

Conclusions

Independent pacifist movements in East-Central Europe and the Soviet Union have become a main channel to voice social discontent and to transcend political alienation. Their birth and evolution have been favored by the maturity of the oppositional counterculture and, as in the case of the GDR, by the support provided by nongovernmental (religious) institutions. People involved in unofficial peace activities have discovered a common ground for nonviolent resistance to an oppressive state machine and an alien ideology. To contain the pacifist infection, authorities have resorted both to harsh measures and apparent concessions. The future of these independent peace movements depends on domestic and international factors, but they are now a major component of the growing civil society and it would be extremely difficult for the authorities to suppress them. It can be projected that these groups will continue to develop and undermine the self-serving peace ideology of the ruling elites.

The dynamics of the independent peace movements in Eastern Europe and the USSR bear out the thesis that anti-militaristic attitudes in Soviet-type regimes necessarily evolve toward confrontation with officialdom. The "gray area" between the state and the citizens cannot remain long neutral. The communist regimes cannot acquiesce in the creation of parallel centers of civic life, for the autonomous, self-generating activities jeopardize the Communist party's grip on power. But the example set by Charter 77 shows that a community of people interested in living in truth and dignity can survive even under extremely unpropitious circumstances. Certainly, challenging the official cynicism and duplicity is an undertaking full of risks. But peace and human rights have emerged as the basic issues whose defense cannot be automatically discarded as "fomenting anti-socialist conspiracies."

As East German and Hungarian activists realize, one cannot dissociate war and peace issues from the general oppositional approach. Semi-dissident activities are either assimilated into the official discourse or turn into genuinely oppositional attitudes. This is, however, a long and tortuous process of self-assertion. It is a search for political identity whose tempo depends on dissident traditions in a given country and the level of political repression. The fact, for example, that there is no autonomous pacifist and/or ecological subculture in Romania is certainly related to the preservation of a staunch Stalinist dictatorship there.

Independent pacifism should be seen as a step toward the reconstitution of the civil society in Eastern Europe and the Soviet Union. It is neither the ultimate form of political protest, nor the backbone of a self-sufficient social movement. As long as they remain hostages of a self-styled political narcissism, independent peace groups cannot become more than marginal discussion communities. However, the trend seems to be toward the politicization and radicalization of these movements. Freedom and Peace in Poland is only the most evident case of politically militant pacifism, as is recognized both by its members and the authorities. It is thus important to emphasize that maintaining a hidden agenda, refusing to broach human-rights issues, and pretending to be interested in peace *per se* has not helped the Hungarian group Dialogue survive. On the contrary, such an attitude makes the group vulnerable to government manipulation and suspect to oppositional circles. Exactly as one cannot artificially oppose peace to human-rights issues, it is senseless to establish borders between independent peace and human-rights groups.

The unofficial peace groups have significantly contributed to the growing interest expressed by Western anti-nuclear activists in human-rights issues in the Soviet bloc.[149] Even more important, the philosophy of democratic peace has helped activists from Central Europe to close ranks and develop an international vision which challenges bloc logic and seeks the unification of a democratic Europe: "The issue of peace could become, slowly, the international strategic focus of all East European oppositions. . . . In East Germany it could be different because of the German issue, but in Poland, Czechoslovakia and in Hungary the issue of peace will be more and more identified with the whole democratic movement. It will be inseparable from it."[150]

East European and Soviet pacifism has persuaded many Western activists that being unilaterally anti-nuclear is a delusion. One must reflect on the political uses of weapons in different social orders. Whereas Western activists can safely reject their governments' strategic options, similar stances in Eastern Europe and the Soviet Union can be stigmatized "high treason." To their credit, these unofficial groups have not been deterred by this risk and have continued to oppose the growing militarization of their societies.

Independent peace groups will continue to emerge in the Eastern bloc. Their dynamics are intimately related to systemic political developments: The more liberal the body politic, the more radical these groups will tend to be. At the same time, they can exert continuous pressure on the rulers to stop human-rights violations and demilitarize society. A major component of the blossoming civil society, the independent peace groups will not limit themselves to anti-war propaganda. They are bound to explore ideas critical of the military and police establishments, and challenge thereby the repressive institutions, including the Communist party. Their activities contribute to the democratization of these societies. In the long run, independent peace movements can generate a new state of mind along the younger generation in communist countries. Unofficial peace activities can also exert a major impact on the morale of armed forces there and encourage grass-roots criticism of official expansionist designs.

From the viewpoint of Western foreign policy, these groups represent a positive development. Their activities contribute to the democratization of Soviet-type regimes and the erosion of their militaristic ideology. If conscientious objection is eventually recognized as a basic human right in the Soviet Union and Eastern Europe, one can expect major problems for the Warsaw Pact's drafting capacity. At the same time, these movements advocate fundamental human rights whose observance would make the communist regimes significantly less dangerous for world peace.

NOTES

1. With regard to the Polish struggles for the restoration of the civil society, see Neal Ascherson, *The Polish August: The Self-Limiting Revolution* (New York: Viking Press, 1982); John Rensenbrink, *Poland Challenges a Divided World* (Baton Rouge and London: Louisiana State University Press, 1988).

2. See Adam Michnik, *Letters from Prison and Other Essays* (Berkeley: University of California Press, 1985), p. 147.

3. A term introduced by Czechoslovak dissident thinker Václav Benda in an essay written in May 1978 and published in *Palach Press Bulletin* (London, 1979).

4. See Havel's essay, "The Power of the Powerless," in Václav Havel et al., *The Power of the Powerless: Citizens Against the State in Central-Eastern Europe* (Armonk, N.Y.: M.E. Sharpe, 1985), p. 67.

5.   Quoted in "Is an 'Anti-Crisis' Pact Possible," *Radio Free Europe Research*, Polish SR/5, April 11, 1988, p. 16.

6.   For the role of dissident groups in the resurgence of the civil society see Fernando Claudin, *L'opposition dans les pays du socialisme réel* (Paris: Presses Universitaires de France, 1983); Jane Leftwich Curry, ed. *Dissent in Eastern Europe* (New York: Praeger, 1983); Rudolf L. Tőkés (ed.), *Opposition in Eastern Europe* (Baltimore and London: Johns Hopkins University Press, 1979; Ludmilla Alexeyeva, *Soviet Dissent: Contemporary Movements for National, Religious, and Human Rights* (Middletown, CT.: Wesleyan University Press, 1985); Cathy Fitzpatrick, *The Moscow Helsinki Monitors: Their Vision Their Achievement The Price They Paid May 12, 1976–May 12, 1986* (New York: Helsinki Watch Committee, 1986); Rudolf L. Tőkés (ed.), *Dissent in the USSR* (Baltimore and London: Johns Hopkins University Press, 1975); Valery Chalidze, *The Soviet Human Rights Movement* (New York: The American Jewish Committee, 1984).

7.   See T.H. Rigby and Ferenc Fehér, eds. *Political Legitimation in Communist States* (New York: St. Martin's Press, 1982); *Power and Opposition in Post-revolutionary Societies*, an international conference organized by the group *Il Manifesto* (London: Ink Links, 1979); Maria Hirszowicz, *Coercion and Control in Communist Society: The Visible Hand in a Command Economy* (New York: St. Martin's Press, 1986).

8.   See George Konrád, *Antipolitics* (San Diego: Harcourt Brace Jovanovich, 1984); for similar views, see Christa Wolf, *Cassandra: A Novel and Four Essays* (New York: Farrar Straus and Giroux, 1984).

9.   See Václav Benda, Milan Šimečka, Ivan M. Jirous, Jiři Dienstbier, Václav Havel, Ladislav Hejdánek, and Jan Šimsa, "Parallel Polis, or An Independent Society in Central and Eastern Europe: An Inquiry," with an introduction by H. Gordon Skilling, *Social Research*, Vol. 55, No. 1–2, Spring/Summer 1988, special isuue on Central and East European social research, part 2, pp. 211–246.

10.   See John Keane, *Democracy and Civil Society*, (London and New York: Verso, 1988), pp. 191–212.

11.   For the attempts to restore independent social awareness as a major variable of the political space, see the text of the platform of the Hungarian Democratic Opposition: "The Social Contract: Prerequisites for Resolving the Political Crisis," *Beszélő* (Budapest), June 1987.

12.   See *Sovetskaya Kultura*, April 9, 1988; English translation of Gelman's speech in Isaac A. Tarasulo, *Gorbachev and Glasnost: Viewpoints from the Soviet Press* (Wilmington: Scholarly Resources, 1989), pp. 303–312.

13.   See Cornelius Castoriadis, "The Gorbachev Interlude," in *New Politics*, Vol. I, No. 4 (New series), Winter 1988, p. 60; for Castoriadis' views on the militaristic regime in the Soviet Union (*stratocracy*) and its future, see "Le régime social de la Russie," in Cornelius Castoriadis, *Domaines de l'homme: Les Carrefours du labyrinthe* (Paris: Seuil, 1986), pp. 175–200.

14.   See Catherine Fitzpatrick, *Introduction*, in *From Below: Independent Peace and Environmental Movements in Eastern Europe and the USSR*, A Helsinki Watch Report, October 1987, p. 1.

15.   See Michael Waller, *Peace, Power, and Protest: Eastern Europe in the Gorbachev Era* (London: The Centre for Security and Conflict Studies, 1988), p. 23.

16.   See Vojtech Mastny, *Helsinki, Human Rights, and European Security: Analysis and Documentation* (Durham: Duke University Press, 1986).

17.   See "Excerpts From East-West Agreement on the Protection of Human Rights," *New York Times*, January 17, 1989; for the brutal repression of the mass demonstrations in Prague's Wenceslas Square, see Jiři Pehe, "The Authorities Suppress the Commemoration of Jan Palach's death," *Radio Free Europe/Czechoslovak SR/1*, January 20, 1989, pp. 13–17.

18.   See Abraham Brumberg, ed., *Poland: Genesis of a Revolution* (New York: Vintage Books, 1983); Peter Raina, *Poland 1981: Towards Social Renewal* (London: George Allen & Unwin, 1985).

19.   See Adam Michnik, "The Great Counter-Reformer," *Labour Focus on Eastern Europe*, Vol. 9, No. 2, July–October 1987, p. 23.

20.   See "Jaruzelski Interviewed" (Wojciech Jaruzelski's press conference as reported by Radio Warsaw on January 19, 1989), FBIS-Eastern Europe, January 23, 1989, p. 51.

21. See Václav Havel, "An Anatomy of Reticence," in *Crosscurrents: A Yearbook of Central European Culture*, No. 5, (Ann Arbor: University of Michigan, 1985), pp. 1–23.

22. Ibidem, p. 5.

23. Ibidem, p. 16.

24. Ibidem, p. 17.

25. Ibidem.

26. Ibidem, p. 18.

27. According to Catherine Fitzpatrick, "Were it not for support for these groups by major Western peace organizations, they (Soviet and East European independent peace groups) would have been crushed by state security agencies long ago." (See *From Below*, op. cit., p. 4) Though Fitzpatrick admits the existence of major disagreements between Eastern and Western autonomous peace movements, she tends to credit the latter with too much of a leverage on the policies of Communist authorities. If independent movements are alive in the Soviet bloc it is primarily because they address real issues and their members have heroically resisted repression, smears, and isolation.

28. See Ferenc Fehér and Agnes Heller, *Eastern Left, Western Left* (Atlantic Highlands, N.J.: Humanities Press International, 1987), pp. 161–186; for the Hungarian authors' criticism of the political philosophy of the Western anti-nuclear movement, see Ferenc Fehér and Agnes Heller, *Doomsday or Deterrence? On the Anti-Nuclear Issue* (Armonk, N.Y. and London: M.E. Sharpe, 1986).

29. See Miklós Haraszti, "The Hungarian Independent Peace Movement," in *Telos*, No. 61, Fall 1984, pp. 134–43.

30. See David R. Marples, *The Social Impact of the Chernobyl Disaster* (New York: St. Martin's Press, 1988).

31. Moscow Trust Group, "We Vote to Review Nuclear Power Programs," April 1987, quoted in *From Below*, op. cit., p. 99.

32. See "Why East and East must meet . . ." —an interview of Václav Havel, *East European Reporter*, Vol. 3, No. 2, March 1988, p. 2.

33. See Vladimir Tismaneanu, "Dissent in the Gorbachev Era," *ORBIS*, Vol. 31, No. 2, pp. 234–43.

34. See H. Gordon Skilling, "Independent Currents in Czechoslovakia," *Problems of Communism*, Vol. XXXIV, January–February 1985, pp. 32–49; on the beginning of this initiative, see H. Gordon Skilling, *Charter 77 and Human Rights in Czechoslovakia* (London: George Allen & Unwin, 1981).

35. For the major documents of the East German peace movement, see Wolfgang Büscher, Peter Wensierski and Klaus Wolschner, eds., *Friedensbewegung in der DDR* (Hattingen: Edition Transit, 1982); Eberhard Kuhrt, *Wider die Militarisierung der Gesellschaft: Friedensbewegung und Kirche in der DDR* (Melle: Verlag Ernst Knoth, 1984); for the pacifist-religious symbiosis, see Joyce Maria Mushaben, "Swords to Plowshares: The Church, the State, and the East German Peace Movement," *Studies in Comparative Communism*, No. 2, Summer 1987, pp. 123–36.

36. See "Documents of the Soviet Groups to Establish Trust Between the U.S. and the U.S.S.R.," Compiled, Translated and Edited by the Staff of the Commission on Security and Cooperation in Europe, Washington, D.C., May 22, 1984, p. 51.

37. Jaroslav Sabata, "Pour une alternative démocratique," and Jiří Dienstbier, "Je me sens solidaire de vous," (Letter to the pacifist congress in West Berlin) *L'Alternative* (Paris), No. 24, November–December 1983, pp. 19–21 and 13–15; see also, Jan Kavan and Zdena Tomin, eds., *Voices From Prague : Documents on Czechoslovakia and the Peace Movement* (London: Palach Press, 1983).

38. See *From Below*, op. cit., p. 10–11.

39. See the full text of "The Prague Appeal," in *From Below*, pp. 207–212.

40. Ibidem, p. 211.

41. See "Giving Real Life to the Helsinki Accords: A memorandum to citizens, groups, and governments of all CSCE countries," a memorandum published by the European Network for East-West Dialogue, Berlin/Vienna, November 1986, p. 2. See also *From Below*, pp. 239–58.

42. Ibidem, p. 3.

43. Ibidem, p. 11–12.

44. For the new Soviet approach to Eastern Europe and the reassessment of the "Brezhnev Doctrine," see "East-West Relations and Eastern Europe (A Soviet-American Dialogue)," *Problems of Communism*, Vol. XXXVII, No. 3–4, May–August, 1988, pp. 55–70.

45. See "Dissidents Issue Communiqué on 1956 Events," in Vladimir Tismaneanu, "Dissent in the Gorbachev Era," (Documentation), *Orbis*, Vol. 31, No. 2, Summer 1987, pp. 235–236.

46. See the interview with Jacek Szymanderski, *East European Reporter*, Vol. 2, No. 4, 1987, pp. 57.

47. See Polly Duncan, "A New Generation of Opposition: East and West Activists Convene in Poland," *Sojourners*, Vol. 16, No. 9, October 1987, p. 15.

48. See János Kis, "Can We Have a Joint Programme?" in *East European Reporter*, Vol. 2, No. 4, 1987, pp. 58–59.

49. See "Intent on Democracy: An Interview with Jacek Czaputowicz," *Sojourners*, vol. cit., p. 22.

50. Interview with Szymanderski, *East European Reporter*, op. cit.

51. See the document "Peace and Human Rights," in *East European Reporter*, op. cit., p. 58; for the Warsaw Seminar, see Janet Fleischman, "Beyond the Blocs? Peace and Freedom Hosts International Seminar in Warsaw," *Across Frontiers* (Berkeley, CA), Vol. 3, No. 4, Summer–Fall 1987, pp. 27–28.

52. See Jaroslav Sabata, "Gorbachev's Reforms and the Future of Europe (A contribution to the Budapest Seminar), *East European Reporter*, Vol. 3, No. 2, March 1988, p. 7–8.

53. See Jan Urban, "On East-West Dialogue . . . in Moscow," *East European Reporter*, op. cit., p. 9.

54. See "We want to be more than passive spectators," extracts from Charter 77's letter to the Moscow Seminar, *East European Reporter*, op. cit., pp. 9–10.

55. See Martha Henderson, "Unprecedented Moscow Meeting Tests Glasnost," *Humanitas* (a newsletter published by the International Human Rights Committee, Menlo Park, Ca.), No. 1988; for Timofeev's political and intellectual itinerary, see Vladislav Krasnov, "Lev Timofeev and Soul-searching with the Soviet Elite," *Studies in Comparative Communism*, Vol. XX, No. 3/4, Autumn/Winter 1987, pp. 253–64.

56. See "Protest Against Reprisals in East Germany," *East European Reporter*, op. cit., pp. 66–67.

57. See Barbara Donovan, "Conscientious Objection in Eastern Europe," *Radio Free Europe Research*, RAD Background Report, January 26, 1988.

58. See Miklós Haraszti, "If Eastern Europeans Object to Military Service," *The New York Times*, August 15, 1987.

59. Ibidem.

60. See "Appeal to the Vienna Follow-up Meeting of the Conference on Security and Cooperation in Europe," *East European Reporter*, op. cit., p. 66; John Tagliabue, "In East Bloc, an Expanding Network of Dissenters," *The New York Times*, March 2, 1988; Vladimir Tismaneanu, "Pacifism lives behind the Iron Curtain," *The Philadelphia Inquirer*, April 23, 1988.

61. See the text of Urban's press conference on January 19, 1988, translated in *FBIS*, Eastern Europe, January 20, 1988, pp. 22–24.

62. See Barbara von Ow, "Das Gewissen fordert sein Recht," *Süddeutsche Zeitung* (Munich), January 16, 1989.

63. See the Charter's founding declaration reprinted in H. Gordon Skilling, *Charter 77 and Human Rights in Czechoslovakia*, op. cit.

64. See Jan Kavan and Zdena Tomin, eds., *Voices from Prague: Documents on Czechoslovakia and the Peace Movement* (London: Palach Press, 1983), p. 25.

65. See "Why East and East must meet . . ." (an interview with Vaclav Havel), op. cit., p. 3.

66. See "Chapter 77 and the Copenhagen Peace Congress," *RFER*, Czechoslovak SR/14, October 22, 1986.

67. See *Neue Arbeiter Zeitung* (Vienna), April 1, 1987, apud FBIS, Eastern Europe, April 2, 1987;

for the text of the two letters, see "Charte 77: retrait des troupes et des missiles," *La Nouvelle Alternative* (Paris), No. 6, June 1987, pp. 10–11.

68. See *From Below*, p. 21.

69. See "Charter 77 Debates Its Own Philosophy," *RFER*, Czechoslovak SR, July 1, 1986, p. 13.

70. Ibidem, p. 15.

71. See Peter Martin, "Independent Peace Activity Intensifies," *RFER*, Czechoslovak SR/8, June 3, 1988, pp. 7–10.

72. Ibidem, p. 7.

73. See Jan Jozef Lipski, *KOR: A History of the Workers' Defense Committee in Poland* (Berkeley: University of California Press, 1985), p. 281.

74. See Jan Kavan, "Drawing back the Iron Curtain between East and East," *EER*, Vol. 3, No. 1, November 1987, p. 23.

75. See "A Meeting on the Polish-Czechoslovak Border: Statement of Participants," *EER*, op. cit., p. 24.

76. Ibidem.

77. See John Tagliabue, "Prague Steps Up Hard Rights Stand," *New York Times*, June 23, 1988.

78. See Jan Obrman, "Police Halt Charter 77 Peace Seminar," *Radio Free Europe*, Czechoslovak SR/1, June 28, 1988, pp. 7–8.

79. Ibidem, p. 8.

80. See Miloslav Mlynař, "Pacifists in the Present-Day World," in *Tribuna* (Prague), September 24, 1986.

81. See "Charter 77 Document: 'A Word to fellow Citizens'," *Radio Free Europe*, Czechoslovak SR/1, January 17, 1987, pp. 9–19; for a perceptive analysis of the Charter's renewal in the Gorbachev era, see Jan Kavan, "Prague's Kamikaze Icebreakers," *The Nation*, January 24, 1987, pp. 78–84.

82. See "The future depends on change from below . . . ," an interview with Petr Uhl, *EER*, op. cit., p. 42.

83. For the East German upheaval in October 1989, see Leslie Colitt, "Exodus may hasten reform" and "Opposition calls for dialogue," *Financial Times*, October 3, 1989.

84. See Robert F. Goeckel, "The Luther Anniversary in the GDR," *World Politics*, Vol. XXXVII, October 1984, No. 1, pp. 112–134.

85. For a comprehensive approach to the links between the peace movement and the cultural and political opposition in the GDR, see Karl Wilhelm Fricke, *Opposition and Widerstand in der DDR. Ein politischer Report*, (Koln: Verlag Wissenschaft und Politik, 1984).

86. See Wolfgang Büscher, Peter Wensierski, and Klaus Wolschner, *Friedensbewegung in der DDR: Texte 1978–1982* (Hattingen: Edition Transit, 1982), pp. 242–244.

87. See Roger Woods, *Opposition in the GDR Under Honecker, 1971–85: An Introduction and Documentation* (New York: St. Martin's Press, 1986); Vladimir Tismaneanu "Nascent Civil Society in the German Democratic Republic," *Problems of Communism*, March–June 1989, pp. 90–111.

88. See Emile Noiraud, "La guerre des écussons," *L'Alternative* (Paris), No. 18, September–October 1982, pp. 36–36.

89. See the text of the statement in Woods, op. cit., pp. 211–213.

90. See Eberhard Kuhrt, *Wider die Militarisierung der Gesellschaft: Friedensbewegung und Kirche in der DDR* (Melle: Verlag Ernst Knoth, 1984), p. 62.

91. See Ronald D. Asmus, "Is There a Peace Movement in the GDR," *Orbis*, Summer 1983, pp. 301–341; Emile Noiraud, "Un courant pacifiste en RDA," *L'Alternative*, No. 14, January–February 1982, pp. 51–52.

92. See *From Below*, op. cit., p. 44.

93. Ibidem, p. 47.

94. See *EER*, Vol. 2, No. 1, Spring 1986, p. 61.

95. See "To the Participants in the XII World Festival of Youth and Students in Moscow," *Across Frontiers*, Winter 1985, Vol. No. 2, quoted in *From Below*, op. cit., pp. 34–35.

96. See "Appeal to the Government of the GDR," *EER*, Vol. 2, No. 1, 1985, p. 62.

97.   See Susan Buckingham, "Freedom to think differently . . .: A report on the latest crackdown on GDR independents," *EER*, Vol. 3, No. 2, March 1988, pp. 55–57.

98.   See "Lass ihre Politik scheitern," *Der Spiegel*, No. 5, February 1, 1988, pp. 18–27.

99.   See Serge Schmemann, "A Sympathy Card on East Germany's Birthday," *The New York Times*, October 8, 1989; Mike Leary, "Police take no action," *The Philadelphia Inquirer*, October 13, 1989.

100.   See Leslie Colitt, "East Berlin's Angry Young Activists," *The Financial Times* (London), February 3, 1988.

101.   Ibidem.

102.   See E.P. Thompson, *Double Exposure* (London: The Merlin Press, 1985), p. 62.

103.   See Miklós Haraszti, "The Hungarian Independent Peace Movement," *Telos*, No. 61, Fall 1984, p. 135.

104.   See Ferenc Koszegi, "The Making of the New Peace Movement in Hungary," in Ferenc Koszegi and E.P. Thompson, *The New Hungarian Peace Movement* (London: European Nuclear Disarmament—Merlin Press, 1983), p. 13.

105.   Ibidem, p. 14.

106.   Ibidem.

107.   Ibidem, p. 15.

108.   See Miklós Haraszti, "The Hungarian Peace Movement," op. cit., p. 137.

109.   See for extensive excerpts from the Politburo document, see E.P. Thompson, *Double Exposure*, op. cit., pp. 69–72.

110.   See Miklós Haraszti, "The Hungarian Peace Movement," op. cit., p. 143.

111.   Ibidem, p. 139.

112.   See E.P. Thompson, *Double Exposure*, op. cit., p. 73.

113.   Ibidem.

114.   See the interview with Father Bulányi, in Hans Henning Paetzke, *Budapest 30 ans plus tard: Entretiens avec les animateurs de l'opposition démocratique hongroise* (Paris: Editions Joseph Clims, 1986), pp. 97–107.

115.   See "Back to basics," *The Economist* (London), July 26, 1986, p. 44.

116.   See "Situation of Conscientious Objectors Reported," (Vienna Domestic Service in German), FBIS, Eastern Europe, December 14, 1987; in 1985, the samizdat journal *Hirmondo* published an open letter by Kiszely to Cardinal Lászlo Lekáy urging him to resolve the situation of Catholic conscientious objectors "who have been imprisoned and vilified on the base of your false information."—*From Below*, op. cit., p. 59.

117.   Quoted in *From Below*, op. cit., p. 57.

118.   See Barbara von Ow, "Das Gewissen fordert sein Recht," *Süddeutsche Zeitung*, January 16, 1989.

119.   See Herbert Reed, "Hungarian Greens' Petition Austrian Parliament," *RFER*, RAD Background Report/96, July 11, 1986, p. 3.

120.   See Jackson Diehl, "Danube Plans Rile Hungarians," *The Washington Post*, December 15, 1985; for eco-politics in Hungary, see the documents published in *Across Frontiers*, Vol. 3, No. 4, Summer–Fall 1987, pp. 7–13.

121.   For impact of *Solidarity* and the militarization of Polish society in the aftermath of Jaruzelski's coup on December 13, 1981, see George Stanford, *Military Rule in Poland: The Rebuilding of Communist Power, 1981–1983* (New York: St. Martin's Press, 1986).

122.   Quoted in *From Below*, op. cit., p. 73.

123.   For the legacy of *Solidarity* and the emergence of new forms of social activism, see Bronislaw Misztal, ed., *Poland After Solidarity: Social Movements versus the State* (New Brunswick: Transaction Books, 1985).

124.   See Michal Kolodziej, "The Freedom and Peace Movement in Poland," *RFER*, Press Review/3, April 13, 1987, p. 5.

125. Ibidem, p. 6.

126. Ibidem, p. 9.

127. Ibidem, p. 10.

128. Ibidem, p. 11.

129. Ibidem.

130. Ibidem.

131. See "The Freedom and Peace Movement in Poland," op. cit., p. 15.

132. Ibidem, p. 18.

133. They also suggested that "given a situation in which two military blocs exist side by side, no proposals (should) be made if their implementation would lead to unilateral disarmament. One must take into consideration the real possibilities of arms control. In the case of the Soviet Union, where all the information is under the strict control of the authorities, this is rendered very difficult."—ibidem, p. 20; *From Below*, op. cit., p. 75.

134. See "The Peace and Freedom Movement in Poland," op. cit., p. 22.

135. See "An Open Letter from Piotr Niemczyk," *New Politics*, Vol. I, No. 4, (New Series), Winter 1988, p. 205.

136. See "The Peace and Freedom Movement in Poland," op. cit., pp. 22–23.

137. See "An Open Letter from Piotr Niemczyk," *New Politics*, op. cit., p. 207.

138. Ibidem. For an excellent collection of "Freedom and Peace" statements, see *Wolnosc i Pokoj: Documents of Poland's "Freedom and Peace Movement* (Seattle: World Without War Council, 1989).

139. See *From Below*, pp. 107–108.

140. See "Appeal to the Governments and People of the USSR and the USA," in *Documents of the Soviet Groups to Establish Trust Between the U.S. and the U.S.S.R.*, Compiled translated and edited by the Staff of the Commission on Security and Cooperation in Europe, Washington, May 22, 1984, p. 2.

141. See *From Below*, op. cit., p. 109.

142. Ibidem, pp. 110–111.

143. Activist Aleksandr Shatravka, 36, was the only member of the "Trust Group" to be tried for the group's peace activity *per se*. Shatravka was arrested in July 1982 and sentenced to three years of labor camp for circulating the "Trust Group" 's petition in a forestry work site in Siberia where he was employed as a seasonal worker.—ibidem, p. 112– 113.

144. Ibidem, pp. 124–125.

145. See the complete text of the declaration, ibidem, pp. 225–232.

146. Ibidem, p. 231.

147. See "Interview with Nikolay Khramov," *Humanitas*, no. 1, op. cit., p. 2.

148. See Bill Keller, "In Russia, Some Ideas Are Still More Equal Than Others," *The New York Times*, May 15, 1988.

149. See Brian Morton and Joanne Landy, "East European Activists Test Glasnost," *Bulletin of Atomic Scientists*, May 1988, pp. 21–26.

150. See "Interview with Miklós Haraszti," *Berkeley Journal of Sociology*, Vol. XXXI, 1986, pp. 159–160.

2

The Independent Peace Movement in the USSR

Eduard Kuznetsov

By its nature, the Soviet system strives to maintain maximum control over all the forms of activity in which citizens are involved. Sometimes the system is fairly successful at this; at other times, it is forced to make compromises. The latter usually happens during rare periods of "thaw." The reasons for "thaws" are complex, but they in no way testify to radical changes in the essence of the system. They are characterized particularly by an increase in the number of informal groups or organizations whose creation has not been officially sanctioned. The Soviet mass media now admit that groups of this kind began to appear about twenty years ago. Although there were few of them then, today Soviet newspapers acknowledge their number to be in the thousands. Most are groups of rock- and pop-music fans. Another widespread type of informal association are the sports, usually soccer, fan clubs. Then, of course, there are groups of punks and hippies. There also exist such associations as the Lyubers,[1] who propagate force and order "purging the country of bourgeois influences." To judge from indirect evidence, they enjoy the backing of the authorities; with police encouragement, they beat up punks and hippies.

Also fairly widespread are groups that protect historical monuments and the environment. The most well-known of these groups is the Moscow *Pamyat* (Memory), whose open anti-Semitism and extreme Russian chauvinism, although criticized from time to time by the Soviet press, have so far not led to any administrative, much less judicial, measures against its members. In addition, like mushrooms after rain, thousands of diverse amateur clubs have appeared; in Moscow alone there are nearly 700.

In the fairly recent past, in the rare times the Soviet press tried to explain the appearance of these informal associations, it would usually say that they had to do with the psychology of young people, their desire to be original and stand out from the crowd, and also with the poor organization of their leisure time. But since the appearance of glasnost, when calls for self-criticism have become popular, a number of Soviet journalists have suggested that the emergence of such groups is connected with serious shortcomings in Soviet society. In March 1987, for example, an article in *Pravda* speculated that the emergence of informal groups reflected the desire of some youths to isolate themselves from Soviet reality. The gap between deed and word, which became, from all indications in the Soviet press, particularly noticeable in the years of Brezhnev's rule, has, in a sense, turned off many young people from official public activity. They see too much hypocrisy in it.

It is not always easy to draw the boundary between the plethora of informal groups and the strictly dissident associations. To put it somewhat simplistically, informal groups can be said to be less interested in political issues, speak less critically about Soviet reality (or else not criticize it at all), and frequently are not as cohesive and organized as the dissident associations. As it happens, however, the repressive policy of the authorities leads to a situation in which groups that began as apolitical turn into more or less openly dissident groups.[2]

Some informal associations are undoubtedly a potential reserve for strictly dissident groups and movements like the peace movement. In this sense the evolution of the Soviet hippies is interesting. As recounted in a samizdat article, "The Ideology of Soviet Hippies: 1987,"[3] in recent years hippies in the USSR have begun to take a critical attitude toward their Western counterparts, reproaching them for "losing their revolutionary spirit," sinking into drug addiction, and having such slogans as "Better to get into mud than politics," said to denude Western hippies of their "activism and spirit of struggle." Referring to peace and disarmament issues, the document states:

> In order for a policy of disarmament to move, first and foremost what is needed is trust between West and East. As a first step we propose establishing cultural contacts between various countries, to provide the opportunity for free travel to Western countries. . . . We demand the founding of a public monitoring group that would oversee the agencies of power and the repressive apparatus.

Although as a rule the attitude of the authorities toward independent peace groups was decidedly negative, it sometimes happened that the actions of such groups did not automatically entail repressive measures. This is apparently explained by the type and intensity of their activity. For example, in June 1987 the newspaper *Komsomolskoye znamya* published, in fairly neutral tones, an excerpt of an article of an unofficial group in the Crimean city of Gurzuf. The newspaper quoted a member who confirmed the group's pacifist program. With the exception of this newspaper article, however, the Gurzuf group did not publicize its existence in any other way. This is possibly the reason for the neutral tone adopted in the official mention of it. The authorities' attitude toward active independent pacifist groups is completely different.

The status of unofficial peace groups, as a rule, is in a gray area. Although they try not to flaunt their dissident attitudes, and at times even deliberately emphasize in their statements their loyalty to the existing Soviet system, such attitudes are not alien to them. Thus the authorities view them as strictly, or at the very least, latent dissident groups. Accordingly, they do not leave them untouched by their repressive solicitiousness.

The most interesting of the informal peace groups are the Moscow Group to Establish Trust Between East and West (the Trust Group)[4] and the Dolgoprudny group Friendship and Dialogue.[5] In 1982 the Trust Group made a public announcement of its existence, but its roots go back as early as 1980, when about fifteen scientists organized seminars that met more or less regularly in various private apartments in Moscow and Dolgoprudny. At first, they mainly discussed questions of psychological testing of various segments of the population, then the range of topics grew significantly wider. In particular, one of the seminar initiators outlined the notions that became the impetus for the activization of the group and the expansion of its sphere of contacts. This person read a paper on how the complex bureaucratic system functions according to its own logic and is virtually uncontrollable even by its own formal leadership. Therefore, the bureaucratic machine should not be trusted with anything serious, much less questions of war and peace. Independently thinking people should take it upon themselves to resolve these issues, and the best way to accomplish this was through contacts between ordinary people in various countries in spite of and outside of the bureaucratic system. On this basis, after long discussion with "people from the outside" (the Muscovites Sergei Batovrin and Oleg Radzinsky and others) the Trust Group was born on June 4, 1982, at a press conference with the participation of eleven "founding fathers" and fifteen representatives of the foreign press and wire services, the Group announced its founding. The Group's first document, with an exposition of its purposes, was signed by seventy-three people.

The stream of new people, increasingly oriented toward some kind of more definite action than scientific seminars, brought the Trust Group out on the streets. The group began to make more and various peace appeals to the Soviet government and Western publics, to organize peace demonstrations and collect signatures on appeals for peace and bilateral disarmament, to pass out leaflets, put up posters, and stage hunger strikes. The hostile attitude of the authorities, primarily the KGB, to the Group's activities increased markedly; the homes of Group members were systematically searched; demonstrations were broken up with force; virtually every third seminar was closed down with the help of the police and "people in plainclothes"; the telephones of Group activists were disconnected, various provocations were staged; Group members were taken to the police station on trumped-up pretexts and sentenced to fifteen days' jail for "hooliganism" or "insubordination to law-enforcement agencies"; Group members and their relatives were intimidated and fired from their jobs, and so on.

The persecution increased—a number of activists, seven, did not escape forcible psychiatric detention, and nine people were imprisoned in concentration camps. Moreover, the activists were not officially prosecuted for peace activity; instead, charges were fabricated like "leading a parasitic life-style;" "not paying alimony"; "resisting officers," and so on.[6] As a result, the sphere of the Trust Group's activity was involuntarily enriched—it began to organize regular demonstrations in defense of its persecuted colleagues.

The extensive coverage of the Group's activity by foreign media attracted the attention of a number of peace organizations in the West, primarily in West Germany, Holland, the United States, England, and Australia, whose representatives, traveling by official invitation to the USSR, began more and more frequently to look for opportunities to make contact with the Group. Foreign radio stations that broadcast to the USSR in the languages of the Soviet peoples, including Radio Liberty, the BBC, Voices of America, German Wave, and Voice of Israel, began to air frequent and detailed reports about the Group's activity. This made the Group fairly well known inside the USSR and attracted people wishing to join it.[7] At the end of 1982, the Trust Group officially applied to the Moscow Party City Executive Committee for registration, but received an oral response that "In order to fight for peace, you don't need to register in our country."

The Trust Group's first task was to promote mutual trust between the people the people of the USSR and the USA by organizing what they called a "four-sided dialogue" between the two countries that would include on an equal basis the independent public of both countries in the dialogue of the politicians. From the moment of its inception, the precepts on which the Group's activities were based did not allow for radical changes[8], although in past years they have been enhanced by a number of new aspects. These precepts are reflected most completely in a document drafted in the beginning of 1987 with the title "Group to Establish Trust Between East and West: Declaration of Principles." The following are excerpts from this document:

Peace and Mutual Trust: . . . the reasons for the current tension in the world . . . are rooted in the lack of trust between countries and peoples. . . . [It is essential] to have the peoples of both countries come to know one another . . . eradicate in people's consciousness the stereotype of the "enemy" imposed on them, and overcome the "barricade mentality." . . . it is essential to expand contacts between ordinary people in the East and West, eliminate governmental, political, ideological, and other barriers to East-West cooperation, and jointly resolve common problems. A cardinal increase is needed in the exchange of ideas, people and information. . . .

Therefore, we are appealing to the governments of the USSR, the US and other countries of the East and West with a call to take such measures as the following. . . .

• a tourist program for inexpensive travel in the countries of the East and West;

• a program that would enable people to receive books and subscribe to journals both from the West and from the East;

• a program to exchange children between Soviet and Western families during school holidays;

• [the] exchange of hired workers;

• [the] exchange of a network of permanent cultural centers;

• television discussion between the politicians of both sides during which television viewers from West and East would have the opportunity to address questions to them over the telephone;

• clinics for joint medical practice.

• [etc.]

We see our purpose as follows:

• to break down anti-Western sentiments and to oppose the expressions of xenophobia and chauvinism in our country;

• to cooperate closely with activists in the peace movements abroad in order to overcome mistrust of the peoples of the USSR. . . .

• to oppose the growing militarism of public consciousness, first of all, the system of so-called "military-patriotic education of youth";

• . . . [to seek] the anti-militaristic raising of children. . . .

• . . . we . . . are opposed to the presence of foreign troops in foreign territories, first of all, the presence of Soviet troops in Afghanistan.

• . . . Genuine détente is possible only from below, through the growth . . . of grass-roots peace initiatives.

Human Rights and Peace: These two issues . . . are inseparably linked. It is impossible to speak about peace without also discussing human-rights issues. In the same way, it is unacceptable to be involved with the struggle for human rights while relegating to second place the problem of preserving peace. . . .

. . . The mistrust that is experienced towards a government that violates human rights is also extended towards ordinary citizens . . . we are for opposing all violations of human rights in any corner of the globe.

In our own country, we consider the following to be essential:

• irreproachable adherence to the constitutional rights and freedom of citizens;

• amnesty for all prisoners of conscience . . .;

• changes in the legislative and judicial-executive practices in the USSR with the objective of preventing opportunities for the persecution of people for their convictions;

• complete abolition of the death penalty;

• guarantee of the "right to pacifism," that is, establishment of alternative civilian service for persons who are unable, for reasons of conscience, to serve in the army;

• . . . the right to freedom of movement and choice of residence both outside one's country (unimpeded departure and return) and within one's country (the dismantling of the system of obligatory resident permits). . . .

Protection of the Environment, Problems of the Third World, and Domestic Problems: . . . The immense resources which are presently being spent on producing the newest types of weapons could be successfully applied to resolve these ecological problems.

. . . joint international programs . . . could serve as the most effective means of establishing trust in the world.

The catastrophe at the Chernobyl nuclear power station . . . forced us to re-evaluate the dangers ensuing . . . from atomic reactors used for peaceful means . . . we feel it is essential, at a minimum:

• to review all current programs of atomic energy for the purpose of adopting more effective safety measures;

• to shut down and cease construction of any new reactors of the RBMK type.

• to guarantee the accessibility of atomic energy to international oversight by both governments and publics.

• to allocate additional resources for the creation of alternative non-nuclear energy sources. . . .

Conclusion: The Trust Group is an informal association of citizens who share the above principles. It is not an organization and does not presuppose "party discipline," or strict membership, or the presence of a leader. It does not have an obligatory program of action. The degree of activity of each person is determined by himself or herself, both concerning actions taken in the framework of the Group as well as actions taken individually, by one's own desires. By the same token, the degree of responsibility the Group takes for each of its activists is determined separately in each concrete instance.

The Trust Group came together during a period of harsh repression against all varieties of opposition movement in the USSR. The Group's founders proceeded from the assumption that if the Group took on a traditionally oppositional identity, it would be crushed very rapidly. Therefore, although they understood the necessity for serious structural changes in Soviet society, they did not declare such ideas but rather the opposite. In every possible way they emphasized that the purpose of the actions was not to criticize the existing system, but rather to avoid conflicts with the authorities that would interfere with the Group's struggle for peace.[9] The Group's founders surmised that by mobilizing as broad a mass of people as possible and attracting their attention to such vital issues as the questions of war and peace, they would awaken people's interest in social problems as such and would thus encourage phenomena that could lead to significant changes in the Soviet system.

By the end of 1982, the number of people who regularly participated in various Trust Group activities grew to several dozen people. As their actions became more irritating to the authorities, repressive measures were unleashed against them. Evidently, some of the Group members who had been intimidated decided to break off into an independent group. In January 1983 five of the eleven "founding fathers," including Viktor Blok and Boris Kalyuzhny, founded the Dolgoprudny group, Friendship and Dialogue. The group's active nucleus consisted of about forty people—almost exclusively members of the intelligentsia. Friendship and Dialogue proclaimed their goal to be:

> development of human contacts between citizens of various countries, as well as the improvement of the population's political and general culture through popularizing knowledge and attracting attention to human rights by non-trivial demonstrative activity.

The Friendship and Dialogue Group's chief form of activity was conducting seminars. In this group's framework, practically every week there were seminars held by groups called Peace and Social Research as well as Historical-Philosophical Research. There were also other active groups: Round-Table Meeting Club (also known as the English Club) and the Hebrew Conversation Club (Dibur). Once in a while, Friendship and Dialogue would invite foreign guests to read papers at the seminars. The range of topics at the seminars included: ecological research and technical issues, which were of wide interest and, let us note, embarrassing for the authorities, for they covered such subjects as improving interference protection for radio sets and do-it-yourself construction of Geiger counters. There were also such topics as experimental research with "acid rain"; mathematic models of the interaction of military and civilian sectors on the reliability of several types of nuclear reactors; a study of the biological consequences of environmental pollution; and a lexicographic-semantic analysis of articles in the Soviet press.[10]

Up to about one hundred people regularly take part in Friendship and Dialogue's activities. The group maintains contacts with an analogous group in Leningrad. A similar group arose in Stavropol, but it broke up after the arrest of its leader, A. Samoylov. In the same manner, a group in Novosibirsk resembling Friendship and Dialogue was not able to launch itself.

Animosity, however, developed in relations between the Trust Group and Friendship and Dialogue. This was chiefly because in January 1983, having decided to split off and work independently, representatives of Friendship and Dialogue announced at a press conference that the independent peace movement in the USSR was not being subjected to any particular persecution by the authorities. Later, this time in 1986, Friendship and Dialogue tried once again to reintegrate with the Trust Group, but the latter rejected these attempts, fearing that various disagreements would intensify as the result of such a merger. There already were a fair number of such disputes. The problem was that a certain G. Samoylovich, one of the oldest activists of the independent peace movement, founded a sort of parallel Trust Group.

The attempts to split up and/or subject informal associations to their influence are normal tactics of the authorities in general and the KGB in particular. There are plenty of testimonies about this.[11] In the opinion of a number of the representatives of the majority of the Trust Group, an active nucleus of the Samoylovich group began at some point to realize something that the Trust Group had long feared, that the authorities would try to create a pseudo-independent peace organization. Therefore, A. Korostelev and A. Nelidova, members of the main part of the Group, appealed on December 6, 1986, through Alexander Ginzburg, a Russian émigré in Paris, "to all who receive the Trust Group's documents." The following are excerpts from this appeal:

> The KGB has conceived a major new provocation against the Group. People have been found who are interested in the splitting of the Group, that is, in its destruction. . . . These people are writing filthy, slanderous statements and signing them as the Trust Group. They hold parallel seminars. There would be nothing wrong with this if these seminars were not called Trust Groups seminars. And their level is very low. And we know that foreign peace activists, who mistakenly end up at these seminars, say that the Trust Group is completely disintegrating. . . . The real Trust Group is horribly persecuted and fights for each of its oppressed activists through demonstrations, letters and statements—as much as it is able. The pseudo-group is not harassed and does not fight for anyone. Therefore we ask you . . . to pay attention to the signatures on the Group's documents. We fear that the KGB could plant documents defaming the Group.

On December 23, 1986, at a meeting of the faction of the Trust Group in which twelve people took part, G. Samoylovich announced that such actions of the Trust Group as demonstrations, and such appeals in connection with the Chernobyl catastrophe as the proposal to provide individual Geiger counters, were unconstructive and only provoked the authorities' irritation. Samoylovich also criticized the group for not coming forth with support for a single peace initiative of the Soviet government—for example, the moratorium on nuclear testing. Then G. Samoylovich and a certain O. Sternik, who had not long prior to this meeting joined the peace movement and before the meeting in question not had any influence in it, brought to the attention of those present a statement containing the following:

1. The Group had done what it could to contribute to the creation of an atmosphere of trust between the USSR and the USA.

2. At the current stage, the struggle for trust could only be carried out on a national scale.

3. Since the Group could not operate on a national scale, it would announce its disbanding.

4.   The group revoked all statements granting persons who had left for the West the right to represent its interests.

Despite the fact that only five people signed the statement and the majority of the Group was not even informed about the meeting, on the next day, December 24, 1986, it had already been brought to the attention of Western news agencies. Thus, in the future, when speaking of the Trust Group, we will have in mind only its chief part, which remains alive and well.

With the beginning of a period of relative liberalization in the country, the Trust Group began to be more open in its statements about a number of political problems, such as the presence of Soviet troops in Afghanistan. Its sphere of activity was also enriched with the call to introduce alternative civilian service for people who could not serve in the army for reasons of conscience. This was a very dangerous appeal from the point of view of the authorities, and soon the first victims of the struggle for alternative service for conscientious objectors appeared among the Group members: Dmitry Argunov, Lev Krichevsky, and V. Filipyev. They were forcibly drafted into the army despite medical exemption from service. Krichevsky, for example, had lost 97 percent of the vision in his right eye.

The Trust Group maintains very close contacts with analogous, although less active and numerous, groups in Leningrad, Minsk, Lvov, Kiev, Kuybyshev, Novosibirsk, and Vilnius. The groups in these cities arose either as a result of preliminary personal contacts with the Moscow Trust Group or on their own, after they learned about the Trust Group's activity from foreign radio broadcasts and from samizdat materials. With the strictly oppositional movements the Trust Group had virtually no real connections.[12] On the other hand, the contacts with various youth associations have become closer—in particular, with the group called *Mukhomory*, the Toadstools. The history of this group is interesting in its own right, particularly because pacifist sentiments are fairly strong in it.

The Toadstools grew out of a group called Antaris, founded in 1975 in Moscow by Ilya Smirnov. Antaris was a pacifist and decidedly pro-Soviet group. It was made up mainly of high-school seniors and students at professional technical schools. It staged various types of demonstrations, one in front of the American Embassy, for example, in which they threw jars of ink at the embassy walls. There were about a hundred people in the group who had their own style of dress and their own banner. The activity of Antaris at times took the form of street rumbles, which provided the authorities with a reason to break up the group rapidly. In 1980, however, a number of former Antaris participants, headed by Konstantin Zvezdochetov, founded a pacifist-oriented group called the Toadstools, whose members also called themselves "Moscow Conceptualists." There are about ten to twelve people who are active members of the group, but around them there are always a lot of young people, mainly from artists' circles and from the theater world. Besides exhibits of unofficial artists and various types of events held in apartments, the Toadstools are famous for what they call "Actions." Actions are a kind of public event, a type of unique socio-psychological testing of the public. For example, one of the Toadstools' Actions consisted of enacting an execution on Serebryany Bor, a suburban Moscow beach. They brought two "convicts" under military escort, put blindfolds on them, and "executed" them in a completely realistic manner. They then carried away the "corpses." One of the people sunbathing on the beach fainted, but the absolute majority of the people reacted to the "execution" completely calmly, although with curiosity— as if this were in the normal course of events on a beach.

In 1986, Konstantin Zvezdochetov and another Toadstool activist, Sven Gundlakh, were drafted into the army, despite the fact that they had exemptions on health grounds. They were drafted after refusing a demand by the KGB to "stop their activity," and were sent to the Far East. Three months later, Zvezdochetov came down with a stomach ulcer, and then in a local newspaper an article appeared above his signature, in which he condemned his "mistakes." At the time of his recantation he weighed about 103 pounds.

Beginning in 1986, the Trust Group's activity sharply increased. It widely publicized its program and broadened its contacts with Western peace movements. Beginning in January 1987, the Group began to issue a monthly information bulletin.

For a characterization of the Group's activity, it is worth recounting, in a somewhat abbreviated form, the contents of a bulletin taken at random, No. 4, issued in April 1987:

April 4. The Krivovs' telephone is shut off. Their apartment is where the Group regularly holds its meetings.

April 5. Two Group activists, Nikolai Khramov and Alexander Rubchenko, speak in a public hall at a branch of the Central House of Architects before participants in a "Conference of the Common Cause"—a semi-official ecological, religious and philosophical club of Moscow intelligentsia. There were about 200 people in the audience. The Group's Declaration of Principles provoked great interest among those attending the meeting, and after a discussion of it, fifteen people announced their adherence to its premises.

April 7. Regular meeting at the apartment of Krivovs, a married couple. A representative of the West German Green Party from Bonn spoke about the Greens' activities.

April 10. Group members Vladimir and Zinaida Glezer emigrated from the USSR.

April 13. For the first time, direct contact is established with the Polish independent peace movement Freedom and Peace. . . . As was reported previously, the authorities refused an exit visa for Krivov to Poland in order to attend the Freedom and Peace seminar on the problems of defending peace and the environment.

April 15.   A regular meeting of the Group took place at the apartment of Grigory Yakobson. . . .

April 17.   A working meeting of the Group took place with representatives of a support group from West Germany.

April 18.   A meeting took place with a family who are members of a delegation of the Swedish Christian peace movement. . . . Problems in cooperation between West and East European independent peace movements were discussed. . . .

April 21.   A regular meeting of the Group. Representatives of a Quaker church group spoke about their activity. At the meeting, the text of a letter to the government of Yugoslavia was passed along with an Appeal to the Participants of the Freedom and Peace Warsaw Seminar.

April 24.   At 14:00, six Group activists made an attempt to visit the Yugoslav Embassy in Moscow and submit a letter by the Trust Group in defense of six Slovenian pacifists, who are threatened with lengthy prison terms for refusing to serve in the army for reasons of conscientious objection. The police obstructed their passage into the Embassy, after which all six unfurled posters saying "Legalize the Right to Pacifism!" . . . The demonstration lasted about three minutes: police reinforcements who hurried to the scene tore the posters into bits. They pushed the six demonstrators into a car and took them to the police station. Within about two and a half hours, all six were released . . . Police Captain Shamba threatened that the next time these "law-breakers" would face harsh punishment.

April 26.   On the anniversary of the Chernobyl catastrophe, the Trust Group held a demonstration with slogans: "Chernobyl Must Never Happen Again!" "We Demand Safe Nuclear Power Stations!" "We Vote for Review of the Nuclear Energy Program in the USSR!" Seven Group activists were detained on their way to the demonstration by police in various parts of the city and taken to the police station for three hours. . . . Seven other Group activists successfully staged the demonstration. It lasted for about two and a half hours. They gathered at the Lenin Library, gave an interview to Soviet and Western journalists, marched along Kalinin Prospekt in the direction of the Arbat, and collected signatures among citizens to support the Group's demands. The demonstration attracted a large number of citizens who expressed solidarity with its participants. In the course of an hour on the Arbat, the Group members collected about 230 signatures. Agents in plainclothes incited hostile attacks, interfered with the gathering of the signatures, openly intimidated and threatened the citizens, and interrupted the shooting of the scene by the American television company NBC, breaking their equipment. The demonstration was broken up by a street-cleaning machine . . . almost all the demonstrators were detained by the police for identity checks.

Thus, during April 1987, there were ten significant actions, and this month was not an exception.

In a period of relative thaw, it is difficult for the authorities—without direct orders from the highest echelons, at any rate—to take harsh measures toward a fairly large group, particularly one that is attracting increasing sympathy from ordinary people. For them, the struggle of dissidents for some of human rights is not very comprehensible, but slogans about peace, or, for example, the Chernobyl disasters hit much closer to home. What complicates the situation for the authorities even more is the fact that the Trust Group has strong support from various peace movements in the West. Moscow does not want to ruin relations with such Western groups who in their own way influence those with whom Moscow has certain political stakes. The authorities' plight is further complicated by the fact that effective persecution of the people demonstrating with slogans for peace and international trust would require inventing a plausible cover of legality for these measures while adhering to propaganda clichés.

Gradually, representatives of Western peace organizations began to change their positions. Previously, they had spoken only against the policies of their own governments and the United States. During the first years of contact with the Trust Group, they reacted to any hint of a critical relationship on the part of Trust Group representatives toward the Soviet government with surprise and even animosity. They called on their interlocutors to "fight for peace and nothing else," and "not to take too fault-finding an attitude towards the Soviet government, since the main thing was that it also fought for peace." With the passage of time, some Western peace organizations became convinced that the persecution of the unofficial peace movement in the USSR was not an invention and took an increasingly critical attitude toward Moscow.[13]

How Western peace activists who travel to the USSR gradually came to see the true face of the Soviet system is best illustrated by a concrete example. From June 15 through July 8, 1987, there was a "Soviet-American Walk for Peace" along the route from Leningrad to Moscow. The American participants in the march supposed that, just as in their march from California to Washington, they would meet with ordinary people without obstruction. The march did not, however, take place on foot, but in buses, and the marchers only managed to communicate with official "representatives of Soviet society." Seven Trust Group activists tried to join the march, but they were detained by the police. Only one independent peace activist, Andrei Mironov, displayed resourcefulness and managed to hook up with the march—but seizing a moment when the Americans were not nearby, the police abducted him, put him on a plane, and sent him to Moscow. Only when the marchers arrived in Moscow did the Trust Group members succeed in making contact with them. "When we told them how all of this looks from the side," writes Irina Krivova in an article "Where Is Their True Face?"[14] "they couldn't understand how to put together the external charm of the Soviet marchers with what we were telling them about the Soviets."

Nevertheless, the Americans remained firm and insisted that the Soviet authorities permit the holding of an official meeting with representatives of the Trust Group on July 7, 1987. This took place in a conference hall at the Solnechny campgrounds. The Group brought eighteen people. It was virtually a press conference, at which representatives of the Group tried to talk about their activities and answer questions from American participants in the march. They only "tried to" because the "representatives of Soviet society" kept interrupting them by stamping their feet, whistling and shouting remarks like "You're criminals!" "Hooligans!" "Reaganites!" During the break, the leader of the Soviet side of the march—a certain Filin—swooped down on the Group representatives with coarse, uncensored swear words and threats.

"And this is the very same Filin," writes Irina Krivova, "whom the Americans came to love so and saw in him the incarnation of the friendly Soviet people. . . ."

Before we left [Krivov writes] the Americans once again surrounded us. There were no exclamations, as before, but strong handshakes and saddened eyes:

"Hang in there! You're great! But the Soviet marchers? . . . But during the whole walk they were so friendly, so caring. What was happening the whole time? And where are their true faces?"

What could we answer? For we do not even know if they even have a face at all.

Beginning in 1987, the authorities were forced to make formal contact with representatives of the Trust Group, which virtually constitutes if not a form of legalization for the Group, at least recognition of the difficulties in which the authorities found themselves. In May 1987, at the insistence of Western peace activists, Irina Krivova was permitted to represent the Group in speeches at the Fourth International Meeting Dialogue in Moscow. Soviet authorities viewed this concession as a shameful defeat, and at the first opportunity they will undoubtedly try to recoup their loss. The most indicative example of this occurred when five Trust Group activists were invited to the Sixth END (European Nuclear Disarmament) Convention in Coventry, England. OVIR, the Soviet Visas and Registration Office, refused to give the activists permission to go, stating that petitions for such a trip had to come from the Soviet Committee for the Defense of Peace (SCDP). Since the organizers of the END Convention had stated that the SCDP could take part in the conference only if independent peace movement representatives also could come, the SCDP was forced to negotiate with the Trust Group. In the course of these negotiations, however, the SCDP put forth a number of unacceptable conditions, in particular that the Group must support the position of the SCDP in everything and condemn the doctrine of nuclear deterrence, condemn SDI, and so on; and that it must submit in writing detailed information about its activities in all the years of its existence, and agreed to have only one representative go to England. Although the Trust Group agreed to have only one representative, Yury Kiselyov, go to Coventry, they rejected the rest of these demands.

Meanwhile, articles began to appear in the Soviet press about how the Trust Group had announced its disbanding during the previous year. And on July 13, 1987, there was a TASS dispatch stating that the Trust Group had split into several factions and an agreement with one of these factions had been reached about including its representative in the SCDP delegation to the END Convention in Coventry. The representative upon whom the solicitious attention of the SCDP alighted turned out to be Olga Sternik—the same Sternik who was one of the initiators of the statement about the Trust Group. At the conference, speaking in unison with the official Soviet delegation and not saying a word about the independent organizers, she stated that next time no official delegations from the East block should be invited.

In connection with this, on July 13 the Trust Group wrote a letter to the END Convention in Coventry:

> At the present time the Trust Group is stronger than ever before; it is putting out a monthly bulletin, it is conducting great cultural and ideological work, and has grown in number. There can be no question of any weakening or any splitting. The Trust Group unanimously elected Yury Kiselyov as its representative for the convention. There is no other representative from the Group and there cannot be one. Any other person calling himself a Group representative is a provocateur and liar and is pursuing a goal of causing harm to the Trust Group and the world-wide peace movement as a whole.

Various charges against the Trust Group appear in the press from time to time, and the authorities are not averse to spreading rumors slandering the participants of the international peace movement in the USSR. The most common assertion is that people wishing to obtain permission to emigrate are exploiting the pacifist movement. Since, in the course of the last two decades, the concept of emigration is almost automatically associated with the label "Jewish" in the mind of the average Soviet Union citizen, it is evident that one of the goals of such a charge is to play on the anti-Semitism of a certain part of the Soviet population, and in general give the mass reader the impression that the independent peace movement in the USSR is made up only of Jews. This is not true, although it is true that among the members of the movement there are quite a few people who have been seeking exit permits from the Soviet Union for quite a long time. It is also fair to say that a significant number of the peace movement activists have emigrated, although far from all of them did so willingly; some were forced to emigrate in order not to wind up in a concentration camp or a special psychiatric hospital. There are also those who refuse emigration, despite the fact that the authorities pressure them to leave. Logically, it is true that there are others who joined the movement with the hope that by taking part in a cause for which at least for now it is not easy to jail someone, they can force the authorities to permit them to emigrate. In a country where the problem of emigration is so acute, people will naturally use various techniques in order to leave. But that does not define the image of the independent peace movement in the USSR. In general, the desire to emigrate does not deprive anyone of his or her right to take part in any movement and even more so, cannot compromise any movement.

It is all the more strange then that recently a number of Western peace organizations have also seized on this charge. Very likely this is explained by the fact that they have become disenchanted by the activists of the independent peace movement who emigrated to the West. Some interesting notions in this regard are contained in the June 1987 issue of the Trust Group's information bulletin *Day by Day*, where there is an article by Group activist Aleksei Myasnikov, "Without Trust We Cannot Survive (on the Memorandum of C. Fitzpatrick)."[15]

> Some of the Western peace activists complain that Trust Group members who wind up in the West join up with the "right-wingers". . . . What does "right-wingers" mean? Western peace activists call "right-wingers" adherents of the strategy of nuclear deterrence or disarmament on the basis of parity. But what do the "left-wingers" propose—unilateral disarmament? . . . The success of pacifism in one of the superpowers could lead to a heavy defeat. The destruction of the balance of deterring forces and unilateral disarmament will not bring us closer, but farther from universal peace.

Until recently, the authorities' policy toward the independent peace movement was dominated by silence about the movement's existence combined with attempts to crush it with repressive measures. Recently there has been a clear activization of the authorities' efforts to place at least part of the movement under their control using a more sophisticated approach: Articles appear about the unofficial peace movement's activities, but these are as a rule slanderous and vociferous. These methods are accompanied by the same repressive measures as before. That the unofficial groups alarm the authorities is illustrated by recent proposals in the Soviet press to create in each district and regional Komsomol committee special departments for monitoring the activities of informal groups. In July 1987, an organization affiliated with the Soviet Committee for the Defense of Peace was created to protect the environment, using the name Green Peace—apparently with the hope of seizing part of the initiative from the unofficial peace movement.

Judging from information coming out of the USSR, the independent peace movement is gaining more and more adherents. Now and then news appears about previously unknown groups. For example, information appeared that on

September 20, 1987, a demonstration of local pacifists took place in Lvov—about thirty people came out on the streets with the slogans "Peace, Freedom," and "USSR—America: Nuclear Disarmament." In Moscow in October 1986, a religious group called Fellowship and Dialogue announced its formation of a movement to create an all-union society of religious believers to fight for peace.

It is hard to guess what kind of future the independent peace movement in the USSR has, since the future depends not so much on the dynamics of the movement as on the general situation in the country. The fate of the movement and of its active participants will depend on *how* the "thaw" period ends. But for as long as "thaw" has not yet been replaced by "Siberian frosts," it can be supposed that such a dynamic element as the Trust Group will gather more strength, some of it from the growing interest of a number of apolitical informal groups in social problems. The paradox, however, is that the more varied and numerous the ranks of movement members, the narrower the field for tactical maneuvers by its leaders, and the more insurmountable the forces and circumstances that will push it to greater politicization. These tendencies are already emerging. Thus, it becomes more likely that the authorities will resort to decisive repressive measures. Because, Glasnost or no glasnost, the Soviet system can hardly reconcile itself to something that threatens to become a real oppositional force; under fortuitous circumstances, this is what the independent peace movement could become.

NOTES

1. "Lyubery" are named after the suburban Moscow town of Lyubertsy, where this type of group first emerged.
2. Thus, for example, was the case with the Georgian rock group Phantom. It arose in 1984 and was almost indistinguishable from other groups of its type. But because some of its members began to participate in the activity of the Georgian Helsinki Group, a series of repressive actions were unleashed against Phantom. As a result, it acquired the nature of a "dissident organization."
3. A type of programmatic document that is signed "Initiative Group of Hippies of Moscow, Kiev, Lvov, and others cities of the USSR."
4. Until 1986, it was called the Group to Establish Trust Between the USSR and the USA.
5. Dolgoprudny is a suburb of Moscow where several scientific research institutions are located.
6. With the exception of the case of Alexander Shatravka who was tried for collecting signatures to one of the Group's documents.
7. Since the Group's various publications are of the samizdat-type and, consequently, are distributed primarily among trusted people and acquaintances, and since the Group had no opportunity to inform a wider circle in advance of its actions, it was not so easy for a person outside the circle to get into contact with it. For example, for his involvement Sergei Svetushkin, a future activist of the Group, sentenced to six months' imprisonment, took more than a year to finally make contact with the Trust Group.
8. As distinct from the practical interpretation of these precepts, which, in the glasnost period,

has the tendency to become politicized and to become more critical with regard to various aspects of the Soviet system and its policies.

9. For reasons unknown to us, in one of their letters to Alexander Ginzburg (written in approximately December 1986), Viktor Blok and Boris Kalyuzhny, who had emigrated to the West, emphasized that the Trust Group was a political group from the very beginning. This assertion is in no way proved by them and is decisively rejected by other participants in the peace movement in the USSR and is not confirmed by any documentation. See for example, a document by the Group such as "Letter to the Canberra Peace-Makers," (1987) where, in particular, they say: "From the moment of our founding . . . our movement has refrained . . . from criticism of both the movement and other public organizations."

10. An account of one of the seminars by Viktor Blok in an interview (with M. Nazarov, Italy, 1987) gives an idea of their level. "In analyzing the tone of Soviet newspaper articles, we discovered that the sharpness in the tone with regard to tension in one region, for example, in the Middle East, in a strange manner would be carried over to covering events in other parts of the world, for example, in China. The same expressions would be repeated, such as "sharks of imperialism" and so on. We explained this repetition by the fact that the people responsible for writing such articles receive general information at some sort of meetings, where they are pumped up, and the level of tension connected with some region of the globe is unwittingly transferred to the perception of situations in other regions."

11. One of the characteristic accounts can be found in an article by Sergei Grigoryants, the editor of the independent information bulletin *Glasnost*, "Public Political Clubs in the USSR" (see *Russkaya mysl*, September 9, 1987, Paris). Grigoryants writes how the KGB proposed to one young man that he join an informal group and gave him the following task: 'We don't need any information about the group, we have enough of our own people in it already, but you will say what we advise you to say in the meetings.' "

12. But judging, for example, from the materials of such a reliable source as *Glasnost* (nos. 2–4, June 1987, Moscow), recently a number of Trust Group members are undertaking joint actions with dissidents—in particular, signing various statements which do not have an immediate relevance to the peace movement. Despite all this it is difficult to understand if this is a programmatic reorientation of the entire Group or only the individual initiative of specific members.

13. Of course a number of other factors played a role in this, such as the repeated exposure of Soviet agents manipulating a number of Western peace organizations, and of course, the refusal of the USSR to withdraw from Afghanistan.

14. Trust Group information bulletin *Day by Day*, July 1987, no. 7.

15. The article is an answer to a letter in May 1987 to the Trust Group by the American pacifist C. Fitzpatrick. Although it is addressed to the Group, entitled "Answering the Hard Questions," was distributed, however, as a memorandum among peace organizations in various countries. In this letter C. Fitzpatrick summarizes various rumors and accusations concerning the Trust Group members.

3

The Beginnings of Civil Society: The Independent Peace Movement and the Danube Movement in Hungary

Miklós Haraszti

Introduction: What Has Happened Since Their Demise

At the time of this account, the spring of 1988, Hungarian society is showing signs of increased political activity. A short description of the current situation should clarify the paradoxical relationship of the previous decade's limited movements to politics and the main characteristic of the evolving civil society—that is, political activity free from the dictates of the party.

An observer might have gotten the impression in 1987 that a great number of independent political initiatives were being undertaken in several areas all at once. Indeed, 1987 was the first year in which the sheer number of initiatives seemed to provide a guarantee that administrative measures, including police action, could not crush all of them. Those in power could check this tendency only by openly declaring war on society. This does not mean, of course, that from now on revolutionary change is inevitable, especially not in post-1956 Hungary. But for society, the crossing of this quantitative dividing line was the essential objective of the 1980s; for the party-state, the greatest fear. Now begins a new era in which the myth of the party-state's omnipotence will be dispelled and society will experience its own strength.

The Age of Alliances, the publication of one of the characteristic initiatives of our time, the club movement, is a representative product of the new era. Published by a group that is officially an institution's youth club, using printing facilities provided by the American Soros Foundation and paper obtained in all sorts of ingenious ways, the journal is available to other clubs as well. The host institution interferes with the club's activities only when concrete instructions come from the political authorities or from the police. While the journal's articles express moderate views, they show no sign of self-censorship. They explain that the club's primary interests are democracy in Hungary and the plight of the

Hungarian minorities in neighboring countries. They also report that they face bans and administrative sabotage and that their forums of debate are open to functionaries of the Communist Youth League's Central Committee and activists of the opposition. The list of subjects reads like the table of contents in some samizdat publication. It includes all the important issues of the independent initiatives—from the protection of the environment to the protest against the new tax law, from the plight of the Transylvanian refugees to the expectations concerning the National Assembly. At the end of 1987, a Council of Clubs was elected to coordinate the activities of about thirty similar such clubs.

This rather unexpected grass-roots acceptance of the opposition's themes was one of the novelties of 1987; the other was the emergence of openly political reform programs advanced by groups of eminent intellectuals.

The economists published "Reform and Change," the journalists published "The Reform of Public Forums," the party intelligentsia of the Pozsgay circle circulated politology professor Mihály Bihari's reform proposals, and, finally, at the meeting at Lakitelek the populist writers lined up their followers and tried to establish a bridge to Imre Pozsgay, the Patriotic People's Front, and thus to legality. The Hungarian Democratic Forum, the shared pulpit of these groups, was set up with the help of this last-named connection. However, at its first public session at the Jurta theater, since it was impossible to exclude the opposition from the Forum's work, the party members, at the order of the party, had to leave the organization.

In the context of this list the political program of the democratic opposition, *Beszélö*, is barely more than one voice among many. Its manifesto, "Social Contract," proposes a limited reign of the party along the lines of a constitutional monarchy, as an intermediate step toward overcoming the political crisis. This program, as in all likelihood all the others, has practical importance only inasmuch as it popularizes the new mode of conduct: the public demand for radical reforms within the one-party system.

The significance of this change is not diminished by the fact that the increased daring on the one side and the growing indecision of the party on the other were fueled by the open struggle for succession to the aging Kádár's post. Indeed, the growing courage of the intelligentsia is an irreversible process caused primarily by the fact that Kádárism had gone bankrupt, with or without Kádár's departure.

Two of the pillars of Kádárism collapsed at the same time: First, the party was forced to acknowledge that the time of growing prosperity was over and that for an indeterminate period the standard of living would fall. The Hungarian regime is now threatened with the same debt-crisis known to the public from the Polish example. The other strength of Kádárism, which was also based on a comparison with the neighboring communist systems, was its relative liberalism. But recently, both the news of Gorbachev's campaign of glasnost and the worsening economic situation have induced the intelligentsia to be more bold in its demands for reform and for the party to be less resistant to those steps. In terms of liberalism,

Hungary is comparable only to Poland; but public opinion is no longer satisfied by this. It demands more.

Everyone is demanding legal rights instead of case-by-case concessions and guarantees instead of the unwritten law of customs. Moreover, many people do this in public. The criticism and demands focus on four primary areas: economic reforms, the right to assembly, freedom of the press, and parliamentarism.

Organizations of self-protection like the National Union of Small Businessmen and the Alliance of Large Families, and village plebiscites which restore local self-government seem almost harmless compared to initiatives that openly criticize the political system, such as the Union of Academic Workers. This organization rejects the government's policy on science and leaves it up to its members' vote whether or not to remain in the official trade union.

The latest development is the emergence of clubs, circles, and organizations with discernible ideological identities. The Bajcsy-Zsilinsky Circle evokes the former Small-holders' Party, the Péter Veres Circle, the National Peasant Party; the circle around the periodical *Valóság*, which is headed by Rezsö Nyers, evokes the Social Democratic Party.

A Warning: The New Era Might Be Long as Well

In the last two years the fences of fear have collapsed in a spectacular manner. However, although it is the beginning of a healthy evolution, this breakthrough is still far from freeing society from the party-state's grip of power. Civil society has not yet been born, if we mean by this term the existence of nonofficial institutions that convincingly represent ideologies, interests, and autonomies and juxtapose their massive presence to the legitimacy of the party-state.

Although the fear of initiatives and independent action dissolved, it did so only within a segment of the intelligentsia, professionals, and young people. The former philosophy of the intelligentsia—"Careful with actions, because it could only get worse"—has now lost its validity.

Although the change in the intelligentsia's attitude was motivated by the change in the mood of society as a whole, in the case of other important strata, e.g., industrial workers, it is still only their contentment that has dissipated. And it is not certain that the fear that "it could only get worse" has gone with it. People live in a state of schizophrenia. At informal places they openly criticize the regime and feed on the new sensation of openly expressed hopelessness. At the same time they perceive both action and protest as hopeless. For the time being, the other component of post-1956 psychology, which has been passed on from one generation to another as the lesson of the great defeat, still steadily and forcefully exerts its influence: the fear of political authorities. It is now clear that behind the relative prosperity and freedom the real force of depoliticization was fear.

When the limited movements emerged in the early and mid-eighties, every initiative had to articulate its relationship to this fear before it could start to address its own specific issues. "Is it worthwhile at all?"—was the primary question.

The Evolution of Youth Movements: A Pure Paradigm

The pre-"Dialogue," failed attempts to form an independent youth organization represent an edifying paradigm. Such attempts were seldom made, and manipulation, blackmail, and brute coercion always forced the participants to retreat. Still, there was some gradual progress as to the sort of limits within which the initiators imagined their own independence.

The first such attempt took place within the Communist Youth League. This was not only because the participants were afraid to challenge the League's monopoly; the neo-Marxist illusions of the sixties also played a role. As a delayed reaction to the Western student movements of the previous year, in 1969 the students of the Philosophy Faculty and the Economic University got as far as the convocation of a "General Assembly," and passed a resolution calling for 51 percent student participation in the University Council. On the first afternoon of the assembly the police simply moved into the building and tore down the bulletin boards. On the following day the assembly was not allowed to convene.

Twelve years later, in November 1981, students in the humanities were trying to organize an independent body of student representatives. It was evident that such an undertaking would have been hopeless within the Communist Youth League, although they could have known nothing of the failure of the 1969 attempt. This effort led to a series of meetings—camouflaged as negotiations—to discourage the participants. The organizers simply got tired of receiving broken promises, barely masked threats, and refusals to provide public forums. The idea that they could organize themselves without official permission did not even cross their minds.

"Dialogue" was born in the following year. The first independent youth movement came into being, however, in a roundabout fashion, since the organizers originally set a completely different objective. They chose a direction that the establishment could not officially condemn: they joined the peace movement. By using the regime's own propaganda, for a while they imposed their existence on the officially sanctioned peace movement. In the end their movement was terminated by police force, but even then the participants did not deviate from the original, "loyal" interpretation of their movement.

The recent initiative of the Union of Youth Democrats (FIDESZ) provides a happy ending to the paradigm. After so many failed "loyal" initiatives of the post-Stalinist era, FIDESZ wants simply and without any disguise to be the Union of Young Democrats, a rival of the Communist Youth League. Nothing is a more certain signal that a new era has begun than the fact that, in spite of police warnings that their existence is illegal, the founders of the union, referring to their constitutional rights, keep holding their assemblies and the popularity of the union continues to grow.

The First Independent Youth Movement:
The "Dialogue" Peace Group.

The proposal—"Let us organize an independent peace demonstration"—was put forth in November 1981 at a session of the Budapest Student Parliament. The proponents of the idea turned directly to the police to obtain a route; they were, of course, sent back to the Communist League and the Peace Council. But the activists had already become fired up by the fact that although the authorities tried to dissuade them they did not punish them. They started to study the peace movements of the West, which are lavishly praised in the Hungarian press, and began to correspond with them. For their first discussion the participants met at a private apartment and in July 1982, as private individuals, they showed up at the END (European Nuclear Disarmament) convention in Brussels.

Foreign recognition greatly contributed to the fact that they developed beyond correspondence; in September 1982 they registered themselves as an organization. The members sensed the confusion being caused by their activity at home and were able to take advantage of it.

Their objective was to receive official recognition while retaining their independence. Until then nobody had managed to achieve such recognition, but the peace movement appeared a suitable possible vehicle.

The government might consider it in its interest, thought the organizers, to assume the role of mediator between East and West by recognizing the Eastern imitation of the Western peace movement; in exchange it would receive guarantees from the domestic peace movement that it would not become an oppositional force. The party-state, they reasoned, even without Solidarity's example, was justifiably concerned that any independent organization might become a gathering place for forces striving for autonomy.

The support provided by the politically judicious branch of the Western peace movements, e.g., by END, which thinks in terms of all-European interests, was promising indeed. END understood that communist states would not allow the existence of independent peace movements and that the Western peace movement would remain defenseless against the criticism of the "Party of Deterrence" that believes that the movement can help only the Soviet Union while it weakens the West.

Thus a situation emerged in which both the State Peace Council and the Western peace movement could use the independent Hungarian initiative to its advantage. A complex threefold relationship which was in effect a system of subtle coercion came into existence. This leverage made possible Dialogue's survival, but not its dramatic expansion or its use of radical slogans.

Dialogue was not a unilateral movement, and in essence it repeated the official Hungarian peace slogans. At the same time, however, Dialogue insisted on its independence, internal democracy, and youthful style. In reality, Dialogue was more a rival of the official youth organization, the Communist Youth League, than of the sanctioned peace movement. In order to keep their growth inconspicuous they avoided such rebellious techniques as an independent press, flyer distribution, and mass action. They edited a typewritten bulletin for internal use which they unfailingly submitted to the Peace Council.

The expected official recognition, nevertheless, failed to come; the press was not allowed to report about the group's activity. The fact that state officials occasionally received members of Dialogue—most frequently in the presence of Western peace movements' representatives—barely amounted even to a "de facto" recognition. When the group's membership reached five hundred, the success of this youth organization with a Western orientation caused anxiety in those in power.

In March 1983 the Politburo passed a resolution about Dialogue. Afterwards, as a result of a leak, the samizdat press reported about this secret document. The flirtation with the idea of an independent peace movement came to an end. What Dialogue sensed from all these behind-the-scenes events was the launching of a press campaign against it. At the universities, high schools, and at the workplaces of the members' parents, "conversations" of intimidation took place. In the end their summer camp was overrun by the police. Four representatives of the famed Greenham Common women were expelled from the country. The authorities could not have shown in a more spectacular way that the time of hesitation was, indeed, over.

The police action immediately detached from the movement those members who had joined in the hope that it would provide them with an officially authorized sphere for autonomous activity. The movement shrank to a small group of activists and was abandoned even by those leaders who would have been capable of maintaining its international contacts. It should also be remembered that the Warsaw Pact did not install nuclear weapons in Hungary, which made the rhetoric of the primarily anti-nuclear movement somewhat abstract.

The remaining activists finally had to face a dilemma: They either had to turn into an oppositional force, at the cost of likely persecution for defying the official ban on international activities, or cease their activities. Those who preferred the former course did become soon thereafter activists with the traditional opposition, involved with human rights and samizdat.

The Danube Movement:
The Problem

After the dissolution of Dialogue it was just two years until the emergence of another single-issue movement: the protest movement against the Hungarian-

Czechoslovakian-Austrian Danube project. The potential participants were all poised to take action, including the dispersed following of Dialogue, the samizdat readers, the signers of petitions organized by the opposition, and the frustrated technocrats who had been shying away from direct participation in politics.

It had been a cliché for years in Hungary that environmental protection was needed, but it remained a cliché and nothing else. There was an Environmental Protection Office, but it was out of the question that spontaneous groups, local governments, or elected representatives come forward with their own position vis-à-vis the office, or that they could even call attention to hitherto-unrecognized problems. "The matter was discussed and resolved" was the only form in which the press mentioned ecological issues, while at the same time it extensively reported the struggles of Western environmentalists and "Green" parties. These reports, like the duplicity concerning the peace movement, only made the readers realize that nature in Hungary was also being devastated and that Western demands had their domestic equivalent here.

In 1984 János Vargha wrote an objective account in *Valóság* about the Danube dam project. He demonstrated the project's anachronism and, citing expert opinions, listed the anticipated ecological damage. A far more outspoken article ("The Great Slovak Canal"), which analyzed the project's political implications, appeared under a pseudonym in *Beszélő*. The samizdat periodical also published the secret—since it had been critical—opinion of a special committee of the Hungarian Academy of Sciences.

It is a rare moment in the life of a communist country when a gigantic fiasco can be pinpointed even before it is perpetrated. The agreement between Czechoslovakia and Hungary to transform the Danube has been in existence since 1977; probably it was not only a lack of funds, but bad conscience as well, that prevented the start of construction. The project was the brainchild of Soviet specialists in the darkest years of Stalinism, and strategic considerations may have contributed to it. Even the servile Hungarian government of the time considered the plan unacceptable and instructed its specialists to revise it, a fact proven in an issue of *Beszélő* including the minutes of a 1953 meeting. The objections put forth then by Politburo member Ernö Gerö were identical to ecologists' present objections. The project, nonetheless, remained unchanged.

According to the project, a 125-mile stretch of the Danube above Budapest would be transformed. Below Bratislava the Danube would be turned into a huge man-made lake, then it would be diverted to Czechoslovakia through a concrete canal while the original border river along an eighteen-mile stretch would become a small creek. The diverted water would be twice daily discharged onto the turbines at the Gabcikovo power station. Upon its return to the Danube the water would surge to Budapest as a fifteen-foot-high swell, except that after a seventy-five mile run it would be stopped by another power station at Nagymaros.

The length of this article would not be enough to list all anticipated damages. The deforestation of the flood zone and the annihilation of the natural habitat of thirty animal species shrinks into insignificance next to the cumulative effects of the dam's redirecting of the river's course and the creation of the swell: the biggest drinking-water resource of Europe would partially dry up and become polluted; the agriculture of the Danube basin would be left without subterranean water; Esztergom, the capital of Hungarian Catholicism, would be partially flooded; Visegrád, the historical Hungarian capital and the beautiful "Bend of the Danube" would be destroyed by the power station at Nagymaros.

In themselves, the ecological and cultural damage would be sufficient to prompt a national debate, but when the economic balance sheet is considered, the project becomes simply incomprehensible. The completed system would result in a mere 2 percent increase in energy production, at the cost of a huge capital investment that not even an economy far healthier than that of Hungary could afford.

The History of the Danube Movement

The subject of the dam was discussed in what was to be an open debate in February 1984 in a club of the Patriotic People's Front. Only one side, however, Vargha and the critical experts, accepted the invitation. The other side, the government and the water conservation agency, did not send their representatives. (This is what they have been doing ever since: They stay away from all "debates." The only difference is that since then they also ban press reports of counter-arguments.) There was enormous interest in the subject at the club, and a committee was formed then and there for the protection of the Danube.

The Danube movement emerged at a frantic pace, as if "civil society" wanted to punish the party-state for previous intimidations and make up for lost time.

The new committee called meetings at universities and professional circles. In this way information and the movement were spreading simultaneously, proving what until then neither the limited movements nor the samizdat press could prove—that is, that independent initiative could be directly effective. The saving of the Danube appears to be important to several social groups; even more significant, it is a political issue that makes open representation possible.

While the Academy of Sciences accepted that the government would treat its objections as a secret document, the Union of Architects wanted in vain to make its condemnation of the project public. This disagreement was the first precedent for an official organization of professionals to take a stand that differed from the government's.

The Danube cause mobilized professional and lay environmentalists simultaneously. The latter were a variety of groups with different backgrounds. The destruction of the Danube Bend, the diversion of the Danube to Czechoslovakia, and the demolition of Hungarian villages in that area outraged defenders of national values. The suppression of civil initiative, on the other hand, called to arms even the most cosmopolitan democrats. Economists considered the case an example of autocratic wastefulness. The Danube movement provided all these groups with a sense of the euphoria of participating in a joint action and of witnessing the birth of public opinion.

In a short time, more than ten thousand signatures were collected on the petition demanding open public debate. Before that, the opposition's most successful petition campaign—on behalf of Miklós Duray, the jailed defender of the rights of Hungarians in Slovakia—had produced a mere three hundred signatures. It goes without saying that without the moral and political example of previous actions by the opposition, the Danube petition drive could not have succeeded. But mass participation was motivated, at least in part, by the fact that the petition was not initiated by the opposition; although it asked for the revision of a government decision, it did so on the basis of professional and not political arguments.

Signatures of opposition leaders were also on the list, and afterwards, as the conflict sharpened and took on a more openly political tone, their ratio grew higher on subsequent, shrinking lists. This movement, nevertheless, was not born of laymen joining the opposition but rather of the opposition joining the laymen's cause.

Hope played the greatest role. The negative stance taken by the experts was unanimous. (Only the water-conservation lobby supported the project, and not without dissension within its ranks.) Even laymen could see that the project was harmful, and the government could neither line up arguments on its behalf nor try to refute the critical opinions. Hope did not wane even in 1984, when the government ordered a strict press ban concerning the project. This action only raised the hope that silence was necessary to give the government time to rethink the project and avoid the appearance that the new decision was made under the pressure of public opinion. But on August 15, 1985, the government broke its silence, announcing that the original project would be executed. From that time on the ban applied only to that part of public opinion that was critical of the project, while an avalanche of propaganda articles was launched in unabashed praise.

During the year of silence the government ordered an environmental study. Not only the opponents of the project, but also the official environmental experts were not invited to participate in its preparation. The government's study was prepared by the project designers, its future contractors, and water-conservation specialists. The study approved the original plan and asked for some additional funds to deal with some ecological problems, but it did not respond to the most important objections. The censors forbade the public criticism of this ecological study.

At that point the hitherto-loyal civil initiative became a protest movement. Still it was not oppositional in the Eastern European meaning of the word, which implies not simply protest but hopeless protest. This time, the ray of hope came from the belief that there would be insufficient funds for construction, since in the meantime the Hungarian government had been forced to acknowledge the economic crisis and order an overall halt in capital investments.

During this process new forms of protest were conceived and forms that had earlier been considered oppositional entered the public arsenal. Environmentalist samizdats were launched, the first among them the *News of the Danube Circle*. Its first issue published the secret opinion of the Environmental Protection Office, which had served as the reason for its director's dismissal. This expert opinion proposed the same compromise that most protesters did: Gabcikovo should be a power station of "continuous operation" and not an "apex-principle" station. This way the twice-daily swelling of the Danube would not occur, which would mark the station at Nagymaros—intended to tame the water swell—unnecessary, thus eliminating the most attacked and least economical part of the project.

While the cause of the Danube became a national passion, it also became the first real movement, an archetype of democratic pluralism as rivals of the Danube Circle within the anti-project movement. The "Blues" stepped onto the scene. They placed flyers into mailboxes in villages along the Danube. The Danube Circle rejected this method as "oppositional," just as earlier it had rejected the idea of an independent, unauthorized newspaper—although now it considers it acceptable. The flyers of the Blues were more radical in tone than the paper of the Danube Circle, although it is a valid question whether or not anonymous exhortation is an authentic form of calling for action.

Another group, the Friends of the Danube, was pushing for the compromise— the continuous operation of Gabcikovo—proposed by the experts. This group, also anonymously, considered the Danube Circle too radical because of its rejection of the project in its entirety.

In a sense the Danube movement became a forerunner of true parliamentarism. During the 1985 elections, using some procedural opportunities, the Greens, the Blues, and the opposition tried to nominate a coalition candidate. Naturally, the party quickly deflected the challenge, and no nonofficial candidate received the nomination. The openly oppositional Gáspár Miklós Tamás and Lászlo Rajk, as well as one of the leaders of the Blues, Ferenc Langmár (by now it is no longer a secret that he was a Blue), could do nothing against the crude manipulation of the election process. But the issue of the Danube probably elicited the greatest response of all their common issues at the stormy nominating meetings.

The First Lesson:
Cyclical Development

We can formulate one important lesson here: Inasmuch as we mean its tangible institutions and movements, the political civil society that began in the post-Stalinist era takes shape in cycles, through unexpected leaps; by contrast civil society, in a socioeconomic sense, evolves continuously and is hidden from the limelight. These political leaps manifest themselves in collective initiatives that simultaneously have as their objective and means of action the violation of existing rules of public behavior. Once they take place, these collective violations become public property, part of the common political experience even in those cases in which the experiment is limited to a narrow segment of society. Strangely enough, this is the case even if the experiment remains unknown and thus cannot in a practical sense become a social fact.

We already noticed a proof of this in the youth movements' history of failures: New developments do not start the learning process from scratch. In spite of this, the party-state inevitably succeeds for an extended period of time in suppressing the isolated initiatives. Such experiences hinder the spirit of experimentation and on the surface successfully throw society back into the characteristic state of post-Stalinism: passivity. This is particularly true in such countries as East Germany, Hungary, and Czechoslovakia where the first outbreaks of spontaneity—in 1953, 1956, and 1968—were brutally avenged. As opposed to the "draw" of the Polish '56, in these countries the authorities inflicted complete defeat on society, destroying the people's naive belief in the effectiveness of social action. In spite of this, even if two civil initiatives are a generation apart from each other, the new political initiative is always less naive and more prepared from the start to clash with the regime. It takes off from a higher level of independence, further from the limitations of conformity. The new initiative chooses those forms of self-legitimization that are the most removed from official ideology; that is, it moves from the concept that defines the raison d'être of society in terms of socialist salvation, closer to a concept based on the principle of a democratic constitutional state.

The cyclical evolution of political independence is, of course, related in some broad sense to increased socioeconomic autonomy; but this linkage is not by definition mandatory. Reform periods and government crises obviously favor the growth of political courage; but the leading role belongs to the process of political learning and the alleviation of fears of initiating social action.

The History of the Danube Movement II

The fighting spirit of the Danube Circle, fueled by the passing of time and the uneasy silence of the government, was dampened at once by the announcement at the end of 1985 that the project would be financed and built by Austria and paid for by electricity.

In a democracy the real scandal would have started at that moment, since the deal with Austria stripped the Hungarian government of its only argument: the minimal economic advantage the project promised. According to the contract, in payment Hungary is to supply Austria for twenty years with more electricity than the projected output of the Nagymaros station.

The deal was prepared in secrecy with Austrian companies, which had their own share of troubles. Austria had planned to build a similar hydroelectric station on the Danube at Hainburg, but because of protests had to give up the idea; thus a huge branch of industry became unneeded. The plot they then devised was most clever: Austria steers clear of constructing a dam harmful to her environment; instead, she builds it for herself in Hungary, where the Hungarian government ensures that bothersome protests will not take place. Workers do not have to be laid off, huge companies do not have to be shut down, and Austria will receive "*clean* energy."

This outrageous decision did not result in more angry protests in Hungary—just the opposite: All hope was lost. It became apparent that the most advanced, nonofficial civil movement could do nothing more toward its objective than hope for the party-state's favorable decision. When the decision was made, the fight was over.

A series of rearguard actions carried out by the professional keepers of hope, the opposition, followed. Even these rearguard battles created precedents:

The first was the attempt of 2,600 petitioners to call a plebiscite. Surprisingly the secretary of this initiative, Imre Mécs, received a reply from the Presidential Council: a decision not to discuss the petition had been made since the issue in question was a technical one. In any case, the right to petition for a plebiscite had been acknowledged.

On the domestic front everything pointed to defeat. The only ray of hope appeared on the Austrian front with the renaissance of the concept of Central Europe through the efforts of international Green solidarity and foreign public opinion.

The Danube Circle received the 1985 Right Livelihood Award, the so-called alternative Nobel Prize. With the help of the Austrian and West German Greens, the Circle organized its first press conference in a public place and not an apartment—appropriately, in the Green Tree Restaurant.

On February 8, 1986, the Danube Circle called for a silent protest on the banks of the Danube in Budapest. The Austrian Greens were expected to participate in this event, but by the time they arrived, other troubles had occurred.

The debate concerning the Circle's relationship to politics became more intense. The police summoned the organizers of the silent protest and, using threats, coerced them to cancel it. They would not offer the official press's help to announce the cancellation, so at the place of assembly, on Batthyány Square, the organizers had to ask the participants one by one to go home. In spite of this, the police attacked the leaderless groups, including the Austrian participants. It became clear that the continuation of the initiative, if there were one, would have to take the form of true oppositional politics, not against "bad decisions" but against the regime.

The last-ditch effort in this campaign was openly political: The movement took aim at Austrian domestic affairs. The alternative Nobel Prize won by the Danube Circle carried a $25,000 award, a sum that could have provided for a highly visible campaign. In principle, the Danube Circle agreed with the plan, but in the end it did not dare to purchase a full-page advertisement in *Die Presse.* The text of the proposed ad was written by myself. It aimed at reawakening the democratic conscience of the Austrians rather than only at promoting ecological considerations. After all, our only hope was that the Austro-Hungarian deal, which was extremely advantageous to Austria, would become *politically* untenable. But to the Danube Circle, since its members still had an uneasy relationship to politics, this aspect of the text might have appeared too sharp an attack on the Hungarian government.

The advertisement was eventually financed by various donations and made a great impact. The issue has been on the Austrian domestic agenda ever since; if there is still some hope, despite the commencement of construction, it can at least partially be attributed to this fact.

The Danube movement as an independent phenomenon withered away, and its place was not taken—even after Chernobyl—by any other similarly strong environmentalist movement with a similarly heterogeneous following. The Green groups, which in 1987 found shelter within various clubs and associations, in 1987 and 1988 made an attempt to legalize themselves by submitting an application to charter a national *Environmental Protection Alliance.*

According to the grapevine, János Kádár said that "In Hungary there will be no 'Green' Party." We know that the Politburo instructed the appropriate organs to reject the application—something that could have been done only by violating the law, for all necessary prerequisites had been met. When even jurists challenged the legality of this action, an *Alliance for Environmental Protection,* headed by an apparatchik, was secretly created and then announced in a putschlike manner. This "Potemkin" organization took the government's position on the issue of the Danube project without any debate.

As of today the Danube movement limits itself to expressing the general national sentiment that the country still opposes the project, and if the economic situation does not force the government to discontinue its construction, the dam will stand as a monument to dictatorial government.

The Fertile Illusion of a Middle-of-the-Road Position:
The Social Movements of Post-Stalinism

It is a paradoxical feature of the Hungarian—and most likely of every consolidated post-Stalinist—regime that while the opposition remains isolated, it actually reflects the unarticulated consensus of society, and its activities have considerable influence on the modus operandi of official institutions. Of course, the opposition makes its influence felt not with its message but with its very existence: There is a community of people committed to the voluntary transgression of "forbidden" boundaries. As a result of their transgressions, which have made these boundaries visible for the first time, the participants in official public life and the public at large may now move with more daring toward those boundaries.

This does not mean that independent political conduct found more followers: Society's major groups retained their awe of taboos. But courage in attitude has greatly increased.

A few years of samizdat publications, many human-rights petitions, and, let us add, the fact that oppositional activity was left relatively unpunished, have led to the emergence of single-issue, limited movements. Those devote part of their political energy to differentiating themselves from the opposition, an act (which for a large number of members represent a basic philosophy) that is not a mere tactical consideration. These movements draw a line between themselves and the opposition, even though their causes can get published only in the samizdat press and even though the opposition regards them with sympathy.

While the opposition's status is by definition hopeless, these movements stake everything on their legality. They are movements of criticism; therefore, if we limit out understanding of state socialism to its past—i.e., Stalinism—it is difficult to understand what is the hope of these movements. Nevertheless their founders hold to the view that if they pledge not to add to the forces of negation, narrow their focus to one single issue, and limit their methods, then the regime may accept them.

It may be remarked that the failure of our two concrete examples, Dialogue and the Danube Circle, does not necessarily disprove this chain of reasoning. It is quite possible that the opposition's influence will manifest itself in exactly this way, by facilitating the middle-of-the-road movements' acceptance by the regime.

It is easy to state that these single-issue movements, which emerge in the period of post-Stalinism and fill the space between the opposition and the party-state, are shaped by fear. It is more difficult to recognize that this difference in moral quality between the two approaches is not necessarily a negative phenomenon. The significance of these movements goes beyond the fact that they signal a ripening in the situation. They indicate the political profile of a new generation, promise new concepts in the realm of macropolitics, and anticipate moderate but steadfast efforts. It is probable that, in those countries that are either in the Soviet sphere of influence or are formidable for some other reason, a civil society will emerge in exactly such middle-of-the-road movements and ideologies—rather than in forms of complete opposition. This civil society will be led by forces other than those standing for fundamental democracy. The creativity of societies living in fear finds its expression in these movements.

Naturally, without the previous and continued efforts of the fundamental opposition, assuming that the pattern of disintegration experienced by Dialogue and the Danube Circle is not repeated, the assimilation by the system of these middle-of-the-road movements would be unavoidable. But the "excessive" success of the fundamental opposition—I refer to Solidarity—may blur the fact that middle-of-the-road civil society, the true vehicle of democratization, has not yet been formed. In the wake of possible defeat, the nostalgia for total confrontation may dissuade the opposition from providing the assistance the "middle" movements need, and thus hamper the formation of civil society. Another lesson can be learned from the Hungarian example: Without the help of the opposition, even single-issue movements that differentiate themselves from the opposition cannot come into being. This assistance is important, since political civil society can constitute itself only through concrete, one-time initiatives that take the form of leaplike events.

Phases in the Evolution of Civil Society

The incident of the phony Alliance for Environmental Protection belongs to the new era I mentioned in my introduction: The previously apolitical organizers turn to the government with a legal challenge, and they no longer argue about the Danube; rather, they debate constitutional guarantees. And the government is forced to react to civil society's pressure in a defensive, manipulative manner, since a simple "No" can no longer prevent organizational activities.

Three eras are taking shape before our very eyes. The first is called post-Stalinism. The party-state becomes more liberal: It reduces oppression to the "necessary" level; it permits a certain degree of consumption and perhaps some measures of decentralization in the economy. As for culture and ideology, while both remain controlled, the importance of directives decreases and that of taboos increases. In this era society contents itself with making use of the openings proffered by the system. The opposition remains isolated; the single-issue movements that emerge toward the end of this period—in the mold of Dialogue and the Danube Circle—move toward the center, not toward the opposition, before they become dispersed. Nonetheless, political experience accumulates even if it does not find a steady vehicle. The essential quality of this first era is the struggle against fear and the rise of independent initiatives, independent opinion, and social activity free from the party-state.

Civil society in the true meaning of the term emerges in the second phase. This phase can be called post-totalitarian, and is characterized by the presence of an authoritarian regime—inasmuch as the party-state's ideology collapses but its structure remains in place and its existence is sustained through open oppression. It is no longer a system in the true meaning of the word—in any case, not more than a system in decay, since it consists of clearly heterogeneous elements and is no longer able to reproduce itself. Democratization replaces liberalization as the central issue of politics; and while the latter was dictated by the will and timetable of the party-state, democratization takes place under the pressure of emerging public opinion. The regime is on the defensive. There is an official attempt to put the economy on a pragmatic foundation, and therefore there is a struggle against the old structure even within the establishment. Culture is no longer under strict controls, the existence of self-censorship becomes felt, and unacceptable and real censorship takes over. The life of society is characterized by legal and other battles—by conflicts in the areas of democratization of everyday life, individualism, pluralism, the principles of popular representation and minority rights. The fear of our own actions dissipates and large masses acquire the ability to accept conflict openly and also to manifest self-limitation in regard to these conflicts.

The third phase is post-communism: only a hypothesis, but an inevitable one. Having lost its rationale, the party-state must collapse in its macrostructure. True democracy emerges, which builds on the forms, energies, experiences, and pluralization that were already given shape in civil society. It is a secondary issue whether this process takes place along the lines of Juan Carlos's Spain, as an orderly transition, or through smaller or larger revolutionary shocks. It is also immaterial whether this transition occurs in the context of a European reorganization or prior to it in a more hasty manner. What is significant is that without the evolution of civil society in the preceding two phases, this transition cannot be successful.

This classification considers the Hungarian evolution as a representative model. It is not a negligible lesson that post-1956 Hungarian development represents a classical pattern regarding the central question of civil society—that is, the nature of fear and its dissipation. As a result of the total defeat in 1956, Hungarian society started from point zero; the total impact of the 1956 defeat provides proof that even after such a fierce anti-totalitarian explosion it is possible to restore the regime if the explosion was not preceded by a gradual growth of civil society. (The failure of the Prague Spring proves the same point.)

The Hungarian evolution is model forming because Kádárism did create a consensus; it consolidated post-Stalinism that was rooted in liberalization after the 1963 amnesty of political prisoners. Until the end of the seventies the regime did not even have to reckon with an opposition; afterwards, as a result of the opposition's isolation, a special transition occurred, from the tactics that had been dictated by fear to the open struggle for civil society.

As for other countries, the Yugoslav evolution is muddled by the inner division of nationalities. In Czechoslovakia, consolidation based on liberalization did not occur even after 1968; therefore, under the influence of Gorbachevism the inevitable rehabilitation of 1968 will swiftly and stormily grow into the demand for democratization and the open formation of civil society. As a result of this, in Czechoslovakia the period of conflicts and the middle-of-the-road movements that I described will be shorter. Poland deviates from the Hungarian model in the other direction: After 1956, in ideological terms, the church survived the defeat, as did the small farmers in economic terms; therefore the opposition did not partake in politics in an atmosphere of total fear but could serve as a point of crystallization. Since 1981, Poland has been at the end point of possible political evolution, in a prolonged stalemate caused by geopolitical factors. This stalemate could be broken from within if the middle-of-the-road progress of civil society were more advanced and had the strength to shatter the legal customs and modus operandi of the party-state. This breakthrough will undoubtedly take place in Poland if in one or two other countries a similar development of the authoritarian state and civil society occurs.

The case studies of Dialogue and the Danube movement are probably most useful in forecasting probable civil conduct within the Soviet Union in the era of Gorbachevism. In that country, the Stalinist oppression that lasted for decades has created psychological conditions comparable to the impact of the total Hungarian defeat. Therefore the post-Stalinist integration will, in all likelihood, be just as lasting and successful as it was in Hungary. The Soviet intelligentsia, like the Hungarian after 1956, expects improvement not from opposition, but rather, almost exclusively, from the paternal, enlightened party. For this reason the Soviet intelligentsia's adoration of post-amnesty Kádár. Another similarity is that Gorbachev, just like Kádár after 1956, attempts to raise the standard of living. The surfacing of the problem of nationalities may, however, very well thwart the realization of this pure formula and accelerate the crisis of post-Stalinism.

4

Anti-militarism and the Independent Peace Movement in Czechoslovakia

Milan Hauner

The Antecedents of the Peace Movement

In spite of its reputation for democratic traditions, no distinct pacifist move-ment developed in prewar Czechoslovakia. After rejecting the militia option based on the Swiss model, the parliament of the First Republic (1918–38) voted for a constitution that made military service compulsory for all male citizens regardless of ethnic or religious background. Refusal to perform military service was punishable with imprisonment ranging from three to twelve months.

The official ideology of the state did not provide room for genuine pacifist attitudes. Individual pacifists and Christians who took the commandments of their faith very seriously fell into conflict with state authorities and were prose-cuted without exception. The inborn anti-militaristic and anarchistic inclination of many Czechs, "Svejkianism," as identified with the novel *The Good Soldier Svejk*, written by Jaroslav Hasek in reaction to World War I, remained confined to the sphere of artistic expression rather than civic behavior. During the 1930s, in anticipation of Nazi aggression, Czechoslovakia became a heavily militarized country where objectors to conscription were treated as traitors and prosecuted accordingly. Members of the Jehovah's Witnesses eligible for military service, for instance, were subject to routine prosecution for their refusal to answer the call-up, in spite of the fact that otherwise their sect enjoyed full religious freedoms.[1]

As a moralist philosopher, T. G. Masaryk was believed to be a pacifist, but as president of the new republic he was also commander-in-chief. During World War I Masaryk approved of armed struggle for the sake of national independence, and for this purpose he organized military formations abroad among Czech and Slovak ex-prisoners-of-war, called Legions. During the First Republic, the Legionaries became the most visible symbols of the country's newly acquired militaristic tradition. Genuine pacifists were looked down upon. The International Fellowship for Reconciliation (IFOR) had a rather meager membership in Czechoslovakia, and intellectual pacifism opposing militarization and rearmament during the 1930s was weaker than in most West European states.

Among the intellectuals, if Professor Rádl, chairman of the YMCA in Prague and the founder of the Czechoslovak League for Human Rights, had been interested in creating a strong mass following, he might have become a real challenge to President Masaryk's popularity. Despite the fact that Rádl's name and legacy have fallen into oblivion, he remains an inspiration to many supporters of the semi-illegal human-rights movement in Czechoslovakia today, such as the members of Charter of 77.[2] Less well known today is Premysl Pitter, who was an active member of IFOR. He was a deeply motivated anti-militarist inspired by Tolstoy and the Bible, who was arrested and sentenced during World War I for conscientious objection to military service. After the war he founded a humanitarian organization that cared for neglected children in Prague. He continued to write articles in which he defended refusal to conscription on conscientious and religious grounds. When he was arrested and charged, Romain Rolland wrote on Pitter's behalf to President Masaryk—but to no avail.[3]

The Legacy of Anti-militarism and Communist Reality:
The Case of Conscientious Objection

The Great War of 1914–18 was a decisive watershed in European history. The pacifist movement was seriously paralyzed by the betrayal by socialist leaders, who at the outbreak of hostilities and in that atmosphere of national hysteria abandoned overnight their anti-war stand.[4]

One might have expected that after the victory over Nazi Germany pacifist ideas would have generated strong support, especially among those nations between the Elbe and the Volga, which suffered most from the war. Here, however, the territorial overlord was Stalin's Soviet Union, where "bourgeois" pacifism had no place. Although after 1945 in Czechoslovakia a special legal commission worked on amendments to military-service legislation that would have acknowledged the right of conscientious objection, this initiative was discontinued as soon as the communists established their dictatorship in 1948. Ironically, Soviet Russia had set a judicial precedent for conscientious objection to military service within socialist legal theory: A revolutionary decree of January 1919 exempted religious objectors from conscription and offered them alternative civilian service. This progressive legal provision, however, was removed in 1939, when the new Universal Military Service Law was introduced. Marshal Voroshilov, the People's Commissar for Defense, justified this by arguing that not a single request for exemption from military service on account of religious conviction had been received in 1937–38.[5]

Almost without exception the communist states of Eastern Europe have not accorded legally recognized status to conscientious objection to military service. The partial exception is the German Democratic Republic, which, under pressure from the Lutheran Church, introduced in 1964 legal provisions for unarmed, albeit still militarized, service for those conscripts who objected from "a religious standpoint or similar reasons." However, for a determined and deeply motivated conscientious objector, this is not a satisfactory solution. "Construction soldiers" *(Bausoldaten)* have to wear uniforms, swear an oath to military authorities under which they continue to serve, and participate in military construction projects.[6]

No other East European country has had legal provisions such as those in the GDR, but several have since the 1950s followed certain unpublished regulations according to which members of some religious sects, conscripted together with others termed as politically unreliable elements, have been assigned service in special unarmed military units employed in the coal mines or on road construction; in Czechoslovakia these "PTP" units are called "Black Battalions."

Indeed, one would look in vain in any of the languages of Eastern Europe for an adequate translation of the term "Conscientious Objector" (the only exception is the cumbersome German term *Wehrdienstverweigerer*); it does not appear in any works of constitutional or legal character. This omission has ideological reasons stemming from the communist doctrine of "Just War": A communist country is always conducting a just war defending itself against the aggressive onslaught of imperialism.[7]

Because they were modeled on the 1936 Stalinist Constitution of the USSR, the constitutions of practically all East European states thus stipulate the "supreme or sacred duty" as defense of the socialist fatherland.[8] The GDR Constitution of 1949 is an exception only for historical reasons. Originally, it had no provision for regular service. It was amended in 1955 after the introduction of the voluntary military service, with a relatively anodyne phrase "honorable duty"; compulsory conscription was finally introduced immediately after the construction of the Berlin Wall in 1961. The provision for universal obligatory military service derives from the duty to defend one's communist fatherland. Thus, all East European constitutions carry a clause to the effect that no one may be exempted from military obligation on the grounds of religious belief. Since "defense of the socialist fatherland" and military service have become more or less identical in the constitutional theory of the East European countries, it follows that individual resistance to war in general, or refusal to take up arms during the military service in particular, amounts to "the betrayal of socialism, of the forces of peace." It may even be twisted into "support of the enemies of peace."[9]

In contrast with all three of its Soviet-bloc neighbors, the situation of the conscientious objector in Czechoslovakia, both legally and in the public mind, is worse for reasons of ignorance. Until very recently, this indifference combined with lack of support from the churches and independent human-rights groups.

According to Article 37 of the 1960 Czechoslovak Constitution, "the defense of the country and its socialist order is the supreme duty and matter of honor for every citizen." Evasion or refusal of military service can be punished with imprisonment from six months to five years and up to fifteen years or death in a state of emergency. Although reduction in the length of military service or even deferment has occasionally been applied to special categories of workers such as miners, no exception has ever been made for genuine conscientious objectors.[10] A letter of inquiry by the London-based organization War Resisters International received a firm reply from the Czechoslovak Embassy in London, dated October 19, 1972: "No deferments are granted for religious or ethical reasons."[11] Most cases of imprisoned conscientious objectors in Czechoslovakia involve members of small religious sects such as the Jehovah's Witnesses (the most numerous among the prosecuted), Adventists, and Nazarenes.

The Soviet-led invasion of Czechoslovakia in 1968 was the largest military action in Europe since the end of the Second World War. It is therefore not surprising that official definitions of peace and socialism meet with indifference and hostility. The crushing of the "Prague Spring" and the subsequent "normalization" brought a small group of intellectuals together to establish the Charter 77 human-rights movement. Thanks largely to these courageous individuals, documented cases of conscientious objectors are more numerous today and they receive publicity both at home and abroad. These cases mostly involve students of theology. One of them was Frantisek Matula, who refused military call-up on religious grounds and was tried in December 1975 by the military court of Prague. Because in the end Matula agreed under pressure to serve in the army, he was given a relatively mild sentence of fifteen months imprisonment, suspended for three years. Fearing that the suspended sentence for conscientious objection could have established a legal precedent, the ministry of defense called on the supreme court to quash the verdict and reexamine the case. The outcome was inescapable: In June 1976 Matula's sentence was changed to two years' unsuspended imprisonment.[12]

Several similar cases followed; perhaps the best known among them has been the case of Matula's colleague from the Comenius Theological (Evangelical) Faculty in Prague, Ales Brezina, who was sentenced in 1977 to two and a half years imprisonment. Brezina was one of the first signatories of Charter 77. He was immediately suspended from his studies and faced a series of petty intimidations by the authorities. Three months later he received his call-up order, which he refused to follow. Brezina summed up the reasons for his refusal in a letter to the military authorities.

All that [list of harassments] has convinced me that the Czechoslovak People's Army does not serve the defense of a particular community, not does it protect the individual and his rights, but serves the suppression of his rights instead. I am convinced that the truth is on the side of fights for human rights, who are defending human dignity without weapons.

Brezina signed his letter with the routine official greeting "Let Peace Succeed" (*Míru zdar*), which must have sounded to military ears like a mixture of irony and defiance. In less than three weeks he was arrested. He refused to answer his interrogators, as he explained in his final speech before the military tribunal which sentenced him in June 1977 to two and a half years' imprisonment: ". . . the circumstances of my refusal to serve in the army (which itself is unimportant to me) are trivial. The really important question is: why did I refuse?"[13] In the summer of the same year, a group of young people organized a protest march in Moravia, during which they declared their solidarity with Matula, Brezina, and a few other cases of conscientious objectors; they demanded the introduction of a civilian service as an alternative to military conscription.[14]

This important episode received some publicity in Czechoslovak samizdat publications and protest songs, as well as in the Western media, so the plight of conscientious objectors was not forgotten; a few courageous priests like pastor Milos Rejchrt defended the cause when in their prayers they criticized the militarization of the society and the submissive attitude of its members.[15]

Rock Counterculture and Peace

Although only a few courageous individuals have engaged in conscientious objection, a larger audience of outsiders has also expressed their sympathies as a gesture of indirect participation. In the specific circumstances of the post-1968 repression, this function has been performed by the unofficial culture, especially as personified by rock-music bands. These include the "Jazz Section," which has been notoriously at loggerheads with the authorities, and by the independent human-rights movement as represented by Charter 77. In actual fact, if the term "movement" may be used, it should be applied to the spontaneous "Dionysian" spirit of the teenagers, intoxicated by the rhythm of rock music, rather than to the "Apollinian" minds of the inner circle of Charter 77.[16] This can be seen best in the extraordinary event of December 8, 1985.

It was the fifth anniversary of John Lennon's assassination. Several hundred Prague teenagers, mostly high-school students and apprentices, gathered under the historic Charles Bridge on a small island called Kampa, in order to commemorate the dead musician as they had done on four previous occasions. This time, however, they turned an improvised music festival into a full-blooded anti-war demonstration for "Freedom and Peace," shouting such slogans as: "When will there be peace, John?" "We want freedom!" "Give peace a chance!" "No missiles are peaceful," "Flowers, not weapons," "Scrap the army!" "Red bourgeoisie out!" "SS-20s Out!" About three hundred "Lennonists" signed a petition that must have alarmed the authorities: "We reject the stationing of any nuclear weapons on either side of Europe!" The petition was also sent to the Soviet and U.S. embassies. The police arrested and interrogated several of the spontaneous Lennonists, but all were later released and no serious persecution followed. Several months later, however, when a group of young people requested official permission to establish an organization called Young Art for Peace, supported by a petition bearing over five hundred signatures, the authorities turned it down. Several petitioners were interrogated by the police, who accused them of being "the young blood of Charter 77."[17]

The spontaneous youth demonstrations of December 1985 and the Young Art for Peace initiative during the following summer showed that young people wanted to express their feelings about war and peace outside the official channels. Their reaction also reflected their attitudes toward military service, an issue that had been discussed both domestically and internationally: Only two weeks before the Lennonist demonstration, the supreme council of the Evangelical Church of the Czech Brethren, the synod, had urged the Czechoslovak Parliament to initiate legislation leading to the introduction of an alternative civilian service for conscientious objectors.[18] Moreover, on January 24, 1986, spokesmen for the GDR independent peace movement had addressed an appeal to their government requesting the discontinuation of paramilitary education in schools and the legalization of a genuine alternative civilian service for conscientious objectors outside the military structure.[19]

Charter 77 reacted to the spontaneous youth demonstration against militarism calling it "a unique event in our capital . . . and a challenge to us all," and by issuing in March 1986 a document entitled *Space for the Younger Generation.* It urged the Czechoslovak Parliament to let young people travel abroad, to establish international summer camps, to "let them live their own life . . . and listen to their own music bands and singers." Further, the document addressed for the first time the sensitive issue of compulsory military service, suggesting that it be reduced from twenty-four to eighteen months as it is in Hungary and the GDR, and that labor service be introduced for conscientious objectors. "Society could make good use of this service without weapons," the document stated, "particularly in forestry conservation and environmental protection in general, as well as in the care of the aged and disabled."[20]

A further step in this direction was undertaken by Jan Svoboda, a Charter 77 signatory. On March 3, 1987, he addressed a long letter to the Czechoslovak Parliament that contained a comprehensive list of suggestions elaborating on some of the ideas regarding military service reform proposed by Charter 77 a year earlier. The reforms proposed that the length of compulsory conscription be reduced, that there be various legal provisions to alleviate the plight of conscripts who are the heads of households, and that there be an alternative service for conscientious objectors outside the given military structures. Jan Svoboda's call for an open nationwide discussion on compulsory military service and the army's moral struck an immediate response among young people. Within less than three weeks his petition attracted over one hundred signatures.[21]

The Charter document on Czechoslovak youth, together with Jan Svoboda's petition, constitute a qualitatively new initiative in influencing public acceptance of conscientious objection as a basic human right. Although these two initiatives are not similar to more radical actions undertaken several years earlier in the GDR, Hungary, and Poland, the more cautious Czech initiatives should nevertheless be considered part of the pressure "from below" that is spreading throughout Eastern Europe.

Following the 1987 Warsaw Seminar, Charter 77 announced the launching of a work group to "systematically deal with questions of peace and their link with human and civil rights, as well as with the demands for the observance of civic rights in the army and during military service." However, the Chartists have neither enthusiastically embraced all the anti-militarist demands unanimously endorsed in Warsaw, nor have they put forward their own, as they suggested, "more precisely formulated" proposals. Charter's only specific objection was against the article opposing military service for women, which did not seem relevant for Czechoslovak conditions. On the other hand, they felt that most of the points were "very close to us."[22]

Charter 77 and Western Peace Movements (1980–84)

Conscientious objection by individual pacifists epitomizes the anti-militarist attitude in its purest and most concrete form, and it also has broad ramifications on the noisy stage of international politics. The late 1970s and early 1980s saw the reemergence of pacifist movements in the West, first in response to plans introducing the neutron bomb into the NATO nuclear arsenal, and then against the deployment of "Euromissiles" (Pershing II and Cruise).[23] The Soviet Union retaliated by stepping up its earlier deployment of SS-20 missiles and by upgrading its other shorter-range missile systems in Central Europe.

To many observers it seemed as if the Soviets were conspicuously successful in manipulating the Western peace movements during this initial stage and seducing them to take a radical anti-U.S. and anti-government stand.[24] It would have been a serious mistake, however, to assume that Moscow had fundamentally changed its view of pacifism. Soviet officialdom made it brutally clear that no criticism of the country's own nuclear buildup was to be tolerated. Members of the independent Moscow Trust Group, created in June 1982 for the purpose of "establishing trust between the USSR and the USA," faced constant harassment and harsh persecution.[25]

While Soviet propaganda provided detailed descriptions of NATO's nuclear might and its power to obliterate mankind, no word was allowed about Soviet nuclear strategy. Pacifism was strictly for export to the West. Nuclear-disarmament activists visiting Moscow were unable to speak in public about Soviet nuclear deployment, let alone to display banners calling on the Kremlin to dismantle its missiles or to terminate its war in Afghanistan.[26]

The Marxist-Leninist doctrine holds that true peace can only be realized within the communist system and that wars are products of the class antagonisms and internal contradictions inherent in capitalist societies. It follows that the "Struggle for Peace" under Soviet leadership is an important part of international relations. The official coordinating body for Soviet peace propaganda has been for many years the World Peace Council, founded during the first Western anti-nuclear movement in the early 1950s at a time when the U.S. possessed an unchallenged superiority in nuclear weapons. The Soviets had little to lose in demanding the abolition of thermonuclear weapons.

Along with other official peace organizations like the Christian Peace Conference and the *Pacem in Terris* movement, the Soviet leadership decided to locate the headquarters of the World Peace Council in Prague, where it has been headed for many years by its indefatigable president, the Indian communist and Lenin Prize winner Romesh Chandra. Since official definitions of peace and socialism in Czechoslovakia are of necessity consciously or unconsciously associated with the Soviet-led invasion of August 1968, apathy and cynicism toward peace propaganda of all kinds have dominated the behavior of ordinary Czechoslovak citizens.

In January 1977 this vicious circle of indifference was broken by the appearance of Charter 77. The group is regarded as the most active human-rights movement in Eastern Europe—not because of its size, which is only around 1,300 signatories after ten years of existence, but because of its unusually wide range of activities. Frequently acting as the unofficial moral authority of the Czechoslovak people, Charter 77 grew out of a strong domestic need to oppose injustice. In one concrete case, persecution of two rock-music groups by authorities brought together ex-Communists, Christians of different denominations, and a variety of independent thinkers such as the famous Czech playwright Václav Havel and the leading Czech philosopher Jan Patocka. The major external factor which stimulated Charter 77 was undoubtedly the signing of the Helsinki Final Act on "Security and Cooperation in Europe" by thirty-five governments. The act's importance for Soviet-controlled Eastern Europe has never been fully appreciated in the West; it meant the public acknowledgment of the official commitment of the East European and Soviet governments to internationally accepted standards and norms of human rights. In admitting that human rights and peace were inseparable, the communist leaders unwittingly legitimized independent civic initiatives from below.

Three additional major events followed the Helsinki Final Act and the formation of Charter 77. First, there was the emergence of the Solidarity movement in Poland with its ten-million membership. There had been nothing like it before, and probably shall never be again.[27] Second was the emergence of the Western peace movement, which was to exercise a very strong influence upon the independent social and cultural movements in Eastern Europe. Finally, the nuclear disaster at Chernobyl took place in April–May 1986, with its still incalculable consequences for the morale and future behavior of the East Europeans.

Given the intensity of the Western peace movement, a number of observers wondered at the relative delay with which Charter 77 reacted to the new wave of anti-nuclear pacifism just across the border. It was almost as if Charter 77 viewed the issue of war and peace as a somewhat profane diversion from the concern for human rights and basic freedoms.

Although individual Chartists condemned the 1968 military invasion as illegal and demanded the withdrawal of Soviet troops from Czechoslovak territory, Charter documents usually failed to do so in the late seventies (e.g., in 1977 on the anniversary of the invasion). However, on the decennial Charter spokesmen denounced 1968 as contrary to the Helsinki provisions and questioned the legitimacy of the continuing presence of Soviet troops in Czechoslovakia.[28]

Historians are often uncomfortable if they cannot establish the beginning and end of a chronological chain of cause-and-effect relationships. Since we are to relate the Western peace movements with the independent human-rights activities inside Czechoslovakia, we ought to ask ourselves: Who inspired whom, and when? In my view, however, it is not important to establish which side was the prime mover. As Vilem Precan and H. Gordon Skilling, the two most scrupulous chroniclers of Charter 77 activities, have rightly observed, it was the opening of the second Conference on Security and Cooperation in Europe (CSCE) in Madrid during 1980 that provided Charter 77 with a stimulus to appeal to the Czechoslovak government to honor its obligations under the Helsinki accords.[29] In September 1980, Charter 77 spokesman transmitted a letter to the President of the Republic, Gustav Husák, in which they expressed hopes that the Czechoslovak delegation at the CSCE meeting in Madrid would not only press for the reduction of armaments but for the promotion of human rights, especially in his own country, as well.[30]

Had he taken the issue of human rights less cynically, President Husák, being himself a former political prisoner,[31] might have found the Charter letter discomforting. It urged him to cancel the unjust jail sentences imposed on the leading Chartists and "VONS" members[32] Otta Bednárová, Václav Benda, Jiří Dienstbier, Václav Havel, Jaroslav Sabata, Petr Uhl, and others, and to terminate criminal proceedings against Rudolf Battek and others. The letter also urged that the signatory states agree at Madrid to "legitimize and to support the citizen-initiative groups," in order to monitor each signatory's human rights record.[33] Moreover, shortly thereafter, Benda, Dienstbier, and Havel, who had been confined to the same prison, were able to smuggle out a letter addressed directly to the delegates in Madrid, in which they demanded that, as a signatory, Czechoslovakia should observe and implement the Helsinki Final Act and the international human-rights convenants which explicitly forbid imprisonment and other forms of persecution for the defense of fundamental human rights.[34]

Still, "peace" did not figure as the principal demand in Charter 77 documents of that time; rather, it is made conditional to the pursuit of freedom. The Chartists believed that there was not a perfect legal framework for this provided by the Helsinki Final Act, and incorporating the two International Convenants on Political/Civil Rights and Economic/Social/Cultural Rights, all of which were officially endorsed by the Czechoslovak legislation in 1976; hence the main argument in Charter 77 documents that peace and freedom must be considered indivisible. This central argument was already present in the first Charter 77 statement on West European peace movements of November 15, 1981, addressed to Czechoslovak authorities (i.e., Federal Assembly, Government Presidium, Office of the President, Czech Peace Council, Christian Peace Conference, and *Pacem in Terris*):[35]

> The Helsinki document is quite unequivocal in including explicitly as an equal component within the framework of indivisibility respect for human rights without which a policy for peace worthy of the name is unthinkable. The connection is mutual and works both ways. One can hardly believe in the sincerity of peace efforts where people are persecuted for demanding that the undertakings of detente policy in the area of human rights and basic freedoms should be carried out. . . .

In their second document of March 29, 1982, conceived as an "open letter" to Western peace movements, the theme of the indivisibility of peace and freedom was stressed yet again. Although the three spokespersons, Radim Palous, Anna Marvanová and Ladislav Lis, wished to reassure Western readers that they appreciated "the gravity of the international situation and the importance of peace efforts of ordinary citizens," they made a special effort to remind them of the abortive Western appeasement efforts during the 1930s which culminated in the Munich Agreement of September 1938, when "Daladier and Chamberlain gave way under pressure to Hitler and Mussolini, permitting a further expansion of the totalitarian regimes and contributing thereby to the outbreak of the Second World War—all in the name of safeguarding peace in Europe as they claimed. . . ."[36] This warning can also be seen as a safety device against "the naive demand of those who wished to protect life at all cost, regardless of human responsibility to the values which surpass life itself." The Chartists concluded their appeal with a call for "unofficial action by ordinary citizens," both in the East and the West, in order to extricate the pursuit of peace from manipulation and supervision of state authorities; they stated that they would welcome further meetings to exchange views with representatives of peace movements of different countries.[37]

In August 1982, on the fourteenth anniversary of the Soviet invasion of Czechoslovakia, the Chartists issued a statement in which they declared that "the right to live in peace is a fundamental human right" and demanded the departure of Soviet occupation troops from the Czechoslovak territory, as proof of credibility for current Soviet peace proposals.[38]

More letters from Charter 77 to peace movements abroad were to follow between 1982 and 1984: to groups in the German Democratic Republic, to the

Dutch Interchurch Peace Council (IKV), to the International Conference for Europe Without Nuclear Weapons in Western Berlin, to French peace organizations meeting at Larzac, to the British peace movements (CND and END), and to the Conference on European Nuclear Disarmaments (END) in Perugia.[39] However, although invited to attend peace conferences abroad, Charter 77 delegates have so far been prevented by the Czechoslovak authorities from attending every single one of them. In the new documents on peace and peace movements, the Chartists criticized Western pacifist advocates of unilateral disarmament as one-sided and leading toward "peace at any price"; they also rejected the "spirit of appeasement" (with direct references to the sacrifices of Czechoslovakia by the Western powers at the Munich Conference in 1938) and called for the withdrawal from Europe of both Soviet and U.S. forces. They repeated their appeal to the Western peace movements to support the imprisoned human-rights activists. The ultimate vision of the Chartists was to see the creation of a world peace movement, in the East and West, in Europe and overseas, directed not from above by bureaucratic manipulators but built up from below by a mighty democratic coalition of common people.

Many of these ideas were incorporated in the European Peace Declaration issued at Perugia in July 1984. Although the Chartists themselves were not allowed to participate at the conference, their signatures were attached to the declaration, together with those of five unofficial Hungarian delegates and of over fifty representatives of Western peace movements. The official Soviet and East European delegates were not at all pleased and refused to endorse the declaration. The document stressed the long-standing Chartist principle that peace and human rights were indivisible; it condemned the arms race and the deployment of nuclear missiles in both West and East; it called for the withdrawal of foreign troops from all countries, the dissolution of NATO and the Warsaw Pact, and the creation of an nuclear-free zone from Portugal to the Urals. This was a significant achievement for a semi-clandestine group of Czechoslovak idealist intellectuals.[40]

The 1984 Perugia Conference must be regarded as one of the milestones in the evolution of Charter 77 views on European and world peace. As one of the best-informed observers of the East European situation commented, the Charter 77 emphasis on "unofficial action by ordinary citizens" for the sake of discussing issues of peace and arms control, may have been encouraged directly by the United Nations document of December 13, 1982, which demanded freedom of expression and association for all peace movements.[41]

That the new intimate relationship between "peace and freedom" was not to be an easy honeymoon had been confirmed by the controversial results in the World Peace Assembly held in Prague in June 1983. While individual Western pacifists were warmly welcomed by Czechoslovak authorities, members of Charter 77 were denied access to the conference altogether.[42] However, despite strong police interference and stage-management efforts by the organizers, several

Chartists succeeded in meeting the Western delegates. Together they issued joint statements emphasizing the inseparability of the pursuit of peace and human rights. A Charter 77 communiqué of June 30, 1983, asserted that the brutal action of the Prague police against some of the Western delegates and journalists at their unofficial meeting with the Chartists demonstrated yet again that a state that cannot guarantee the existence of basic human rights as a foundation for understanding between different peoples and nations "is not ready for a peace dialogue," and that such a state "can at best stage world championships in peace of a kind."[43]

An anonymous writer from Prague who satirized the official charade surrounding the "world championship in peace" and the naïveté of some Western delegates unable to see through the state-managed show had a few critical words to say about Charter 77 as well. The Charter manifesto, he commented ironically, reminded us that the pursuit of peace in the world was difficult and complex; but so, too, were the manifesto's ideas full of difficult and complex sentences. The future researcher who survives the next war, the writer continued, will certainly be satisfied with the correctness of the balanced pronouncements contained in the Charter manifesto; but alas, they did not address the contemporary Czech public. "O friends," he urged them, "you, who are our only spokesmen, why do you hesitate to make a further step ahead?"[44]

The leading Chartists saw themselves largely in the role of petitioners or academic discussants, and refrained therefore from demonstrating in public for the cause of peace. However, some 300 young Czechs gathered under the banner "Peace and Freedom" during the last day of the conference, only to have their procession quickly broken up by the police.[45] Surprisingly, the Catholic Primate of Czechoslovakia, Frantisek Cardinal Tomásek, decided to appear at the peace conference in Prague to make a brief but effective statement on the inseparability of peace and freedom, including religious freedom.[46] Although Czechoslovak media suppressed news about these events, Western journalists informed the public and exposed the police repression and official censorship.[47]

Ironically, a mere three months after the Prague "world championship in peace," the authorities announced the deployment of Soviet nuclear-tipped missiles in Czechoslovakia and East Germany. The official Czechoslovak Press Agency alleged that several hundred thousand Czechoslovak citizens demonstrated in various cities in favor of the installation of Soviet missiles in their homeland.[48] Despite police harassment and warning that any expression of opposition against the missiles would be seen as a criminal act and charged accordingly, the Chartists did criticize the installation of the weapons.[49]

There were some signs of protest inside the country itself, although they cannot be measured by Western standards. In Brno, Czechoslovakia's second largest city, several young people initiated a petition against the stationing of missiles "anywhere in the world," which was signed by almost a thousand persons; similar petitions followed in other cities.[50] In November, several employees of the Institute of Geophysics in Prague signed a petition to the president and government of Czechoslovakia protesting the installation of nuclear missiles in their country; threats of dismissal from jobs and police interrogations forced a number of them to retract their signatures.[51] There must have been more petitions of a similar kind, though it is impossible to verify their numbers and signatories: The Czech exile journal *Listy* stated, for instance, that one of such petitions addressed in February 1984 to the same recipients carried over 900 signatures.[52] Moreover, readers' letters to the official Communist party daily, *Rudé Právo*, expressed their doubts about the necessity of the new missile deployments. The fact that the newspaper admitted that its readers expressed this deep concern is an indication that there must have been some muted opposition to the installation of missiles in official circles, too.[53] A major joint protest did not receive any domestic media publicity: On November 22, 1984, thirty East German peace activists and Czechoslovak Chartists signed a declaration protesting the stationing of Soviet missiles in their countries.[54]

The East-West Dialogue on Freedom and Peace

While Charter 77 was exchanging messages with anti-nuclear movements abroad and continuing to appeal to the deaf ears of the authorities, individuals from Czechoslovakia, not all of them associated with the Charter movement, had started an exchange of letters with their Western counterparts. According to Jan Kavan, editor of the *Palach Press Bulletin* in London and one of the best informed journalists on the subject of independent movements in Eastern Europe, the dialogue has marked a qualitative change in Charter 77's attitudes toward the West and its greater engagement in the politico-philosophical debate on the theme of peace and human rights as two equal and indivisible objectives.[55]

The dialogue received what can be now considered its historic baptism in the exchange of letters between "Václav Racek," an anonymous Czech critic of the Western peace movements, and E.P. Thompson, a British social historian, committee member of END (European Nuclear Disarmament), and the most eloquent and critical exponent of "Exterminism," the philosophy of mutual nuclear annihilation between the two world systems.[56] During 1980 E.P. Thompson visited Prague in order to conduct talks with both official and independent peace activists; he failed to make contact with the latter because they avoided him out of mistrust.

On behalf of the East European dissidents, Racek refused to subordinate human rights to the issue of peace, especially under the imperative of an emotional and apocalyptic vision of an inevitable nuclear holocaust. Stating that Thompson's aim of achieving a nuclear-free Europe was both naive and impracticable, Racek implied that had it not been for the NATO nuclear deterrent, the Soviet totalitarian system would have crushed the liberal freedoms of the West long ago. He said that the social system in the East was essentially different from the

Western society in which Thompson lived and was allowed to criticize, and told him bluntly that "your identification of both blocs with 'Exterminism' is unacceptable . . . your END peace movement . . . seems therefore to be an unconscious analogy of the appeasement of the Thirties."[57]

In his lengthy reply, Thompson tried several ways to dispel Racek's fears that the Western peace movement was unconsciously helping to strengthen Soviet control over Eastern Europe—but to no avail.[58] From the time that the indivisibility of human rights and peace had become the cornerstone of Charter 77 statements, Czechs had maintained their reservations about Thompson's END and similar anti-American groups in the West, accusing them of bias in favor of the Soviet Union. While Washington was often portrayed as an aggressor poised to use nuclear weapons, Moscow was frequently given the benefit of the doubt with regard to its heavy military buildup, including the steadily growing numbers of the SS-20 missiles that had been aimed since 1977 at Europe. On the other hand, the Racek–E.P. Thompson correspondence served as a sort of trial balloon for other Czech dissidents anxious to convey their views to their Western counterparts. Thompson's reception in Hungary in 1982 among the unofficial peace activists, for example, and his improvised lecture in the apartment of the writer Miklós Haraszti, reflected a different, much more cooperative, spirit, under what were, of course, significantly less oppressive circumstances than in Czechoslovakia.[59]

Between December 1982 and February 1983, exactly two years after the first exchange of letters, Racek and Thompson wrote to each other again. This time the Czech challenged the Western peace movement to make two radical steps: first, to redefine its attitude to totalitarian systems by identifying themselves with human-rights activities in the Eastern bloc, and second, to "support the military forces of Western democracies as instruments of human rights confronting totalitarian systems."[60] Thompson responded: "I am afraid that you must know little about nuclear weapons if you suppose that these can be 'instruments of human rights.' " He praised the recent statements of Charter 77 and expressed his amazement that Racek had ignored them. "I no longer know who you are," Thompson concluded the exchange, "nor from what position you speak." He recalled the recent arrest of Ladislav Lis, one of the three spokespersons of Charter 77, which occurred, ironically, on the same day that the leaders of the Warsaw Pact countries issued in Prague "a whole bundle of peace-loving proposals aimed at Western opinion." Thompson declared that the arrest of Lis caused the proposals to lose their credibility, and that he was therefore not prepared to accept the invitation from Czech officialdom to attend the much-advertised Peace Assembly in Prague in the coming month of June.[61]

By contrast, Jaroslav Sabata, a Charter 77 activist and a former prominent communist politician during the Prague Spring, distanced himself from Václav Racek's black-and-white approach. In his letter of April 1983 to Thompson, he accepted the fact that in order to be meaningful any disarmament had at the same time to be a human-rights movement. Because he believed that the Western peace movement had "intrinsically the same aim as ourselves," Sabata wanted to offer a "third way," a joint platform between Western peace movements and Easter human-rights groups for the sake of the preservation of peace, the democratic transformation of Europe, and the eventual unification of the continent.[62] Thompson replied in February 1984, offering his enthusiastic agreement. However, he rejected the idea of German reunification. Although, Thompson, too, wanted to terminate the post-Yalta presence of Soviet and U.S. troops in Europe, he vehemently rejected the creation of a new, all-embracing "Euro-state." His vision of transformation was based more on a stage- by-stage convergence between Eastern and Western Europe, gradually freed of nuclear weapons and foreign troops.[63]

Paradoxically, despite the fact that it reached an impasse, the Racek-Thompson exchange had a beneficial impact in other quarters. Independent Czech peace activists began to reexamine their distrust of END and other anti-American groups; they were persuaded to go further than the simplistic Czech tendency to favor American militarism because it was checking the Russian military machine. Thus, around 1981–82 the visits and messages of Western peace activists led to a gradual conviction that a way of bypassing the official Czech peace committees in order to work on a citizen-to citizen basis between East and West should be found.[64]

Milan Šimečka is another remarkable Charter activist who contributed during 1983 to the East-West dialogue. Like Jaroslav Sabata and other leading Chartists, Šimečka was also imprisoned by the Czechoslovak authorities for his writings and independent activities.[65] His essay, "Why We're Not Marching: The Silent Voices of Eastern Europe," was submitted to the peace congress in Prague, but it was circulated primarily in the West rather than at home.[66]

His observations about the ambiguity of the official "peace campaigns" in communist Eastern Europe are similar to the earlier reminiscences of Vladimir Bukovsky:

> Plenty of our people are aware of the devastation that threatens the entire globe. Still, whenever those people feel they ought to do something about it, they are quickly discouraged by the way contributions to the "peace fund" are extorted from them each payday for ostentatious dinners for ostentatious dignitaries at peace congresses in ostentatious palaces . . . The nature of the "peace campaign" in Czechoslovakia makes spontaneity superfluous because it assumes that preserving peace is best left in the hands of the government, the Communist party and the military chiefs.

Turning to the question, why the Western peace movement has failed so far to arouse support among East Europeans, he wrote:

We often look upon peace movements, slogan waving and assorted exaltations with benevolent condescension. In our countries, such spectacles for peace are organized by the state. We have grown used to that; we have lost all the capacity to believe in the spontaneity of any street demonstration, East or West. . . . So we watch footage from protest demonstrations—courageous young women chaining themselves to the gates of military installations and throwing themselves in front of military vehicles—with disdain. Sad to say, we cannot avoid the malicious thought: Just come and try here, at a Czech or a Soviet base! You'd never know what hit you! They'd fix you so fast it would be years before anyone heard of you again! Such cynicism does not predispose one to participate in mass demonstrations for peace.

According to Šimečka, "the structural crisis of Eastern Europe socialism is also a peace crisis." If we can imagine the next war, he speculates, it will begin as a civil war within one East European state, presumably Poland, which will then escalate into a war between two different social systems. "The greatest responsibility for preserving peace lies with the Western democratic societies," he argues, because they are not in danger of facing "explosions of social hate," like the totalitarian societies in the East. Thus "responsibility for peace is not equal"; not only has the West a greater responsibility than the East, but the developed countries have a greater responsibility than countries struggling against hunger.

Ladislav Hejdánek's essay "What Peace Do We Actually Want?", written in the spring of 1983, was another important contribution to the East-West dialogue. A religious philosopher and a pupil of the late Jan Patocka (regarded by many as the spiritual father of Charter 77), Hejdánek himself is a distinguished representative of the Christian group inside Charter 77. He said he refused to support a "false, bogus, frail peace," because such a peace would inevitably lead to another war. If disarmament were limited to Europe only, it would create greater superpower competition in other regions. The release of military resources and their diversion from Europe to Asia, for instance, would make the Chinese and Japanese increasingly nervous. Furthermore, he wrote:

> European disarmament would mean capitulation; Europe would give up its authentic voice in relations with the USA and the Soviet Union. At the same time it would shift the burden of threat to other settlement . . . it would be catastrophic for Europe itself. Sooner or later it would lead to the permanent division of Europe or its domination by one or other of the superpowers (geopolitically, most probably the Soviet Union) and its relegation to one of the spheres of influence. Are we sure that such a course would be the most reliable path to peace? Either we can trust the superpowers to go on avoiding a world conflagration, in which case there is not point in mass peace demonstration, or we cannot trust them, in which case why should European disarmament mean a step toward peace rather than war.

The main thrust of Hejdánek's argument was the emphasis on internal peace within societies both in the East and West, whose absence, he was convinced, remained the single most important source of tension leading to wars.[67]

As we have seen, the views of Czech peace activists are far from identical. Hejdánek's Christian argument that there must be "values which surpass life itself," can be contrasted with Jiří Hájek's warning that while there may be "values for which it is sometimes necessary to sacrifice life, it is hard to invoke this argument when we are talking of the entire human species . . . that would lose any meaning in a depopulated world burnt out by a nuclear war."[68] Among the Czech dissidents Hájek, an ex-Communist academic and former foreign minister, is one of the strongest supporters of Western peace movements; he may appear even too soft on what many dissidents perceive as the risk of a "second Munich of 1938." However, the Czech peace activists are united in seeing human-rights and peace issues as indivisible.

In addition to Hejdánek, other Christian laymen and clergymen became interested in establishing dialogue with nonbelievers and believers in both parts of Europe. In 1984, thousands of signatures were collected for a petition supporting Cardinal Tomásek's invitation to the pope to participate, in July of the following year, in a major religious commemoration in Czechoslovakia. In August of the same year a group of eight prominent clerical Christians, deprived of state consent to preach, addressed a letter to the participants of an international seminar in Budapest, "Working Toward a Theology of Peace," in which they protested their exclusion from international gatherings.[69] The following spring Rev. Jakub Trojan from the Evangelical Church of Czech Brethren drafted the more-than-5,000-word "Contribution to the Discussion on Peace," the most comprehensive and thought-provoking document to be found among the individual appeals from Czechoslovakia.[70]

Trojan stated that he believed in the necessity of cooperating with the Western peace movement, and he accused Charter circles of having neglected peace issues in their early years. In his view, having been understandably engrossed in their difficulties as a semi-illegal group of conspirators, with usually half of their prominent members in prison, the Chartists had become dilettantes with regard to peace questions. Trojan rejected the appeasement analogy with the 1930s ("Munich"), of fifty years ago, believing that peace could have been saved by militarization against Nazism, whereas there is no such hope in the 1980s because of nuclear weapons. Trojan favored unilateral nuclear disarmament and was a resolute opponent of any form of militarization. Even in democratic societies, militarization could conceal totalitarian tendencies (e.g., McCarthyism). Peace under a totalitarian regime, in his view, was still better than total destruction in a "battle for freedom."

The ex-communist journalist Jiří Dienstbier began to circulate his essay "Pax Europeana (About the Thinkable and the Unthinkable)" several months before Trojan's treatise on peace. Inspired by a vision of a united Europe whose cornerstone would be the reunification of Germany, Dienstbier launched himself into a spirited defense of "Finlandization" as a model of friendly ties between the Soviet Union and the states of Europe, including a united Germany. While advocating the dissolution of NATO and the Warsaw Pact, together with the withdrawal of all foreign troops from European countries, Dienstbier wanted the European states to maintain modest armed forces strictly for defensive purposes— which will, nevertheless, still require safeguards in the form of a Euro-American treaty and "the protection of the strategic nuclear potential of the superpowers."[71] While much of his essay is full of contradictions, Dienstbier's thoughts about informal contacts between citizens' groups are worth reading.

This account would not be complete without mentioning what is perhaps the most influential contribution to the East-West dialogue of all, Václav Havel's "Anatomy of a Reticence." Czechoslovakia's best-known playwright and oft-persecuted Charter 77 former spokesman prepared his 8,000-word essay in April 1985 for the forthcoming European Disarmament Convention in Amsterdam (July 1985).[72] After exposing the "reticence" of many Western peace activists toward the dissidents in Eastern Europe, Havel analyzed his own "reticence" about being portrayed with his Chartist colleagues in the domestic media as "Western fifth columnists." The word *peace*, Havel noted, has become meaningless in our part of the world. For thirty-seven years the official propaganda hammered down the people's throats such phrases as "By building the motherland you will strengthen peace," "The USSR is the guarantor of world peace," and so forth. Not only has the Czechoslovak public become apathetic from such overdoses, it is also frustrated by the fact that in the official newspeak "the struggle for peace" is invariably directed against "Western imperialists."

In a passage devoted to those Western activists demanding nuclear disarmament in both East and West, Havel tried to explain why the East is not West in terms of opportunities to dissent and repercussions for demonstrations against the installation of nuclear missiles in one's own country. Any tolerance of blatant violence by Western anti-war activists makes their attitude toward peace extremely dubious, as in the example of Afghanistan:

> How much trust or even admiration for the Western peace movement can we expect from a single sensitive citizen of East-Central Europe, when he has noticed that this movement did not ever at any of its congresses or any of its demonstrations with hundreds of thousands of participants get around to protesting emphatically that one important European country five years ago attacked a small neutral neighbor and since that time has been conducting . . . a war of extermination that has already claimed a million dead and three million refugees? Seriously, what are we to think of a peace movement, a European peace movement, that is practically unaware of the only war being conducted today by a European state?[73]

Havel then enumerated several points on which independent peace groups in East and West should reach an agreement: recognition that the division of Europe was the fundamental cause of the present tensions; initiation of a "restructuring of the political realities that lie at the root of the current crisis"; an insistence on the respect for human rights as both precondition and "sole genuine guarantee" of real peace; recognition of the right to German reunification and to the demand for the withdrawal of foreign troops from Europe. Many of these points appeared in other individual messages discussed earlier; and in statements on peace issued by Charter 77 and by independent peace groups in the GDR, Hungary, and Poland. They were brought together in the most ambitious and comprehensive text on peace at about the same time Havel's "Reticence" appeared—the *Prague Appeal.*

Charter 77 and Peace Movements in East and West (1985–87): The Prague Appeal

Given the collective and private endeavors of the Chartists during the first half of the 1980s, there was every hope that their concentrated intellectual energies might lead to a significant and original contribution to the East-West debate on peace. The *Prague Appeal,* a document drafted for the Amsterdam Peace Congress (July 1985) and signed on March 11, 1985, by almost fifty prominent Chartists, realized that hope.[74]

The authors of the *Appeal* moved even further from the practical day-to-day discussion of disarmament topics into the realm of long-term ideals. Apparently, they believed that European unification was the purpose of the Helsinki Accords signed ten years earlier. Although the original dominant theme of inseparability of peace and human rights was certainly not abandoned, questions of international relations, both with regard to East and West and with regard to the Soviet Union were not incorporated. In the Chartist view, the reunification of Europe must be based on its transformation into a community of free and independent nations through a slow process of exchanging guarantees and assurances, rather than by threatening to destabilize the balance, which the Chartists believed had been the negative pattern of East-West relations in Europe for some time.

The document reiterated the faith of Charter 77 in the Helsinki Final Act and the CSCE follow-up talks in Madrid, which were seen as "not just an acknowledgment of the status quo, but of a program of European and Euro-American cooperation." According to the Chartists' vision, the evolution would have to progress in two stages: first, by creating the necessary "framework of cooperation and dialogue" formed by "individual citizens, groups of citizens or nations" rather than state governments. The second phase was to be characterized by spontaneous negotiations to deal with various disarmament initiatives and the creation of nuclear-free and neutral zones. Through the widest grass-roots pressure network, governments should be compelled to reach agreements on nonaggression and renunciation of force, both conventional and nuclear, and to become instrumental in the rapprochement of the two economic blocs dividing Europe: the EEC and the CMEA. Moreover, this widespread, populous, all-European citizens' initiative, having brought about the solution to the problem of an imminent nuclear war, should devote itself to the solution of other outstanding problems such as the environmental question.

Along with the proposals for the withdrawal of foreign troops from Europe, the dissolution of NATO and the Warsaw Pact military organizations, the removal of all nuclear weapons "either sited in or aimed at Europe," and the scaling down of armed forces in all European countries to "a level eliminating the risk of aggression from any quarter," the most daring "taboo" proposal was that concerning the reunification of Germany. "If our aim is European unification", the *Prague Appeal* argued, "and no one should be denied the right to self-determination, then this applies equally to the Germans." Realizing how delicate the subject of frontier revision in Europe was, the Chartists hastened to "declare unequivocally that no solution shall be sought through a further revision of European frontiers." Paradoxically, however, they declared on the one hand that they did not believe in frontiers, which "should gradually lose much of their significance."

The *Prague Appeal* reached its climax in the final paragraph:

> We do not seek to turn Europe into a third superpower, but instead, to overcome the superpower bloc structure by way of an alliance of free and independent nations within the democratic and self-governing all-European community living in friend-ships with nations of the entire world. Only freedom and dignity of individual citizens can provide the guarantee to the freedom and self-determination of nations. And only sovereign nations can transform Europe into a community of equal partners which would not pose the threat of a global nuclear war, but instead, serve as an example of real peaceful coexistence.

"Perhaps this ideal sounds like a dream," the Chartists admitted in the following sentence. Sure enough, the *Prague Appeal* was subject to criticism both at home and abroad among the Czech exiles, especially from among the Social Democrats who were skeptical about the whole Helsinki process and opposed the idea of German reunification.[75] But as far as the overall impact on peace movements was concerned, the Western groups' reactions was on the whole favorable.[76] Charter 77 received replies and comments from Britain (Labor Party, Liberal Party, CND, END, National Peace Council, and East-West Peace People), Holland (IKV), Denmark (*Nej til Atomvaben*), West Berlin (Group for East-West Dialogue), Norway (*Nei Til Stomvapen*), France (CODENE, *Association Initiative pour le Dialogue Est-Ouest*), USA (Humanitas International), and the Belgrade *Praxis* group.[77] There was also a letter from Roland Jahn, a founding member of the Jena Peace Community, who wrote to Prague from a West German prison where he was serving a thirty-day sentence imposed for his picketing activities at the NATO base in Bitburg (having been expelled from East Germany in June 1983). His message was followed by a long letter signed by twenty-one GDR citizens, including Pastor Rainer Eppelmann, who in 1982 had issued the

"Berlin Appeal" calling for a rapprochement between the two German states and the removal of all nuclear weapons from Germany. From Poland, the Committee for Social Resistance (KOS) replied.[78]

The GDR peace group, while expressing its reservation at the Charter's positive appraisal of the CSCE post-Helsinki process, enthusiastically embraced the "German Question" as formulated by the Czechoslovak activists. It is interesting to note that the Germans themselves did not mention the term "reunification" in their text; their letter referred cautiously to the "German Question" and the importance of solving it through a peace treaty "with both German states." The KOS letter from Warsaw disagreed in even stronger terms with the *Prague Appeal's* rosy picture of the Helsinki process, but supported the idea of German unification and of the inviolability of European borders. Moreover, KOS was not afraid to spell out the inevitable implications of Charter 77's utopian views of the principle of self-determination. They pointed out that the *Appeal* had ignored the fate of subjugated free European nations within the Soviet Union such as the Lithuanians, Latvians, Estonians, Belorussians, and Ukrainians. Because of these two major reservations, KOS refused to sign the *Prague Appeal.*[79]

A much more detailed criticism of the *Prague Appeal* arrived by the end of the year from János Kis, a leading Hungarian social critic. The Budapest philosopher disagreed with the Charter's description of the present European status quo (the state of "non war") and with its symmetrical description of the East-West polarity. The very different geographic location of the two superpowers with respect to Europe, explained Kis, should have made it rather obvious to the Charter 77 authors that the Soviet Union is in fact a Euroasian power. As a result, Soviet power would only increase as a consequence of bilateral disengagement by both superpowers.

Kis was also deeply skeptical about the Chartists' dreams for achieving "European unification," for he felt that it is assumed that the Soviet presence would somehow evaporate in the process. "What is to become of the empire built by the tsars and then rebuilt by Lenin and Stalin?" asks Kis, "should the Ukraine, Belorussia, Estonia, Latvia, and Lithuania regain their independence and enter as sovereign partners the all-European community? . . . Can we realistically anticipate a Soviet state integrated into a democratic and self-governing all-European community of equal and independent states?"

It is impossible to follow up here in all details the East-West dialogue triggered by the *Prague Appeal* of March 1985, which was to go on for more than a year. It provided the spark on both sides of the ideological divide for subsequent discussions coordinated through the "European Network for East-West Dialogue," a loose group of volunteers formed at the 1984 END Conference in Perugia. Inspired by the *Prague Appeal,* the Network circulated by the end of 1985 the first forty-page draft entitled *Giving Real Life to the Helsinki Accords.* While Charter 77 activists were preoccupied with their comments on the first draft, a second amended version was already in circulation by the time the

Network convoked a conference in Milan by mid-May 1986. This time, a wide variety of comments from Eastern Europe was available: from the Polish "Freedom and Peace" group (Janek Minkiewicz), from the Ljubljana peace group (Gregor Tomc), from the GDR peace activists (Roland Jahn), and from two Hungarian dissidents (János Kis and György Dálos). A prominent figure of the Hungarian Democratic Opposition, Kis voiced his belief that before a genuine democratic transformation of Europe could take place, the East-bloc countries must first change into liberal democracies with respect for human rights; furthermore, he would maintain that as a geopolitical entity, Soviet Eurasia did not belong to Europe.

By contrast, the Chartists argued in their document submitted to the Milan Conference that a transformation of the Soviet Union "into a truly democratic federative entity which would be linked with the process of all-European economic and political integration" was still feasible. On the other hand, they stated that Europe could not be neutral or nonaligned, as the Western pacifists maintained, as long as both the Soviet Union and the United States kept their armed forces there. A democratic evolution of Europe could not proceed without solving its fundamental problem, which in Charter's view was the German partition (ignored in the Network's proposal).[82]

By the time the Third Helsinki Review Conference (CSCE) met in November 1986 in Vienna, a third version of the Network's document, referred to as "Memorandum" was ready. Among the thirty-three signatories from Czechoslovakia were seventeen who have been or are Charter 77 spokespersons; the number of signatories from the GDR, Hungary, and Poland is even huger. Altogether over 400 persons from CSCE countries signed the Memorandum, which in itself is a remarkable testimony of an East-West cooperation to revive the paralyzed Helsinki agreement by confronting the mutual prejudices of peace activists from both East and West. Thus, through this frank encounter with the "reticence" existing on both sides of the ideological divide—as Jan Kavan put it so adequately by borrowing Václav Havel's term of preference[83]—the real basis for a genuine East-West dialogue "from below" was cemented.[84]

What Does the Average Czech and
Slovak Think of War and Peace?

If Charter 77 has been recognized as instrumental in initiating joint statements among independent peace movements in Eastern Europe as well as in promoting East-West contacts, and if a number of prominent Czechoslovak intellectuals initiated dialogue with their Western counterparts, one may ask legitimately: What does the average Czech and Slovak think of war and peace?

Although there are ways of measuring this, such as opinion polls, we cannot normally apply them today inside communist-controlled Eastern Europe. However, in the case of Czechoslovakia we are extraordinarily lucky to possess the results of a remarkable survey carried out clandestinely during the first half of 1985, seventeen years after the last public-opinion poll was conducted there.[85] Close to 350 Czechoslovak citizens answered long and complex questionnaires consisting of eighty-five questions, which included such sensitive issues as their attitude to Marxism, Soviet imperialism, the future neutral status of "The Central European Confederacy" and the German Question, and inescapably, war and peace. However, although the poll asked detailed questions about unofficial educational and free-time activities outside the control of state authorities, a number of specific questions pertinent to the anti-war theme, such as the stationing of nuclear missiles on Czechoslovak territory or conscientious objection to military service, were not included. Furthermore, the sample of almost 350 answers cannot be regarded as entirely representative of the Czech and Slovak average, because there was a disproportionately high level of respondents with a university education living in Czechoslovakia's three largest cities.[86]

In some respects, the Czechoslovak attitude to the Soviet military occupation appears to be a mirror image of the West European reaction to the U.S. military and nuclear presence. To the statement that "the US is a greater threat to peace than the USSR," only 6.4 percent agreed, whereas ten times more (63 percent) disagreed; with the statement that "the USSR is going to protect us from the threat of war," only 5.8 percent agreed, while 54 dissented.[87] In other respects, the survey demonstrated the existence of a strong sentiment, especially among the young people, yearning for a nonaligned "United States of Central Europe," with 30.7 percent agreeing readily and 36.2 only partially.

With regard to West European pacifist movements, two statements were offered: "The peace movement in the West has great significance for the preservation of peace and should be supported," and "The peace movement in the West has undermined the policy of their own governments and is playing thereby into the hands of the USSR." Twenty-one point nine percent agreed with the first statement (23 disagreed) and 23.6 percent agreed with the second one (24.2 disagreed).[88] The voting samples show such a remarkable consistency that a fairly safe inference can be made that in a more representative sample of the Czechoslovak population the popular stereotypes and suspicions that the Western pacifists were naively or deliberately playing into the hands of Moscow would have been much more strongly represented. On the other hand, it would be wrong to think that Czechoslovak observers believe that the peace movement is necessarily identified with neutrality or political emancipation; the prevailing opinion is to see these complex issues as separate.

Voting samples also established that the Western peace movement received very little support from those who declared they were "politically active in independent groups" (which is the nearest thing to saying "supporters of Charter 77," which could obviously not be used for fear that survey volunteers and respondents might be arrested). This is not altogether surprising if one is reminded of the reluctant reaction of Charter 77 spokespersons to the first peace campaigns in Western Europe and in the United States. By contrast, and this again should not be surprising, politically passive citizens declared their sympathies for peace movements in numbers usually twice as high, thus conforming to the pattern of official governmental policy. One can therefore tentatively conclude that the attitude of the Czechoslovak public to Western peace movements is determined not so much by the social forces on the two sides of the border as it is by the ideological tension between East and West. "Among the strongest supporters of Western pacifist movements," says Zdenek Strmiska in his commentary, "there are those who are pro-Soviet and refuse to designate the USSR as an imperialist power, as much as those who are anti-American and consider the United States an imperialist power."[89]

However, a small group of between 3 to 6 percent among this highly selective sample of overeducated city dwellers, abnormally politically active and supportive of dissidents, or at least of independent educational activities, expressed their support for Western peace movements. By age group, the most critical attitude to Western peace movements comes from the middle generation, the most positive one from the oldest. Those with university degrees were least supportive of peace movements (only 14.2 percent among all graduates), which is further evidence of the widely spread skepticism among the educated professional groups, by implication also the most critical segment of the population. On the other hand, a similarity with Western Europe was the high percentage of women supporting peace movements: Only 16.8 percent of all women disapproved, whereas male "reticence" accounted for 28.5 percent.[90]

It is extremely unlikely that the Communist party–controlled Institute for Public Opinion Research in Prague, with its Slovak branch in Bratislava, would have undertaken a similar survey on its own initiative if the Communist monopoly on questions of war and peace had not come under direct challenge from the parallel civil society "from below," and if the Chernobyl nuclear accident of April 26, 1986, had not occurred. After these challenges arose, the institute hastily carried out an official poll, the results of which were published in March the following year.[91] However, the official poll on "Public Opinion in Questions of War and Peace" is far from satisfactory; in no way does it measure up to the professionalism of the independent survey. Out of twelve pages of text, only one deals with the interpretation of "empirical data," and, incredible as it may sound, there is not one single figure. The bulk of the article is nothing but ideological diatribes—a telling example of the Czechoslovak version of glasnost in practice.

Even so, judging by the carefully screened published version of the official survey, the results could hardly make the "champions of peace" happy. As admitted in the text, almost half of those questioned declared that both superpowers bore equal responsibility for international tension. Moreover, the most widespread view was that "all participation in war is bad and immoral," which prompted the official commentator to add his warning that "ideas of pacifism were spreading" because of an "incorrect understanding of the relationship between preserving peace and the struggle for national and social freedom."[92] Another worrying tendency for the party evaluators must have been the strong wish for neutrality in Central Europe.

Similar warnings concerning the blurred notion of national consciousness were voiced by the party authorities in Slovakia, who complained that "there was an increasing number of people . . . indifferent to problems concerning their relationship with their own nation and with other nations . . . most people understand homeland in terms of an empirical perception of their residence or birthplace rather than in a political, economic, or statehood context."[93] Still, both Czechs and Slovaks were willing to support peace talks between the United States and the USSR, but it was the Slovak party members who apparently gave the most "positive" replies and showed themselves less affected by Western pacifism than the Czechs. The most "negative" views on war and peace came from the inhabitants of the two capital cities, Prague and Bratislava. Although most respondents did not dare to question the existence of the draft, they did appear to advocate careers in uniform. However, the principles of "defense of the socialist community" against aggression from abroad and of the country's membership in the Warsaw Pact were not seriously challenged.

Conclusions

That the memorandum "Giving Real Life to the Helsinki Accords" came into existence should be seen as extraordinary proof that an East-West dialogue in the sphere of nongovernmental contacts "from below" has not only been feasible, but could also deepen and improve contacts among the East European peace and environmental groups themselves. It is on these kinds of activities that our attention should focus in the near future.

From the standpoint of the independent peace groups in Eastern Europe, it is important to maintain the momentum already gained in the two major fields of East European antimilitarist and antinuclear activities: the issues of *conscientious objection* and *ecology*. Recent developments indicate that the initiative on these two issues has been passed from the peace groups in the GDR to those in Poland and Hungary, with Charter 77 trailing slightly behind; though the latter is still extremely active and critical of governmental policies on the environmental issue, it remains less radical on the question of military service. The launching of a separate peace working group on Charter's initiative in the summer of 1987, following the Warsaw Peace Seminar, the joint declaration resulting from the Czechoslovak-Polish border encounter in August 1987, and the formation of an independent peace association in 1988 seem to confirm this trend.[94]

The issue of conscientious objection is being seen increasingly as the common denominator of antimilitarist attitudes among young people of Eastern Europe. Recent government decisions in Poland and Hungary suggest that some Warsaw

Pact regimes may renounce their uncompromising hostility to recognizing the right to conscientious objection.

Unfortunately, in Czechoslovakia the post-Husák leadership headed by General Secretary Milos Jakes has not displayed any interest in emulating Gorbachev's policy of glasnost. On the contrary, in January 1989 the regime resorted to brutal methods to disperse peaceful demonstrations organized to commemorate the twentieth anniversary of the death of Jan Palach, a young student who set himself afire to protest the Soviet occupation of his country. Among those arrested and later sentenced to prison terms were well-known Charter 77 activists, including Václav Havel.[95] One of the groups that expressed its solidarity with the jailed activists was the Independent Peace Association. Founded in April 1988, this group of young people has become a major voice for concerns and hopes long championed by Charter 77. It is likely that similar associations will emerge in the near future, taking advantage of both internal and external circumstances.

NOTES

1. *The Watchtower Yearbook 1972*, pp. 125–41.

2. The Christian philosopher Ladislav Hejdánek, a former spokesman of Charter 77, edited Emanuel Rádl's last book of essays, *Utecha z filosofie* [Solace from Philosophy], (Prague: Mladá fronta, 1969).

3. Premysl Pitter, *Unter dem Rad der Geschichte* (Zurich: Rotapfel, 1970), p. 53.

4. F.L. Carsten, *War Against War: British and German Radical Movements in the First World War* (London: Batsford, 1982).

5. D. Prasad and T. Smythe (eds.), *Conscription—A World Survey* (London: War Resisters' International, 1968), pp. 131–35.

6. The new Conscription Law of March 25, 1982, left the status of *Bausoldat* unchanged (see *Neues Deutschland* of March 27/28, 1982, p. 9f).

7. *Grundlagen des Maxismus-Leninismus* (Berlin, 1960), p. 547.

8. J.F. Tríska (ed.), *Constitutions of the Communist Party-States* (Stanford: 1968).

9. J. Weck, *Wehrverfassung und Wehrrecht der DDR* (Cologne, 1970), p. 71.

10. See note 9 above: Amnesty's International unpublished *Report on Conscientious Objectors in Europe* (London, 1976), p. 23.

11. WRI Bulletin: *Compulsory Military Service and the Objector*, 12/1972.

12. *Report on Conscientious Objectors in Europe*, p. 24, *Süddeutsche Zeitung* of 5 August 1976.

13. Author's correspondence with Ales Brezina who lives now in Canada. Brezina's final speech before the military court of June 14, 1977, as well as his letter of refusal to the military authorities dated March 29, of the same year, have been published by Vilém Precan (ed.), *Krestané a Charta* (Cologne: Index, 1980), pp. 149–51. See also *Listy* of October 1977, pp. 10–12 (see next).

14. *Listy* (Journal of the Czechoslovak Socialist Opposition, publ. in Rome), vol. 7, no. 6 (December 1977), p. 20.

15. Ibid., vol. 12, no. 5 (October 1982), pp. 18–19.

16. I have deliberately applied the juxtaposition between the "Dionysian" and "Apollonian" elements, wonderfully depicted in *The Birth of Tragedy from the Spirit of Music (Die Geburt der Tragödie aus dem Geiste der Musik*, 1872), an early but great work of Friedrich Nietzsche's youthful genius, because I believe that it contains a more relevant answer to the problems of mass psychosis of the Czech youth in the mid-1980s than hundreds of pages of sociological research.

17. *Listy*, vol. 16, no. 1 (February, 1986), pp. 12–13; *East European Reporter*, Vol. 1, no. 4 (1986), pp. 27–8; Jan Kavan, "Prague's Kamikaze Icebreakers", *The Nation*, 24 January 1987, pp. 78–81.

18. *Listy*, vol. 16, no. 1 (February, 1986), p. 41.

19. Ibid., vol. 16, no. 4 (July 1986), pp. 13–14.

20. Ibid., pp. 9–12: Charter 77 document 7/86 of March 6, 1986. English version in the *East European Reporter*, vol. 2, no. 1 (1986), pp. 27–9.

21. *Infoch 5/87* (a Czech samizdat press service distributing Charter 77 documents); appendix to Charter 77 document no. 27/87 of March 31, 1978; English version in *Palach Press Bulletin*, 28/29 (1987), pp. 108–15; *East European Reporter*, vol., no. 4 (1987), pp. 64–6.

22. Ibid., Charter 77, doc. no. 40/87 of 3 June 1987.

23. See, for example, among others: Jeffrey Herf, "War, Peace, and the Intellectuals—The West German Peace Movement", *International Security* (Spring 1986), pp. 172–200; Josef Joffe, "Peace and Populism: Why the European Anti-Nuclear Movement Failed," *ibid.* (Spring 1987), pp. 3–40; Harald Mueller and Thomas Risse-Kappen, "Origins of Estrangement: The Peace Movement and the Changed Image of America in West Germany," *ibid.* (Summer 1987), pp. 52–88; Martin Ceadel, "A weak peace movement, but plenty of loyal grousing," *The Manchester Guardian Weekly*, July 17, 1983, p. 4.

24. J.A. Vermaat, "Moscow Fronts and the European Peace Movement," *Problems of Communism* (Nov.–Dec. 1982), pp. 43–56.

25. *From Below*, a Helsinki Watch Report (1987), pp. 107–78.

26. Michael Binyon, writing from Moscow: "Pacifism is a dirty word in Russia," *The Times* (London), April 23, 1982.

27. See Leszek Kolakowski's review of Lech Walesa's book, "A Way of Hope" in *The New York Times Book Review*, December 13, 1987, p. 3.

28. H. Gordon Skilling, *Charter 77 and Human Rights in Czechoslovakia* (London: Allen and Unwin, 1981), p. 164.

29. Vilém Precan, "Charter 77, Its Relationship to Questions of Peace and War and the Contemporary Peace Movements", in Milan Schultz (ed.), *Mír, Mírove hnutí, krestanská etika* (Munich: Opus Bonum, 1984), pp. 75–100. First published in *Listy*, vol. 14, no. 2 (April 1984), pp. 14–22. H.G. Skilling: "CSCE in Madrid" and "Independent Currents in Czechoslovakia", *Problems of Communism*, (July–Aug. 1981), pp. 1–16, and (Jan.–Feb. 1985), pp. 32–49, here p. 45. I am grateful to Drs. Precan and Skilling for sharing their observations with me and for correcting many of my mistakes.

30. Skilling (1981): p. 162–4.

31. Gustav Husák, was arrested as a "Slovak nationalist" in 1951, stripped of all his functions in the Communist Party and government, and sentenced for life imprisonment in 1954. Released in 1960, Husák was rehabilitated in 1963, but was not allowed to assume party or government posts until April 1968, when he became deputy prime minister. Following the Warsaw Pact-led invasion of August 1968, Husák became a Soviet favorite and replaced Alexander Dubček as the First Secretary of the Czechoslovak Communist Party in April 1969.

32.   VONS is a Czech abbreviation for the "Committee for the Defense of Unjustly Persecuted," a group of dedicated human-rights activists, most of them Charter 77 members.

33.   *Listy*, 10/6, December 1980, pp. 65–7; also Skilling (1981), p. 183.

34.   Ibid.

35.   For the full English translation of the letter see: Jan Kavan and Zdena Tomín (eds.), *Voices from Prague: Documents on Czechoslovakia and the Peace Movement* (London: END and Palach Press, 1983), pp. 22–3.

36.   Ibid., pp. 23–5.

37.   Ibid., p. 25.

38.   Ibid., pp. 10–13.

39.   Ibid., pp. 25–8; Precan, *op. cit.*, passim; Skilling, *Problems of Communism* (Jan.–Feb. 1985), p. 48; *RFE/RL Research Bulletin* (Munich), nos. 33 and 36, Aug. and Sept. 7, 1984.

40.   Ibid., *Palach Press Bulletin* no. 25 (December 1984), pp. 15–25, 36–8.

41.   Jacques Rupnik, "Pacifisme et dissidence en Europe de l'Est," *Universalia* (Paris, 1984), p. 239.

42.   Charter 77 document no. 20/83 of June 15, 1983, published in *Listy*, vol. 14, suppl. to no. 2, 1984, pp. 15–16. See also further Charter documents nos. 21 and 22 of 12 and June 14, 1983, demanding to free imprisoned Chartists on the eve of the Prague Conference (Rudolf Battek, Václav Benda, Ivan Jirous, Ladislav Lis, Frantisek Lízna, and Petr Uhl); ibid.

43.   Charter document no. 24/83 of June 30, 1983, Listy, vol. 13, no. 5 (October 1983), pp. 31–3.

44.   Ibid., pp. 34–5.

45.   *The Times* (London) of June 23, 1983.

46.   Skilling, op. cit., p. 44.

47.   Ibid., p. 47.

48.   Jiří Pelikán, "Zít s raketami?" [To live with missiles?], *Listy* vol. 13, no. 6 (December 1983), pp. 1–4.

49.   Charter 77 *Open Letter to Western Movements*, no. 38/83 of November 1983, *Listy*, ibid., pp. 4–5.

50.   Skilling, op. cit., p. 47.

51.   *Listy*, vol. 14, no. 1 (February 1984), p. 11.

52.   Ibid., vol. 14, no. 2 (April 1984), p. 31.

53.   *Rudé Právo* (Prague), of November 5, 1983.

54.   *Listy*, vol. 14, no. 6 (December 1984), pp. 20–1.

55.   Jan Kavan in *Poland Watch* (November 1984), p. 140. I have very much appreciated Jan Kavan's insights and comments.

56.   E.P. Thompson and Dan Smith (eds.), *Protest and Survive* (London: Penguin, 1980); id., *Zero Option* (London: Merlin Press, 1982), *Exterminism and Cold War* (London: New Left Books, 1982); "Breaking the Cold War Ice: East, West—Is There a Third Way?", *The Nation*, July 10–17, 1982.

57.   *New Statesman* (London), April 24, 1981, pp. 6–7.

58.   Ibid., pp. 7–13.

59.   Ferenc Köszegi and E.P. Thompson, *The New Hungarian Peace Movement*, (London: END Special Report, 1983).

60.   See *Voices from Prague*, pp. 13–16.

61. Ibid., pp. 17–21.

62. English version in *Voices from Prague*, pp. 52–70.

63. E.P. Thompson's reply to J. Sabata's letter is to be found in Czech translation in *Listy*, vol. 14, no. 2 (April 1984), pp. 26–31.

64. Ann Martin, reporting from Prague, "Why the Peace Campaign stops at the Iron Curtain", *New Statesman*, June 25, 1982, p. 14. See also Zdenek Mlynář's lecture at the Czech exile symposium at Franken in November 1983, in which he tried to analyze the relationship between the contemporary peace movement and the political left: "Soucasné mírové hnutí a politická levice", *Listy*, vol. 14, no. 1 (February 1984), pp. 7–11; see also Milan Schultz, op. cit. pp. 127–37.

65. Milan Simečka, born in 1930, is living in Bratislava, the capital of Slovakia. Because of his political activities he lost his teaching position in the university in 1970. His best known collection of essays, *Obnovení pořádku* (*Order Restored*, 1979), has been translated into many languages. See also the collection of correspondence with Simecka published by Vilém Precan, *Die Sieben Jahre von Prag, 1969–1976. Briefe und Dokumente aus der Zeit der "Normalisierung,"* (Frankfurt: Fisher Taschenbuch no. 3412, 1978).

66. Published in *The Nation*, July 9–16, 1983, pp. 43–8.

67. *Voices from Prague*, pp. 29–36.

68. Ibid., p. 40. See also Hájek's 1984 essay, "Comments on Peace in Europe", *Listy*, vol. 15, no. 1 (February 1985), pp. 1–6.

69. *Palach Press Bulletin*, no. 25 (January 1985), pp. 49–50.

70. Ibid., pp. 55–65 (summary only). Absence of documentation about the impact and follow-up of this important document abroad prevents us from giving it the adequate coverage it deserves.

71. *Listy*, vol. 14, no. 6 (December 1984), pp. 15–20; English version in *Palach Press Bulletin*, no. 25 (January 1985), pp. 71–7.

72. *Svedectví* 75 (1985), pp. 569–91; abbreviated English text in *The New York Review of Books*, November 21, 1985. See also Ann Ward, "Peace, Politics and Utopia—Havel's Anatomy of Reticence", *East European Reporter*, vol. 1, no. 3 (1985), pp. 38–41. Full English version of Havel's "An Anatomy of Reticence" appeared in *Cross Currents* (Ann Arbor), vol. 5 (1986).

73. Havel's criticism of the Soviet colonial war in Afghanistan is rather unusual for a prominent Chartist. While the tone of collective Charter documents is much more "reticent" on Afghanistan, the Polish underground press, by contrast, has called for solidarity with "fighting Afghanistan" (See Jozef Darksi, "Afghanistan in the Polish Opposition Press"), *Central Asian Survey*, vol. 6, no. 2 (1987), pp. 90–103.

74. *Listy*, vol. 15, no. 2 (April 1985), pp. 3–4; for the English version see *East European Reporter*, vol. 1, no. 1/Spring 1985/, pp. 27–8.

75. *Právo Lidu*, no. 2, 1985.

76. Skilling, "Human Rights and Peace", unpublished draft (1987), p. 34. I am grateful to Prof. Skilling for allowing me to see his text and for his comments on my own draft.

77. *East European Reporter*, vol. 1, no. 3 (1985), p. 36.

78. Ibid., pp. 36–8.

79. Ibid.

80. Jan Kavan, "Helsinki: An Assessment by East-West Independents", *East European Reporter*, vol. 2, no. 1 (1986), pp. 23–4.

81. János Kis and György Dálos, "Thesis on the Post-Helsinki Period", ibid.; see also the message

by János Kis to Warsaw: "Can We Have a Joint Programme?", *EER*, vol. 2, no. 4 (1987), pp. 58–9.

82. Charter 77 document 12/86, in *Listy*, vol. 16, no. 4 (July 1986), pp. 6–12; English version in *EER*, vol. 2, no. 1 (1986), pp. 24–7.

83. See Václav Havel's "Anatomy of a Reticence" quoted above. See Jan Kavan's introduction to the Memorandum, *EER*, vol. 2, no. 2 (1986), pp. 52–60.

84. "Giving Real Life to the Helsinki Accords", a Memorandum drawn up in common by independent groups and individuals in Eastern Europe and Western Europe, publ. by the European Network for East-West Dialogue, April 1987; see also *Listy* vol. 17, no. 1 (February 1987), pp. 18–20. See ORBIS.

85. This was during the Prague spring of 1968–69, see Jaroslaw Piekalkiewicz, *Public Opinion Polling in Czechoslovakia, 1968–69. Results and Analysis of Surveys Conducted During the Dubeck Era* (New York: Praeger, 1972).

86. It took almost a full year to carry out this unusual independent public opinion survey. The questionnaires were sent under difficult conditions in France, to be evaluated with the aid of computers by CRIT (Centre de Recherche Interdisciplinaires sur les Transformations Sociales), under the guidance of Dr. Zdenek Strmiska, until the Soviet invasion of 1968 the Director of the Institute of Sociology in Prague, who published the results in the leading exile quarterly, *Svedectví (Témoignage)*, no. 78 (1986), pp. 258–334.

87. Ibid., pp. 295–8. Compare with the "symmetrical" anti-American reaction in Western Europe shown in the Marplan Poll, conducted about the same time. When it came to basing US nuclear weapons in Europe, the poll demonstrated an almost pan-American chorus of disapproval: 56 percent in the UK, 60 in France, 66 in Germany, and a staggering 78 in Italy. (Cf. David Farhall, "Europe wary of American nuclear stance," *The Manchester Guardian Weekly*, February 22, 1987.)

88. Ibid., pp. 306–8.

89. Ibid., p. 306–8.

90. Ibid., p. 307.

91. J. Herzmann, S. Hampl, L. Friesse: "Verenjné mínení v otázkách války a míru", *Sociologicky casopis* (Prague), no. 1 (1987), pp. 86–97.

92. Ibid. All direct quotes as printed in the *Czechoslovak Situation Report*, RFE/RL Research, April 6, 1987, item 7.

93. *Sociologia* (Bratislava), no. 1 (1987), pp. 9–21.

94. Signed on August 21, 1987, the nineteenth anniversary of the Warsaw Pact invasion of Czechoslovakia, the joint Czechoslovak-Polish declaration stresses three concrete aims to be pursued by independent groups in the Soviet-bloc countries: (1) Conscientious objection in conjunction with the demand for the reduction of the draft and introduction of an alternative service; (2) free travel between all European Soviet-bloc countries; (3) radically new approach to ecological problems. (For the text and names of signatories see *Listy*, vol. 17, no. 5 (October 1987), pp. 52–3. For the new peace association, see Peter Martin, "Independence Peace Activity Intensifies," *Radio Free Europe Research*, Czechoslovak SR/8, June 3, 1988.

95. See John Tagliabue, "7 More Dissidents Convicted in Prague," *The New York Times*, February 23, 1989.

5

The Polish Independent Peace Movement
Christopher Lazarski

On November 8, 1984, Marek Adamkiewicz, a young draftee in the Polish "People's Army," refused to take the military oath. Refusals occurred sporadically, so his was not the first of the kind. In a few similar cases of the late 1970s and early 1980s, military authorities allowed some objectors to complete their service without taking the military oath. Some objectors were dismissed from the army under diverse pretexts; however, others were less fortunate and sent to prison.

This variety of solutions to which the authorities resorted reflects the difficulty of their position. On the one hand, an army oath must be a free act in order to have binding power, and hence its refusal cannot be punishable. On the other hand, the authorities, afraid of a chain reaction, could not admit that such "unpatriotic" behavior was conceivable among draftees. Thus, the objectors were officially deemed either unfit physically or psychologically for service or branded as common criminals. On October 22, 1984, the Military Chamber of the Supreme court seemingly resolved this delicate dilemma. In its interpretation of the law on the military service, the court ruled that refusal to take the oath was tantamount to refusal to serve. This decision, in turn, made the objectors liable to relevant articles of the penal code that stipulate up to eight years of imprisonment for failure to fulfill one's military duty. The Adamkiewicz trial was the first application of this new ruling.[1] On December 8, 1984, a month after his refusal, Adamkiewicz was promptly sentenced by the Military Court of Justice in Szczecin to two and half years in prison. The Adamkiewicz case, however, gave impetus to his friends from the banned Independent Student Union [NZS][2] for an organized campaign in his defense.[3] The period between December of 1984 and April 14 of 1985 was a time of fervent discussion among them in a search for solutions. Ultimately this led to the foundation of the Polish peace movement.

Initially, the possibility of draft resistance being gradually transformed into a peace movement looked unlikely. The reaction of the regime was predictable, for the army is one of the main pillars on which communist power rests, and the authorities could not allow anyone or anything to weaken it. The opposition leaders and society at large did not welcome peace activity either. The former thought that the venture had no chance of succeeding,[4] but that on the contrary it could only bring ruthless reprisals on the part of the government and more imprisoned activists. The attitude of the latter was more complex. Although the army played a leading role in crushing the Solidarity Union, opinion polls indicated that its prestige was still very high.[5] For a nation that has lost its independence three times during last two centuries due to military weakness, such affinity for the army is not surprising. A derivative of the army's popularity was the view that draft evasion was unmanly. Moreover, the Poles were accustomed to regarding pacifism with suspicion. Communist propaganda had irritated them daily with television pictures of Western demonstrations against American armaments. These peace manifestations appeared to the average Pole to be KGB manipulations, because for him, it is Soviet imperialism that poses a threat to peace, not American missiles. As a result, even if the society believed in the good will of the Polish peace activists, it would certainly question their sanity.

In spite of this unfavorable political and social climate, the young oppositionists were increasingly determined not to surrender. For them military service was not an abstract notion. Some had just completed their service, others expected to be drafted soon, and they all understood the deep alienation of draftees who had to face the military machine alone. They were acutely aware of the horrible conditions in the army: "The army is hell . . . officers and older soldiers are allowed to mistreat young recruits. There are frequent cases of nervous breakdown . . . even suicides . . . Let no one kid himself that the army is a school of life; it is often the cause of death."[6] They also knew that the authorities routinely use the service as a weapon against their political adversaries and, for that matter, against any nonconformist draftee. The combination of the standard conditions in the army and the "special treatment" for nonconformists meant that a draftee could hardly expect to survive the service and preserve his dignity. The protagonists of the peace movement had no illusions about the nature of the "People's Army,"[7] which they saw not as defending Poland's independence, but as keeping her dependent. In 1970 and 1981, just as in Czechoslovakia in 1968, it had proved its Soviet imperial functions both internally and externally. It is not surprising, then, that armed service could hardly be regarded by the activists as "honorable duty." Finally, the text of the military oath aroused their greatest indignation, for draftees must swear to: ". . . remain faithful to the *Government of the Polish People's Republic* . . ." and ". . . steadfastly guard peace in fraternal alliance with the army of the *Soviet Union* and other allied armies." This oath was viewed as the symbol of "an entire system of enslavement"[8] and hence had to be rejected "in the name of truth."[9] A modification of the oath's content subsequently became their first demand and was continuously stressed in the future.

The defense of conscientious objectors was a point of departure for the organizers of the peace movement; they quickly perceived the advantages of the concept. The Polish communists, like their comrades elsewhere, present themselves as peace-loving creatures; persecution of an independent peace movement would put them in an awkward position. It would compromise their much cherished "dovish image," useful in "the international struggle for peace," and it would destroy the "liberal image" necessary for the extraction of Western loans. If the regime chose a moderate policy as the activists hoped, an independent peace movement would bring several opportunities. The opposition, strong enough to ensure its existence and too weak to overthrow the regime, could not propose any viable program for the solution of the Polish crisis.[10] This failure resulted in general frustration. The peace movement seemed to offer a new and unorthodox method of weakening the communist state and of reviving the opposition movement itself.

The arms race and the nuclear threat, both of which preoccupy Western pacifists, were not chief issues for the Polish peace movement in its *statu nascendi.* Still, some activists thought that the society's indifference toward these matters and its satisfaction with the deployment of Pershings and Cruises in Western Europe deserved reconsideration. A number of these missiles were directed against Polish territory, hence the Poles had no reason for complacency. Thus, concern for nuclear danger and the need for rousing social awareness also motivated the organizers of the Polish peace movement.

In the final preorganizational stages, Adamkiewicz's friends began a week-long hunger strike in Lesna Podkowa near Warsaw in March 1985 to protest his imprisonment. Throughout, problems of peace and human rights were discussed at daily seminars. Although the protest met with warm reception from opposition leaders,[11] it appears that their endorsement stopped short of support for the peace movement itself. Only the more radical activists of the Confederation of Independent Poland (KPN), irritated by the opposition's procrastination, decided not to wait for official guidance or the blessing of underground patriarchs and published in Cracow, on April 14, 1985, the "Founding Declaration of the Movement: Freedom and Peace" (*Wolnosc i Pokoj, WiP).* Faced with this fait accompli, activists of other opposition centers joined the Cracovian initiative and signed the declaration.

The Cracovian activists announced in the opening statement of the declaration that "the fundamental aim of the Movement is to propagate among Poles and to attract them to a genuine and unadulterated idea of peace." They went on to affirm that "the term 'peace' . . . is . . . generally abused by those who while proclaiming slogans of peace, cooperation and disarmament desire in fact to deprive free peoples of the means and will to defend their liberty."[12] Because of the mass scale of this phenomenon, "the word 'peace' became morally ambiguous and politically foreign" to the Poles. "That is why we want, first of all, to restore the moral and political value of peace activity." In the second part of the declaration, the activists proclaimed that "Freedom is an indispensable condition for peace. . . . There is no peace where . . . there have been created systems of state repression and ideological coercion . . . hence, there is no peace in Poland, under Communists' rule." The peace activists thus wanted to fight for freedom in their country in order to "give peace a chance in Poland." In the last part of the declaration they expressed their desire for "cooperation with all peoples, institutions and movements in Poland and abroad in peace activity based on the principle of freedom."[13]

The Founding Declaration of WiP expressed a peculiar Eastern European or, more accurately, Polish view of peace. Jacek Czaputowicz, a Warsaw activist, who soon became one of the best known of WiP's leaders, said that the declaration stressed freedom too much and neglected peace. Because of this disequilibrium of aims, WiP was threatened with losing its special advantage of being a peace movement and becoming one of many opposition groups in Poland with no separate identity.

The need for a more balanced program was fulfilled by the Second Declaration of WiP, issued on November 17, 1985.[14] This broader and more mature document touches on a variety of problems not broached by its predecessor, and still remains the most significant ideological document of WiP. The Second Declaration is divided into the following seven parts:

1) *Human Rights.* In this section WiP states that civil rights, freedom of expression, full religious freedom, and the unrestricted freedom to organize labor unions and other associations are prerequisite to any other principles. Therefore, these rights form the essence of WiP's struggle. Particularly important in this respect is the issue of prisoners' rights, especially those of political prisoners. "The use of physical and psychological violence against prisoners is inadmissible. . . . We oppose capital punishment which is a disgrace to modern-day legal systems."

2) *National Liberation.* "WiP will support the struggle of nations oppressed by ideologically or nationally alien forces" as well as "the struggle of ethnic groups and national minorities for autonomy." It will also pay special attention to the status of national minorities in Poland and Polish minorities abroad.

3) *The Danger of War, the International Peace Movement.* "In view of the fact that the main threat to the modern world is nuclear annihilation, we will attempt to bring the enormity of this threat to the attention of Polish society. The method "to fight evil is nonviolent struggle . . . [but in a situation] threatening life . . . one has the moral right to resort to force." WiP also endorses the dialogue between the West and the East, especially between the Germans and the Poles, and it proposes "to create a nuclear-free zone in Central Europe which—*if accompanied by the victory of democracy in the East* (author's italics)—would decrease the danger of war." WiP thinks that when a "nation's aims are different from those of the state, the legally sanctioned duty of military service violates human conscience." In the case of Poland, even the military oath

"imposing loyalty to the government" and the "brotherly armies" constitutes such a violation. Similarly, military service often goes against a draftee's religious beliefs, hence WiP demands modification of laws so as to allow for civilian service in place of military duty. Finally, WiP "respects and appreciates the work of many organizations and institutions for world peace. The 'Freedom and Peace' movement wants to become an integral part of these efforts."

4) *The Environmental Protection.* In this part of the declaration, WiP states its strong opposition to "the shortsighted policy of industrialization which causes irreversible damage to the environment" and expresses its mistrust of atomic energy. It also "supports those actions throughout the world whose aim it is to safeguard the environment and ban nuclear testing."

5) *Starvation in the World. Charity Relief,* 6) *Human Development,* and 7) *Tolerance.* In the last three sections of the Declaration, WiP pays homage to the lofty ideas and virtues for which mankind has striven since the emergence of *homo politicus,* leaving no doubt that it stands on the side of Progress against the dark forces of Evil.

In this lengthy declaration, WiP confirms its previous commitment to the cause of liberty while highlighting the importance of issues that are traditionally associated with the cause of peace. In the part devoted to liberty, what is most striking is the attention given to prisoners' rights, to the rights of Polish minorities abroad (for example in the Soviet Union and in Czechoslovakia), and to the right to resort to force in a life-threatening situation. The most interesting points in the second segment on peace are WiP's views on the need for democracy in Eastern Europe (whether this area is nuclear free or not); on the significance of German-Polish reconciliation; and on environmental control—an issue entirely neglected earlier.

A characteristic feature of the East European peace movements is their firm belief in the link between liberty and peace.[15] This is a natural result of the lack of freedom in these countries. An interview with WiP spokesman Jacek Szymanderski further illuminates this conviction: ". . . it is not guns but man who shoots. Totalitarianism is more dangerous than missiles, for it is not enough to supply a man with a uniform and a gun to make him kill. He must also be provided with a false idea and then deprived of a part of his freedom. This is what totalitarianism does. Those who add up megatons choose to ignore this."[16] This last sentence refers to those Western pacifists who concern themselves with weapons only, leading them to demand unilateral Western disarmament. According to WiP, this attitude proves their naïveté and is very dangerous for peace itself.[17] The movement also refuses to cooperate with the official All-Poland Committee of Peace (OKP). WiP regards OKP as a bureaucratic organization whose functionaries are delegated by the communist administration to execute the task of "struggling for peace."[18]

An interesting complement to WiP ideology is the symbolic patron of the movement, Otto Schimek. Schimek, an Austrian Wehrmacht grenadier, was sentenced to death by a field court martial for "desertion and cowardice in the face of the enemy" and executed in Southern Poland on November 14, 1944. These are the only unquestionable facts about the last moments of his life. Schimek was a deeply religious man. In letters to his sister he confessed that faith had saved him from killing anyone during a two-year tour of duty in the Wehrmacht. His sister said that Schimek's friends from the army informed her after the war that he was executed because he had refused to partake in an execution of Polish civilians. Her version coincides with vague rumors that circulated in the Polish underground army; the time and place of Schimek's execution also support these rumors.[19] At any rate, Schimek's grave in Machowa, near Tarnow, had become a place of local worship and pilgrimages even before WiP made him the symbol of its movement. The communist authorities, disturbed by this "German" patron, support the official version of the court martial to the extent that they declared that the sentence was "the only appropriate one."[20] Thus, Schimek, after being executed once by the Nazis is now being defamed by the communist mass media while those who want to lay wreaths on his grave are hunted by the police.

Even if the Nazi court and the communist propaganda are right in that he was a deserter, WiP still maintains he is a fitting symbol for a peace movement. "As a 'plain deserter' Schimek, who did not speak Polish and, therefore, could not count on the help of the civilian population, risked his own life, just as he would have done at the front. From this point of view, his 'apparent cowardice' takes on a totally different form."[21] The letters to his sister, especially the last one, written within an hour of his death, confirm that reasoning. As a consequence Schimek appears to have been a conscientious objector—if not a hero—who ultimately paid the highest price for refusing to kill. This surely is more than sufficient qualification for a symbol of any peace movement.

At the outset of its activity, WiP had a few valuable assets that made possible the survival and the development of the movement. First, the group quickly established a core of about a hundred activists in the main opposition centers— Warsaw, Wroclaw, Gdansk, and Cracow. Most of them had an opposition past and thus experience in underground activity and in dealing with the police. Despite a clear awareness of the risks involved, they were determined to act. The existence of this elite group, which had endured jails, imprisonment, fines, and so on, was a decisive factor for the movement's survival. Second, WiP was able to take full advantage of organized opposition structures. The WiP's elementary task, i.e., to reach the public, was accomplished due to their assistance. Although peace activists sometimes complained about difficulties in getting their own materials published in the underground press, the sheer fact that their texts and news about them were printed and circulated through a nationwide underground network allowed them, in a relatively short time, to become a well-known group. The Committee of Social Resistance (KOS) was especially helpful in this respect. It regularly lent space to WiP in its bulletin *KOS*. Prior to the establishment of WiP's own press in 1986, KOS, with an average circulation of ten to fifteen thousand copies a month, was almost the official newspaper of the Polish peace movement. Furthermore, the opposition movement, by its very nature, served WiP as an umbrella organization. Any persecution of peace activists immediately became an issue in the underground press, and each case entered the opposition's list of grievances automatically. Third, some of WiP's actions generated sizable support. For example, approximately ten thousand people, most of them draft-age students, signed letters protesting Adamkiewicz's imprisonment. Similarly, after the Chernobyl catastrophe, WiP was able to attract a large number of people to the ecology issue.

In September of 1985 WiP initiated an action that challenged the authorities not only in words but, for the first time, also in deeds. In protest of Adamkiewicz's confinement, WiP's activists began returning their military ID's to the minister of national defense.[22] The protesters faced fines and up to three months of jail for this misdemeanor, which in Poland is not regarded as a serious penalty. However, the underground press speculated that the authorities might draft them and sentence them to prison if they refused to serve in the army.[23] It is thus not surprising that only twenty-eight WiP activists decided to participate in that action.[24]

The Second Declaration of WiP devoted an extensive chapter to environmental issues, yet prior to May 1986 the movement did little along these lines. Poles tended to ignore ecological problems. Communism itself was viewed as such an immense disaster that all other problems appeared insignificant in comparison.[25] Moreover, few believed that anything could be done. The opposition frequently published articles on the ecological catastrophe in Poland but was not able or willing to mobilize public opinion to put pressure on the government. The Chernobyl accident, which occurred less than 300 miles from the Polish borders, instantly changed this attitude. In May and June of 1986, WiP organized several demonstrations, supported by hundreds of spontaneous participants, to protest government disinformation about Chernobyl, to demand compensation from the Soviet Union, and to express solidarity with Ukrainians and Belorussians.[26] Furthermore, problems of nuclear energy and the environment became serious matters, now continuously stressed by WiP. As far as nuclear energy was concerned, WiP did not have a clear position. "Some people [in WiP] are against nuclear energy but think that there is no other choice."[27] However, because of obsolete technology and the absence of public control, "all agree that communism is not suited to nuclear energy at all."[28] For that reason, WiP strongly opposed a government project to build a nuclear plant in Zarnowiec and to zone a radioactive waste site in Miedzyrzecze. Environmental protection, in turn, acquired vital importance: "What is most important [for Poland] is the ecology. This country will perish not only because Soviet tanks are stationed here but also because the natural environment is polluted and destroyed. Blaming the communists for everything is blatant exaggeration. In fact, the guilty ones are guys who poison apples in their orchards or sprinkle carrots and lettuce [with chemicals] or [those who] are passive toward such matters as Zarnowiec, Miedzy-rzecze."[29] Since the Chernobyl catastrophe, WiP has provided information about the most drastic cases of industrial pollution and has organized manifestations against them. In one instance, a joint endeavor of the entire opposition and the official press forced the administration to close an obsolete steel foundry in Siechnice near Wroclaw. WiP's outspoken criticism and demonstrations contributed considerably to such a resolution.[30]

The aforementioned return of military documents was followed by an escalation of harassment and persecution of peace activists. On the anniversary of Schimek's execution, in November of 1985, the police detained fourteen members of WiP who wanted to lay wreaths on his grave.[31] This subsequently became a routine procedure. Prior to May of 1987 all such attempts undertaken on the anniversary of his birthday and execution provoked police reprisals.[32] The appearance of WiP also seemed to encourage some draftees to resistance, which, in turn, increased repressions. Refusal to take the military oath was followed by rejection of military service altogether. Among the latter, the case of Wojciech Jankowski became as symbolic for the movement as that of Adamkiewicz. Jankowski was the first draftee during the period of WiP's existence who refused to serve, and he was for that reason sentenced to three and a half years in prison.[33]

In February 1986 the authorities arrested two WiP leaders, Jacek Czaputowicz and Piotr Niemczyk, and charged them with "founding and directing an illegal association known as 'Freedom and Peace,' " which intended "to harm Poland's interests."[34] This was the government's first attempt to penalize WiP members not for taking part in a specific action but for participating in the movement itself, and it opened a most dramatic period for WiP. The authorities seemed to be determined to annihilate the group. Peace activity turned into a very risky venture: "There is no doubt that, unlike in underground activities where you may or may not be caught, membership in Freedom and Peace poses a danger: you will simply have to pay. . . ."[35]

It is evident that WiP would not have been able to withstand persecution for long. The peace movement, however, was only a minor point in a much larger problem that the Polish communists had to deal with. Since crushing the Solidarity Union in 1981, the Jaruzelski regime had tried to overcome the Western political boycott and obtain new financial aid. The Western, especially American, condition for a new rapprochement was the liberalization of Polish domestic policy, which meant the release of political prisoners. On June 17, 1986, the government again attempted to fulfill that condition and declared a new limited amnesty. In August and September it freed more than 200 prisoners, mostly Solidarity activists, but it kept the draft resistors behind bars. WiP did its best to inform foreign and domestic opinion about their fate.[36] This appeared to be the best tactic, for it discredited governmental claims that there were no political prisoners in Poland. The authorities yielded and released them. Ultimately, the prospect of foreign loans was too alluring for the communists to risk losing them because of a few prisoners. This outcome was a great triumph for WiP. The movement had not only attained freedom for all its members but, more importantly, it radically improved its own status. WiP won equal treatment with the rest of the opposition even if it remained the first to be attacked.[37] It became an integral part of the venerable Solidarity opposition, which the communists could not destroy without a thorough transformation of policies in Poland and perhaps even in the entire Eastern bloc—WiP was no longer the "enfant terrible" of the opposition.

In the post-amnesty period, WiP also achieved one more important concession from the government on the question of alternative service. The Jaruzelski regime was faced with the choice of either suppressing the conscientious objectors and losing its fresh liberal image or legalizing alternative service[38] and enjoying the prospect of generous Western loans. The regime adopted the latter course[39] because it had something to gain and not much to lose. Almost two years of WiP activities did not precipitate an avalanche of refusals of military service—what the communists feared most—while the law on alternative service virtually eliminated the possibility of such a development in the future. Even without the threat of imprisonment, the authorities preserved pressure strong enough to induce the overwhelming majority of draftees to serve.[40]

The government also softened its attitude toward Jehovah's Witness draftees, who constituted the considerable majority of prisoner–conscientious objectors and were not freed in the July 1986 amnesty. Since the Jehovah's Witnesses did not defend themselves, their cause was entirely unknown to the public until WiP initiated an information campaign about their persecution. It is difficult to judge how much this campaign influenced the government. Yet the fact is that at the end of 1986 the regime agreed to permit Jehovah's Witnesses to substitute work in coal mines for military service.[41]

Finally, it is worth mentioning WiP's concern with matters of national liberation and minority rights. Soviet intervention in Afghanistan and the struggle of the Afghans are issues that appeared frequently in WiP declarations and appeals. The movement collected signatures on petitions protesting the intervention and displayed street banners expressing solidarity with the Afghans' fight.[42] Furthermore, in response to an appeal by the International Red Cross for medical assistance to the Afghans, WiP issued a series of stamps on the Afghan war and sent the profit to the IRC.[43] The movement often voiced its solidarity with the causes of the Crimean Tartars, Cubans, and Chileans. In Poland it defended Ukrainian minority rights.[44]

Since its foundation, WiP has paid a great deal of attention to relations with Western peace groups. It has sought contacts with those movements that admitted at least some Soviet threat to peace and acknowledged the link between peace and liberty. WiP has developed "good and permanent relations" with such organizations as the Dutch Interchurch Peace Council (IKV); the French

Committee for Nuclear Disarmament in Europe (CODENE); the British European Nuclear Disarmament (END); the Danish No to Nuclear Weapons; the West German Greens, and the American Campaign for Peace and Democracy.[45]

WiP and its Western counterparts share fundamental aims as well as the spontaneity, youth, and idealism of their activists. Still, in many respects they differ profoundly. The former stresses liberty as the highest good, as a prerequisite to any other, regards Soviet totalitarianism as the greatest menace to mankind, sympathizes with the struggle of the Afghans, and protests against violations of the human rights of Crimean Tartars, Ukrainians, Cubans, and others. The latter emphasizes peace, view American imperialism and armament in themselves as the basic enemies of peace, demonstrate against American intervention in Nicaragua, and denounce human-rights violations in South Africa, Chile, El Salvador, and elsewhere. In their dealings with each other, the priorities of each side are acknowledged rather than accepted. Moreover, each side sees the other as somewhat immature and hopes to influence the other's maturation.

An article in *END*[46] about the emergence of WiP illustrates the attitude of the Western pacifists: Its author greets WiP with satisfaction; another country in Soviet Europe has spawned an autonomous peace group. Yet he observes: "So far the group has confined itself to limited objectives, and has not agreed about its strategies in the areas the Western peace movement hold dear—on such questions as first use, multilateral versus unilateral disarmament,[47] and the Star Wars plan." And he writes that ". . . although the groups are becoming increasingly active . . . they still *have to develop the philosophies which would bring them closely into line with the Western peace movement* (author's italics). WiP, for its part, was not prepared to play the role of apprentice. On the contrary, it wished to rectify the course of Western pacifism and to *bring it closely into line with East European movements.*[48] During the initial contact in July 1985 at the Fourth European Nuclear Disarmament Convention in Amsterdam, the Polish pacifists declared: "A man ready to fulfill any order threatens peace more than the neutron bomb . . . States that have authoritarian and totalitarian governments are themselves contradictory to the idea of peace. As long as nations are oppressed, exploited, terrorized and exterminated, there is no peace in the world. Our work for peace should be directed to the liberty of the peoples of Cuba, Indonesia, Afghanistan, Chile, as well as Crimean Tartars etc." Therefore, WiP demanded "to permanently include justice and civic freedoms in the notion of peace and to treat the struggle against totalitarian systems as equal to the efforts toward disarmament." It also unequivocally opposed the idea of unilateral disarmament and suggested regional demilitarization, especially the demilitarization of Central Europe.[49] These disparities in perspectives between the Western and Eastern peace activists sometimes led to paradoxes. In a joint declaration signed in April 1986 by the West German Green party and WiP we read: "We differ . . . in our analysis of the comprehensive nature of the Western military alliance and our analysis of the threat it poses to the Polish people." This statement does not mean that the Poles are afraid of NATO and that the Germans dismiss this threat, as one would guess, but vice versa.

The distrust of "the fatherland of the proletariat," based on Poland's centuries-old experience with first Russian and then Soviet imperialism, made WiP's members truly unorthodox peace fighters. In an open letter to American peace activist Joanne Landy, Piotr Niemczyk asserts that Gorbachev is insincere in his proposal to withdraw all middle-range missiles from Europe. The general secretary knows that the Western governments cannot accept his offer[50] because such a step would endanger the balance of power that has kept Europe in peace for forty years and would leave the Soviets with a "significant predominance in tactical and conventional weapons." Thus this proposal, like many other Warsaw Pact initiatives, does not attempt to achieve an agreement but is aimed at causing disagreement among the NATO governments and at provoking a new wave of anti-American campaigns by Western peace movements. The Polish pacifist expresses his fear of just such a course of events, for "from the point of view of independent peace activities in Poland, nothing is more alarming than a recurrence of the situation whereby the Western peace movement activities become, undoubtedly with no such intention, a tool of Soviet policy and propaganda.[51]

The Western-Polish association includes the exchange of views, joint declarations, WiP's appeals for help against persecution and Western responses to them, participation in international peace meetings, and frequent private contacts. The most spectacular of such activities took place on May 7–9, 1987, in Warsaw, at a peace seminar organized by WiP. In spite of police counteractions,[52] the seminar brought together approximately 250 activists, including about 60 representatives from the West,[53] who debated for three days in the basement of a Warsaw church.[54]

The seminar, entitled "International Peace and the Helsinki Accord" had two basic purposes: first, to find a definition of peace activity acceptable to East and West, and second, to agree on specific actions in the future. A memorandum drawn up by Western and Eastern activists, "Giving Real Life to the Helsinki Accords," served as a common platform for the conference.[55] Four major topics were discussed: a new détente "from below"; peace and human rights; personal responsibility for peace, and ecology a year after Chernobyl.[56] The last two issues did not provoke controversy, yet the first two highlighted contrasts in Western and Eastern outlooks. Although all agreed in principle on the importance of the link between peace and liberty, the participants had different opinions on U.S.-Soviet disarmament negotiations, Soviet or American imperialism, Reagan-Thatcher or Gorbachev's policies, on the problems of Third World countries, and so forth. In view of these differences, it became apparent that the proposition to unify all peace movements into one international organization[57] was at worst unrealistic, and at best premature. However, these controversies, no less than the areas of agreement, served to further the understanding of the nature of East-West relations. The participants realized that if they wished to continue to cooperate, they would have to accept the identity of each movement and its own priorities and methods. Although this conclusion implied that WiP would have to refrain from converting the Western pacifists into "freedom fighters," it was a remarkable success for WiP and a huge step toward the emancipation of East European peace movements.

The autonomy of each group and the emancipation of the East European pacifists can be treated as an unwritten definition of peace activity common to East and West. Thus, the first aim of the seminar was accomplished. The other results included several agreements and joint declarations. The participants agreed to exchange information, to intervene in cases of persecution, to work on the establishment of an International Intervention Center, and to support WiP in its endeavors to establish a nationwide *WiP* bulletin.[58] They also issued an appeal on the International Day of Conscientious Objection and signed an Ecology Declaration.

It is necessary to recall the evolution of the government's attitudes toward peace activity in Poland. Threatened by the growing number of draftees who were refusing to take the military oath, the authorities devised legal restrictions directed against the conscientious objectors. Desiring to resolve the matter of draft resistance once and for all, the Polish authorities created for themselves an even more serious problem. They inadvertently provoked the birth of an independent peace movement in Poland. The growing number of draftees who refused to take the military oath induced the regime to devise the legal restrictions directed against the conscientious objectors. The new ruling, applied for the first time against Adamkiewicz, led in turn to the foundation of WiP.

The authorities' policies toward WiP passed through three stages: (1) indecision and limited counteraction (April 1985—February 1986); (2) full-scale assault (February 1986—October 1986); (3) unofficial recognition and "standard" repressions (October 1986–present). In the first period the regime hardly seemed to take notice of the group's existence. The repressions started in September of 1985 when WiP members began to turn back their military IDs. In the meantime, however, the number of imprisoned conscientious objectors grew. The second phase began with the arrest of Czaputowicz and Niemczyk. In addition to persecution, the government also initiated a propaganda campaign against WiP, accusing it of being in the service of West German revisionists, the CIA, Reagan, and all the other "dark imperialist forces." In the last period, the government reconciled itself to the fact that the independent peace movement existed and was functioning. The price for WiP's destruction appeared too high when attempts to isolate it from the opposition did not succeed. The concessions on the matter of alternative service further reduced the tension. Currently, although the regime seems to abhor the peace movement more than any other opposition group, the existence of WiP is as secure as that of the rest of the Polish opposition.

The Polish peace movement was a reaction to blatant abuses of power in matters of military service. Solidarity with the victims of such abuses became a powerful impetus to young oppositionists to organize a defense movement. This moral concern was strengthened by political considerations. Peace activity appeared to offer a way of striking the communist regime in its weak point and thus overcoming the opposition's impotence. Genuine pacifism was an unfamiliar phenomenon in Poland, and therefore, was not a significant factor in the foundation of WiP. Initially, the peace movement seemed to be a tactical choice for the majority of WiP's members. Soon, however, as the Second Declaration indicates, peace activity *sensu stricto* began to be treated seriously. Although the ideology that WiP developed may not have fulfilled Western expectations, it certainly made WiP a true peace organization.

Unlike other peace movements in Soviet Europe, WiP is not alone vis-à-vis the authorities but is a part of a very powerful—by Eastern standards—anticommunist opposition. Furthermore, as the example of the Warsaw Peace Seminar in May 1987 shows, WiP can occasionally count on the protection and assistance of another institution independent of the government, i.e., the church. Thus peculiar political conditions in Poland enabled it to become a highly visible and dynamic organization in a relatively short time. In the fall of 1986, WiP succeeded in securing its own existence and since then it shares equal (mis)treatment with the rest of the post-Solidarity opposition. Additionally, the movement's pressure forced the government to make a major concession in the matter of alternative service. Even if this problem is still far from being adequately resolved, the conscientious objectors are no longer sent to prison. Other unquestionable accomplishments of WiP are the popularization of "unadulterated" ideas of peace among the Poles, the erosion of the army's prestige, and attention to environmental issues. In relations with Western pacifists, WiP, together with other Eastern groups, has become a mighty voice of nations enslaved by communism. This voice cannot be ignored, and hence some Western pacifists have included, more or less willingly, human rights in their notion of peace. It seems that at the Warsaw Peace Seminar, WiP may also have changed the nature of relations between Western and Eastern peace groups. At least WiP, if not the other Eastern groups, has ceased to be a client begging for financial and political help and become a partner of Western organizations.

WiP has been an essentially successful initiative which has added peace activity to the program of the Polish opposition. Yet the fact that WiP remains a small, elite group constitutes its most significant failure. Its limited size means that the movement has not caught the Poles' imagination and thus has not solved the problems that stem from the opposition's lack of realistic agenda. WiP, along with the rest of the opposition, now bears the responsibility for the general apathy of the Polish society, and one day it may be accused by a new group of young and angry people of belonging to an opposition establishment that has no viable concepts for the future.

Postscript:

I wrote this article more than a year ago. In the meantime, the political situation in Poland has changed dramatically. The pervasive economic crisis as well as the patient grass-roots work of numerous independent activists has finally forced the government to talk with the post-Solidarity opposition. The nature of peace activities and the conditions in which Freedom and Peace acts have evolved too. Neither the regime nor the society now perceives WiP as an immediate threat to communist rule in Poland. Since the regime's concessions in the matters of alternative service, WiP can no longer challenge the government in principle but has to engage in everyday clashes with petty bureaucrats who break the new regulations at the local level. Thus the defense of persecuted conscientious objectors and the dissemination of information about regulations regarding alternative service currently occupy most of WiP's energy. Such activity is naturally less spectacular and, therefore, attracts less attention.

There are other reasons for the general drop of interest in the peace movement as well. The society is not as passive as it was just a year ago. During recent months, the Solidarity Union has been recreating its structures at the factory level: many new professional associations and discussion clubs have appeared, each with its own agenda. During this period of political revival in Poland, WiP has to compete in the market of ideas for its own concerns—not an easy task. Interference in army affairs, defense of conscripts, and demands for nuclear disarmament no longer excite Poles. Another issue, ecology, became part of the national program, and hence the voice of WiP is now only one of many. It remains to be seen if WiP, freed from the unrealistic expectations that burdened the group at its inception, will be able to take advantage of democratization in Poland and expand its narrow base of support.

Washington, D.C., January 1989.

NOTES

1.   Another objector, Miroslaw Zablocki, took the oath after he learned about the Supreme Court ruling.

2.   Adamkiewicz belonged to the pre-Solidarity opposition. A student of physics, he was relegated in 1978 from Wroclaw University for his activity in Student Solidarity Committee [SKS]. See *Gazeta Academicka* (Academic Gazette), no. 2, 1986. His connections with the opposition helped in providing a fast flow of information about his fate.

3.   Legal methods of protests, such as letters to the Parliament and the State Council and open letters with thousands of signatures did not bring any results. See *Freedom and Peace Movement.* Warsaw, May 1987, p. 7; *Tygodnik Mazowsze* (Mozovian Weekly), no. 153, January 9, 1986.

4.   Jackson Diehl, "New Political Movement Confronts Mandatory Military Service," *Washington Post,* Nov. 4, 1986; William Echikson, "Poland's Newest (and Youngest) Protest Group," *Christian Science Monitor,* Dec. 30, 1986; Michael Kaufman, "Hippie Foes of the Draft Handled With Kid Gloves," *New York Times,* Jan. 3, 1987.

5.   In 1984, Polish workers chose the army as the second (behind the Catholic Church) most respected national institution. See Marek Ziolkowski, "Individuals and the Social System: Values, Perceptions, and Behavioral Strategies," manuscript, Poznan University, Institute of Sociology, 1986, pp. 16–17, 20.

6. Z Dnia na Dzien [From Day to Day], no. 14 (358), April 14–20, 1985.

7. Peace activists and the opposition in general were frustrated by Polish society's attitude toward the army. A flood of articles published in 1986 on the role of the "People's Army" shows it well, see for example Robotnik (Worker), no. 113/114; Gazeta Akademicka, no. 2; Wola (Will), no. 3; KOS, no. 90; Nurt, [Current], no. 1; Biuletyn Lodzki [Lodz Bulletin], no. 93.

8. KOS, no. 90, Feb. 23, 1986.

9. Gazeta Akademicka. no. 2, 1986.

10. Underground union activity, the independent press, and patriotic masses and demonstrations could hardly be considered satisfactory. See Solidarnosc Mlodziezy (Solidarity of the Youth), no. 3, July/August, 1986.

11. Lech Walesa sent a telegram to the participants of the hunger strike. Former Solidarity Union advisors, a leader of World War II Jewish resistance in Poland, and well-known writers, scholars, actors, and singers took part in the seminars.

12. A clear reference to the Soviet style of "struggling for peace."

13. The text of the Founding Declaration; a leaflet with no date or place of publication.

14. An English version of the Second Declaration; a leaflet with no publication date or place. I also used an edited version of the Declaration published in Peace & Democracy News, vol. II no. 2, Summer/Fall 1986, pp. 5, 6.

15. The first such public statement was made in 1974 by the Czechoslovak human rights movement in Charter 77 in its Open Letter to the III European Nuclear Disarmament Convention in Perugia, Italy.

16. Przeglad Wiadomosci Agencyinych (Press Agency Survey), no. 32, Dec. 12, 1986.

17. An interview with one of the WiP leaders, Piotr Niemczyk in Robotnik, no. 113/114, Oct. 26, 1986.

18. Solidarnosc Mlodziezy [The Solidarity of the Youth], no. 3, July/August 1986. Wroclaw.

19. Wiez (Bounds), no. 2/3. 1984; Tygodnik Mazowsze. no. 188, Nov. 19, 1986; Freedom and Peace Movement, pp. 16–19.

20. Trybuna Ludu (People's Tribune), March 30, 1986. It is an astounding paradox that Kazimierz Kakol, the chief of the Main Committee for the Investigation of Nazi Crimes, expressed this opinion.

21. Freedom and Peace Movement, p. 17–18.

22. Every adult male in Poland had to carry such an I.D.

23. Tygodnik Mazowsze, no. 153, January 9, 1986.

24. Poglad. [View], February 2, 1986. All of them were jailed or fined. The underground speculations did not materialize, perhaps because the authorities ran out of time. Before the 1986 amnesty, almost all active participants of the peace movement were jailed; therefore, they could not be drafted.

25. An interview of two Warsaw activists of WiP, Jaroslaw Dubiel and Marek Krukowski, in Solidarnosc Mlodziezy [The Solidarity of the Youth], no. 3, June/August 1986, p. 5.

26. Freedom and Peace Movement, p. 9. May 2, demonstrations in Cracow and Wroclaw; June 1, a demonstration in Cracow.

27. Solidarnosc Mlodziezy, p. 3.

28. Ibid.

29. Solidarnosc Mlodziezy, p. 5.

30. Freedom and Peace Movement, p. 24–25.

31. Freedom and Peace Movement, p. 8.

32. In November of 1986 the police detained more than fifty persons, among them three Frenchmen and two West Germans. See *Feniks* [Phoenix], no. 133, November 24, 1986; *Tygodnik Mazowsze*, no. 188, November 19, 1986.

33. *Tygodnik Mazowsze*, no. 153, January 9, 1987.

34. *Freedom and Peace Movement*, p. 9.

35. *Zero*, no. 5, Winter-Spring 1986; "Intent of Democracy, an Interview with Jacek Czaputowicz," no. 9 (*Sojourners*, October, 1987), p. 22—"In our actions the chance of being arrested is 100 percent."

36. Inter alia, a press conference on September 22, 1987 and a sit-in demonstration in Warsaw on October 3, 1987. *Tygodnik Mazowsze*. Jankowski also began a hunger strike.

37. It seems that WiP replaced KPN [the Confederacy of Independent Poland] as the most persecuted but already recognized organization.

38. In fact, to permit the practical application of old legal rules.

39. The legal basis for the alternative service was presented in the official military daily *Zolnierz Wolnosci* [Soldier of Freedom], p. 4, January 7, 1987. A few days later, on January 16, the spokesman of the Ministry of National Defense confirmed that information during a press conference. *Tygodnik Mazowsze*, no. 195, January 21, 1987.

40. The rule does not specify which requirements are to be fulfilled in order for a draftee to be automatically transferred to alternative service. It simply opens the possibility of such service and leaves a decision in hands of the local military commander. In practice, it means that only the most determined draftees are transferred. The rest bow to "petty" pressures such as personal threats, including threats to a draftee's family, employment, career advancement, college education, travels abroad, etc.

41. *Biuletyn Lodzki* [The Lodz Bulletin], no. 102, January 13, 1987. The agreement was reached after confidential negotiations with the Executive Body of the Polish Jehovah's Witnesses.

42. *Tygodnik Mazowsze*, no. 199, February 18, 1987.

43. *Tygodnik Mazowsze*, no. 150/151, December 12, 1985.

44. *KOS*, no. 117, May 4, 1987.

45. An interview with Jacek Czaputowicz in *Wola*, no. 212, February 9, 1987.

46. Peter Lane, "Polish groups risk harassment," *END, Journal of European Nuclear Disarmament*. no. 19 (London, December 1985/January 1986), p. 11.

47. The author apparently did not read the Second Declaration.

48. This ambition is accentuated even more strongly in publications directed to Polish readers. Particular examples are interviews with: Jacek Czaputowicz—*KOS*, no. 87, January 12, 1986; *Metrum*, no. 52, February 26, 1986—and Piotr Niemczyk—"To Cleanse the Word Peace of lies," *Poglad*. no. 231 (Berlin, February 16, 1986), pp. 43, 44; *Robotnik*, no. 113, October 26, 1986.

49. *Nasze Wiadomosci* [Our News], no. 10, January 19, 1986. The idea of a demilitarized nuclear zone in Central Europe was actively recommended by Jacek Kuron, a veteran of the Polish dissident movement.

50. After the December 1987 summit visit in Washington, we know that Niemczyk underestimated the charm of Mikhail and Raisa Gorbachev.

51. *Biuletyn WiP* [Bulletin of WiP], no. 7–8, Warsaw, March, 1987.

52. The police conducted hundreds of "warning talks" and had detained more than thirty WiP members the eve of the seminar. Some participants went into hiding a few days earlier predicting the possibility of preventive arrests. *Tygodnik Mazowsze*, no. 211, May 13, 1987.

53.   Some twenty Western Europeans did not receive Polish visas; two were turned away at Warsaw airport. Only two representatives of Eastern Europe, one from Czechoslovakia and one from Yugoslavia, were able to attend the Seminar. The rest were not permitted by the governments to travel to Poland. *Tygodnik Mazowsze,* no. 211, May 13, 1987.

54.   The church in Poland enjoys "semi-extra territorial rights." The police hardly ever enter church buildings.

55.   The memorandum, which stresses the indivisibility of peace and human rights, was a response to the "Prague Appeal" of the Charter 77 presented in 1985 at the END Convention in Amsterdam.

56.   *Wola,* no. 223, May 18, 1987.

57.   Joanne Landy tentatively made this proposition. *Wola,* no. 223, May 18, 1987.

58.   WiP has only regional bulletins.

6

Against Socialist Militarism: The Independent Peace Movement in the German Democratic Republic

Vladimir Tismaneanu

"God judges the disputes of many peoples: he rebukes powerful nations. Then they forge plowshares from their swords and pruning knives from their lances. They no longer draw their swords, nation against nation, nor do they practice war any longer."

Micah 4:3

For many years the political opposition in the GDR was reluctant to radically question the legitimacy of the existing Marxist regime. In its basic principles, the opposition maintained a "loyalist" approach to the government and underwrote the official doctrine about the GDR as a socialist state of the workers and peasants. In the early 1980s, new social groups and movements emerged that have increasingly criticized the regime's self-image and its repressive policies. Enjoying limited though decisive support from the East German Evangelical Church, these groups have put forward a broad social and political agenda that includes the de-militarization of East German society and the observance of fundamental human rights. Their commitment to radical, neo-Marxist theories and ideals is less marked than was that of their forerunners of the 1960s and 1970s. The independent peace and human-rights movement has thus become the nerve center of an expanding, rapidly growing coalition of groups and associations concerned with the democratization of the East German society. They represent the embryo of the emerging civil society.

A Militaristic Society

Founded with Stalin's blessing in October 1949, the GDR claims to be the first German state of the workers and peasants. Its creation represented a resolute break with the expansionist policies of German imperialism. The self-serving corollary to this assumption was that the East German regime was inherently peaceful. However, the foundation of the Marxist regime was guaranteed solely by the presence of the Soviet Army in what was known for a long time as *die Zone*. As a result, the regime has experienced a dramatic legitimacy problem.[1]

Furthermore, the GDR is the only European communist state established on the basis of a national division. This division has constantly marked the dynamics of authority building there. The ruling party, the SED (*Sozialistische Einheitspartei Deutschlands*—the Socialist Unity Party of Germany) has stubbornly pursued the policy of *Abgrenzung* (demarcation) to preserve and enhance the differences between the two German states.[2] Party dogmas proclaim that, because of class distinctions, there are two German states and two German nations: one socialist and the other one capitalist.[3]

To foster its legitimacy, the Communist state claims to inherit the humanist ("progressive") legacy of German culture. The official ideological apparatus spells out the relationship between the East German political culture and the militant traditions of German socialism, including those associated with such paragons of anti-militarism and opposition to Prussian imperialism as Rosa Luxemburg and Karl Liebknecht. Speaking at a rally in East Berlin in January 1988, Egon Krenz, the then SED second-in-command and General Secretary Erich Honecker's heir apparent, reverentially evoked the two martyrs of German socialism: ". . .we bow to their highest dedication to work, bread, and international peace. We are proud to confirm our loyalty to their revolutionary legacy. We have sworn to Karl Liebknecht and we extend our hands to Rosa Luxemburg in a spirit saying that by word and deed we will serve socialism and peace."[4] The GDR claims to have carried out complete de-Nazification and eliminated the sources of militarism. In its self-image, the East German government appears adamantly committed to peace and international cooperation. But the attempt to impose such a reassuring picture has failed, primarily because of the regime's unabashedly militaristic course.

For a long time, the target of the regime's propaganda was the "revanshist" orientation of West German ruling circles. East German communists brandished the NATO nuclear umbrella and proclaimed their firm commitment to peace. At the same time, particularly after the erection of the Berlin Wall in August 1961, it became increasingly clear that the regime was intent upon eternalizing the division of the German nation along ideological lines.

Of all East European Communist parties, it seems that the SED takes ideological issues most seriously.[5] There is a good reason: for East German Communists, any relaxation (political, economic, or cultural) appears to result automatically in a catastrophic erosion of established socialist institutions. Trapped in its permanent deficit of legitimacy, the SED elite suffers from an excruciating inferiority complex. The East German communists realize that their power rests upon two factors: social welfare and ideological conformity. The accomplishment of the former is the precondition for the perpetuation of the latter.

East German party leaders have not forgotten the June 1953 working-class uprising against Stalinist exploitation (imposition of unattainable production norms and underpayment of those who could not meet them). Instead of loosening the party's hold over society, the SED elite has promoted a techno-bureaucratic model of socialism based on accelerated economic growth, tight political controls, and uncompromising ideological conformity. As a consequence, de-Stalinization has never occurred as a far-reaching political process in the GDR. It is thus worth noting that Walter Ulbricht, Honecker's predecessor and political mentor, was particularly instrumental in persuading the Soviet Politburo to adopt the decision to invade Czechoslovakia in August 1968.[6] At the same time, East German Communists must come to terms with another peculiar feature of their political culture: the continuous flow of information ensured by the exposure of GDR citizens to Western media and ongoing contact with relatives from the Federal Republic. It is quite common for SED functionaries to complain about the presence of the "enemy," i.e., sources of uncensored information like Western TV broadcasting, in virtually every East German house.

To counter the proliferation of reformist-democratic ideas, the regime has strengthened its commitment to a hard-line, utterly conservative vision of socialism. In its recurrent campaigns against internal opposition, the official propaganda has played upon the threat of external intervention. Party-controlled media frequently accuse dissidents of being on the payroll of foreign intelligence services. National cohesion is extolled as a condition for the country's very survival. Militarist values have become a main component of the state-controlled educational system.

The *Nationale Volksarmee* (NVA—National People's Army) was transformed into a regular army in 1965. Since 1970, the role of the army has become so prominent that it is no exaggeration to describe the GDR as a potentially militaristic society. To be sure, the SED still holds total political control over all sectors of the East German system, including the military. But the SED has itself internalized militaristic views and values and imposed them on the whole society. But one cannot neglect or minimize the increasing militaristic tendencies illustrated by the mandatory military education in schools and universities, the government's unflinching opposition to conscientious objection, the cultivation of militaristic symbols and values, and the unbounded celebration of militaristic traditions, including those associated with Junker imperialism. Furthermore, though it is true that the NVA is entirely integrated into the Warsaw Pact system and thereby subordinated to the USSR, the East German military has acquired a major role in the country's power structure. After all, the Polish army's membership in the Warsaw Pact only helped General Jaruzelski prepare his December 1981 coup.[7] As one analyst has noted, "if one focuses on the military as a means of political socialization and assumes that the GDR's military propaganda and premilitary education and training of youth are effective, one can easily come to the conclusion that the GDR is a *militarized* society."[8]

Militaristic education gathered momentum in the late 1970s. In 1978, mandatory military education (*Wehrkundeunterricht*) was introduced in the ninth and tenth grades of the technical high schools. Pupils receive eight hours of instruction each year in the party's military policy, the structure of the national defense system, civil defense, and so forth. In the summer, male pupils attend a two-week camp where military skills are developed, including the use of small-caliber weapons. Theoretical and practical military education has become a "normal" feature of the East German high-school curriculum. Following the Soviet model, paramilitary organizations like the Society for Sport and Technique (*Gesellschaft für Sport und Technik*), which claims a membership of 600,000, contribute to the physical preparation of the youth for the military service. This organization's training programs include small-caliber weapons instruction, diving, driving, rowing, sailing, parachuting, and flying.

In universities, both male and female students must participate in premilitary and civil-defense activities. But the most important form of military-political education is the eighteen months of mandatory military service for East German males. Besides the practical exercises, recruits are strongly indoctrinated: Officers conduct political classes and performances. According to the SED, socialist military education (*sozialistische Wehrerziehung*) should consist of methods and measures to create a "socialist personality" totally committed to the defense of the existing social order. Irritated by the independent peace initiatives, the regime has imposed increased military obligations on the youth. For the SED, the militaristic orientation is a means to maintain ideological regimentation and suppress potential sources of instability. It is an attempt to consolidate the status quo, create a perpetual state of national concern about a potential foreign aggression, and delegitimize the claims of the unofficial peace groups. The ruling elite needs militarism to preserve the foundation myth of the GDR as a beleaguered fortress, the most advanced "Western stronghold of socialism."

Under Erich Honecker, resistance to political change and social liberalization was combined with an emphasis on economic effectiveness. The GDR justifiably boasts that it has the most developed economy of the Comecon. Its standard of living is the highest in the socialist bloc, a fact that has not passed unnoticed in neighboring Warsaw Pact countries.[9]

In its efforts to insert itself into national life, the regime has emphasized the East German national identity. First, it has tried to gain popular prestige through the incorporation into the official ideology of certain uplifting symbols and ideas associated with glorious moments in the history of the German nation. The SED has rediscovered and functionalized some traditional values, including those connected with the Prussian past. Suffice it to mention here the statewide celebrations that commemorated in November 1983 the five-hundredth anniversary of the birth of Martin Luther and in the reassessment of the historical contributions of such personalities as Frederick the Great, Carl von Clausewitz and even Otto von Bismarck.[10] It seems that the government has totally abandoned the traditional Marxist tenets about the "reactionary essence of Prussianism."

Second, the government has sought to convince its subjects that its unconditional solidarity with the Soviet Union is the only solution for the country's survival and the peaceful future of the region. The presence of 400,000 Soviet military on their territory gives most East Germans the feeling that they live in an occupied country, and first Walter Ulbricht and then Erich Honecker went out of their way to try to change this perception. Inculcation of pro-Soviet sentiments remains a major task of the military-educational complex.

For a long time, the SED managed to eradicate the germs of political dissent, but since the early 1980s, it has been confronted with autonomous, grass-roots collective efforts to oppose its militaristic course. Initially apolitical, the East German independent peace movement has rapidly realized that a totalitarian state cannot and will not enter into dialogue with autonomous forces, for to do so would mean to relinquish its very *raison d'être* and succumb to the pressures of society.

Because of its special, suprapolitical position within the East German system, the Evangelical Church has been able to provide the independent peace initiatives and groups with a powerful protective shield. Under its umbrella and with its support, these groups have thrived and have become a significant actor on the GDR social and political scene. The church has successfully mediated the uneasy relationship between the party-state and the groups, which are now a major component of the alternative political culture.

Dissent and Pacifism

Under Erich Honecker, who replaced Walter Ulbricht as the head of the SED on May 3, 1971,* the party has been confronted with strong intellectual dissent. However, unlike their peers in other East-Central European countries, many East German dissidents and critical intellectuals have evinced a remarkable degree of attachment to and identification with the values espoused by the system. Most of the East German opposition is thus intra-, rather than anti-systemic.

To be sure, the opposition also comprises elements who squarely reject the Communist regime. But they usually find ways of leaving the GDR, as did poet and songwriter Sascha Anderson, who emigrated on August 15, 1986. Born in 1953 into an intellectual family, he is typical of a generation who refuse to

---

*Erich Honecker was forced out and replaced by Egon Krenz in October 1989 following a tide of mass demonstrations for political and economic reforms. Krenz was himself ousted in December after only six weeks in power. In the meantime, the SED has abandoned its hegemonic claims and accepted a dialogue with the opposition. As of the writing of this note, the SED chairman is Gregor Gysi, a 41-year old lawyer with close contacts among independent peace and human rights activists.

consider the GDR a "motherland." Their pessimism originates in alienation from prevailing communitarian forms which they perceive as intrinsically specious, in their moral despondency, and an overwhelming sense of *Heimatslosigkeit* (uprootedness). Anderson does not nourish any lyrical hopes about Communism. In this respect, his views differ from those advocated by idealist Marxists like the late professor Robert Havemann or the nonconformist balladeer Wolf Biermann. Anderson belongs to a de-radicalized and totally disenchanted generation of critics. Their position is outspokenly system-rejective. Not only do they not expect the system to humanize itself, but they are actually indifferent to its fate: "I have never taken an interest in the system. . . . I never had an interest in undermining the system from inside. I did not even want to set myself in accordance with the demands of the system."[11]

This radical estrangement from the official ideology has released a younger generation from the mental barriers experienced by the "socialist reformers": "After us comes a generation that I think is even more important. They never chose to join society at all. This is the real difference (between) the situation in the mid-1970s (and now). We still know the system. We even know the language of power. Our aversion to the regime stems from our knowledge of its language, its thinking. The generation after us do not understand the language and the thinking of the regime any more. They are much freer than we. We still had to free ourselves."[12] This radical rejection of the system has resulted in the development of an alternative culture of disaffection made up primarily of rock and punk groups. Its members reject not only Marxism-Leninism but all ideological constraints, including nationalism. To the official ambition to create the "new man of the Communist civilization," these people oppose an iconoclastic disgust and fascination with authenticity. In the words of one young East German punker: "Philistinism turns me off. I am against Germanness. The German is, for me, a *petit bourgeois* and a philistine by nature. I am bothered by this whole pretense, by this mask which is there but which no one removes."[13]

Most of the dissidents, however, have not questioned the existing social order but rather the "distortion" of Marxist principles in the SED's behavior. In many cases, acerbic criticism has come from the humanist left. Günter Kunert, a poet who left the GDR in 1979, describes the moral dilemmas of radical intellectuals who deplore the cultural philistinism of official politics: "I am Jewish from my mother's side and have always been on the Left, so at first I welcomed the East German regime and was delighted to live there. But gradually things began to get difficult. My poems are on very private themes, and I just could not turn out the kind of ideological 'public' poetry they wanted; also, one *Leitmotiv* of mine is the dehumanizing effect of modern technology, and Marxism does not tolerate this kind of pessimism. The Party harassed me and finally refused to publish me. . . . My break with GDR-style socialism was a slow and painful process, since I'd believed in it so much—and I still think the regime has many virtues, but not for an artist. Finally we decided to move here and there was no culture shock at all. I'm still a GDR citizen, I have an exit visa and can pay return visits when I wish."[14]

Other critical intellectuals decided to stay and struggle within the GDR. For a long time, until his death in 1982, physics professor Robert Havemann was the most wholehearted advocate of change from within. His statements and essays summed up the frustrations of intellectuals critical of the absence of political and social democracy. At the same time, Havemann's ideas were instrumental in the awakening and crystallization of a forceful antimilitaristic awareness in the GDR. Together with the writers Stefan Heym, Jürgen Fuchs, Jurek Becker, sociologist Rudolf Bahro, political singer Wolf Biermann, and many others, Havemann denounced the perplexing discrepancy between the regime's humanistic promises and its repressive practice.

A resolute opponent of bureaucratic dictatorship, Havemann belonged to the Marxist revisionist generation. He was convinced that Marxist criticism can decisively affect the politics of the totalitarian system, an illusion that was common in Eastern Europe until it was dispelled by the Communist governments' harsh reactions to their critics in the late 1960s.[15] Havemann's political platform represented an uncompromising repudiation of monopolistic bureaucracy: "The exaggerated sensitivity toward public criticism is a characteristic of Stalinism, which lives in constant fear and is therefore compelled to manipulate opinions and to adapt them to its own security needs; it has only scant respect for theoretical considerations. . . . Under Stalin, Marxist criticism was got rid of by getting rid of Marxist critics. Neo-Stalinism is more radical: it gets rid of Marxism."[16] For Havemann and his supporters, the solution was to reassert the democratic potential of socialism. He defined imagining a communist Utopia based on real equality between citizens as a major task of our times: "There must be no privileged people, classes or groups of any description, but everybody, every person must have exactly the same opportunities, the same chances, and must be equal with regard to each other."[17]

Havemann's anti-Stalinist stances were not futile, for they contributed to the political coming-of-age of a younger generation of intellectuals. Drawing from Havemann's theses, the satirical poet and political singer Wolf Biermann spelled out the need to elaborate a Christian-Communist alternative to the repressive regime: "My entire work has the purpose of advancing the development of a socialist workers' democracy in those countries that call themselves socialist. I voice criticism of the monopolistic-bureaucratic system; and I speak for those forces which, rather than accepting a *petit bourgeois* liberalization forced on them to shut them up by the old bankrupt and neo-Stalinist reactionaries, insist on the continuation of the socialist revolution."[18]

Throughout the 1970s, the critical ferment became more widespread within literary and artistic circles. As mentioned, this ferment was neither nostalgia for the pre-socialist order, unqualified admiration for liberal democracy, nor a wish to do away with Marxist ideology. What permeated was discontent with the

SED dictatorship and the militaristic-bureaucratic course of the government. Paradoxically, this strictly neo-Stalinist regime, with its obsession with ideological purity, had engendered one of the most consistent left-humanist oppositions to really-existing socialism.

The police state did not hesitate to strike back against the intellectual trouble-makers. In 1976, the SED Politburo accused Wolf Biermann of "publicly slandering our socialist State" and deprived him of his citizenship.[19] When noted writers Christa Wolf, Stefan Heym, and Stephan Hermlin protested, the authorities resorted to further repression: Wolf was expelled from the SED and Heym was charged with breaches of currency regulations. Robert Havemann was placed under house arrest, and several other well-known writers were forced into exile.[20]

During the 1978 Writers' Congress, longtime official poet Stephan Hermlin upbraided the government for its growing anti-intellectual policy: "In the absence of real arguments they turn to a demagogy which, when it is a question of belittling the intellectuals, has a long and shameful history in Germany. If literature raises objections, if the intellect expresses cares or sorrow, they point out the pecuniary element in the background with a knowing smile. The bourgeois band of writers has been bribed; the deeper causes are revealed and the wrath of the people is near at hand. Writers have a responsibility, but don't others also have a responsibility, particularly those who possess power?"[21]

The SED leadership only further enhanced its rigid orthodoxy, launched an overall campaign against critical intellectuals and other dissidents. The rationale for this ultradogmatic, Manichaean approach to any form of pluralism was formulated by Erich Honecker in 1979 and has remained valid ever since: "The class struggle has always involved fighting on two sides of the barricade—here the workers' class, there the bourgeoisie, here the socialist ideology, there the bourgeois one. There is no third alternative."[22] This unflinching orthodoxy has been reasserted in recent years in direct contrast to Mikhail Gorbachev's policy of glasnost. For example, speaking at a festive event to mark the seventieth anniversary of the founding of the KPD (Communist Party of Germany), Erich Honecker bluntly rejected suggestions to modify the SED policies in accordance with the wind of change now blowing from Moscow: ". . .we have no reason to copy the practice of this or that fraternal country, apart from the fact that this would be a gross contradiction of the fundamental teachings of Marxism. Peace. . .is served by our foreign policy, it is served by our military policy, it is served by the education of the younger generation, and it is served by the all-round strengthening of our socialist fatherland."[23]

Under these circumstances, a new oppositional strategy had to be devised to take advantage of those areas not entirely permeated with the dominant ideas and values.[24] A reconstruction of the critical discourse was required, and also a rethinking of the possibilities for autonomous social movements in a strongly authoritarian context. The only solution appeared to be to go beyond the merely intellectual opposition, altruistic and heroic but fatally marginal and isolated as it was, and address urgent public issues in accordance with public aspirations, expectations, and needs. In the view of East German critical intellectuals, vital issues included the state's manipulation of the notion of peace and its blatant indifference to environmental degradation. In January 1982, the celebrated dissident thinker Robert Havemann endorsed the "Berlin Appeal," a document that marked the genesis of the unofficial peace movement in the GDR. This statement, whose main author was Reiner Eppelmann, an East Berlin minister involved in youth work, was eventually signed by more than 2,000 East Germans. In many respects, this petition echoed Robert Havemann's political-philosophical views. Before Leonid Brezhnev's visit to West Germany in fall 1981, Havemann had addressed an "Open Letter" to the Soviet general secretary pointing to the division of Germany as a bleeding wound in the very heart of Europe: "What Germany's partition created was not security but the precondition for the deadliest of threats that has ever existed in Europe."[25] The "Berlin Appeal" further elaborated on this alarming premise. In its logical and political articulations, it propounded the main agenda for the emerging independent peace movement. Widely circulated, the "Appeal" ignited passionate discussions among young peace activists. It struck responsive chords among all those who had long distrusted the official peace institutions and pledges.

The main objective of the "Berlin Appeal" was to challenge the government's militaristic propaganda. A slogan frequently reproduced on official East German posters reads: "The stronger the socialism, the more secure the peace." To this, the signatories of the "Appeal" replied: "We propose holding a great debate on the questions of peace, in an atmosphere of tolerance and recognition of the right of free speech, and to permit and encourage every spontaneous public expression of the desire for peace."[26] The authors suggested a broad range of topics to be discussed in such a dialogue. Denying the moral validity of the militaristic course, they asked:

(a)   Oughtn't we to stop producing, selling, and importing so-called war toys?

(b)   Oughtn't we to introduce peace studies in our schools in place of military instruction?

(c)   Oughtn't we to allow social work for peace instead of the present alternative service for conscientious objectors?

(d)   Oughtn't we to stop all public displays of military might and instead use our ceremonies of state to give expression to the nation's desire for peace?

(e)   Oughtn't we to stop so-called civil-defense exercises? As no worthwhile civil defense is possible in nuclear war, these exercises merely make nuclear war seem more serious. Does it not perhaps amount to a kind of psychological preparation for war?[27]

The tone of the "Berlin Appeal" was both hopeful and apocalyptic. Written in the very heart of Europe by people deeply concerned with the danger of a nuclear holocaust, the document challenged East German officialdom in the name of a *new philosophy of democratic peace.* The underlying assumption was that *all* weapons are lethal, regardless of the ideological preferences of those who handle them. "Make peace without weapons," a position voiced in the "Appeal," has become the fundamental demand of the independent peace movement in East Germany: "Make peace without weapons—this does not just mean ensuring our own survival. It also means stopping senselessly wasting our people's labor and wealth on producing the engines of war and equipping enormous armies of young men, who are thereby taken out of productive work."[28] The division of Germany was another of the highly sensitive issues addressed: in unambiguous terms the authors advocated the withdrawal of all occupation troops from Germany and pointed to the need for guarantees of nonintervention in the internal affairs of both German states.

The "Berlin Appeal" was a milestone in the radicalization of East German independent pacifism. By denouncing and publicizing the ceaseless war preparations and the militarization of public education, the document attacked the regime's ideological inconsistencies. Furthermore, the "Appeal" proclaimed the independent struggle for peace to be a major civic duty, an unmistakable allusion to the failure of the official peace institutions to articulate cogent and credible platforms. The "Berlin Appeal" thus consecrated the role of independent peace initiatives from below.

The meaning of the "Berlin Appeal" for the maturing of the East German independent movement cannot be exaggerated. But this document also had an international significance: It emphasized the intimate link between the right of free speech and the success of a true debate on the questions of peace. The "Appeal" contained in a nutshell the philosophy of the unity of peace and human rights which was to become the hallmark of independent peace initiatives in the years to come.[29]

The "Appeal" has proven to have been a detonator for a large number of similar actions. Peace has become the principal integrative value for the development and intensification of unofficial social initiatives in the GDR. Needless to say, the government immediately realized the threat involved in this undertaking and struck back, taking Eppelmann into custody for two days. But unlike similar groups in other communist countries, the East German pacifists benefit from the moral support of the eight decentralized Evangelical Churches with which they have evolved a close symbiosis. The role, influence, and positive attitude of the church have been major factors in the movement's survival and continued development.

The Church and the Peace Movement

As a result of their embarrassing experiences during the Nazi times, East German Protestant Churches have resisted cooperation with the Communist government. However, open conflict has been carefully avoided, and the relation between state and church has been aptly described as "a marriage in which the couple is always fighting—without, however, seriously thinking of divorce."[30] This uneasy relationship has allowed the East German Protestant hierarchy to become consistent spokesmen for peace and to voice constructive criticism of the official militaristic policy. For example, the Evangelical Church of Germany (EKD) advocated the regulation of conscientious objection and civilian service (1955); churches opposed mandatory recruiting for the National People's Army (NVA) in 1961; there was state-church dialogue about religious freedom for soldiers, the oath of allegiance to the flag, and refusal to bear arms in 1962, and about the introduction of unarmed service in construction units of the NVA (started in 1962); the Federation of Protestant Churches made a statement with regard to the international political situation after the NATO decision to increase its military strength and the Soviet occupation of Afghanistan (January 1980); churches sponsored the creation of institutions for peace research, and they endorsed peace discussions and supported independent peace groups after 1981.[31]

This evolution was accelerated by the formation in 1969 of the Federation of Evangelical Churches of the GDR, a measure imposed by the regime in an attempt to break the links between East and West German churches. In 1972, Dr. Heino Falcke, a Protestant Church leader, formulated the philosophy of "the church within socialism": "We will not concede that man's political maturity depends on his liberation from Christ rather than on his being liberated by Christ. . . . We can accept in faith that in a socialist society, too, the lordship of liberating Christ is a reality. . . . So we are set free to reject socialism's rigid view of itself, a view which would face us with the need to reject or accept it totally. We are set free from the paralyzing alternative between outright opposition and uncritically allowing ourselves to be taken over. Thus we are set free to offer practical and discerning cooperation."[32] Based on the belief in the emancipatory role of faith, this conception suggests guidelines for an effective dialogue between the church and the state: The church recognizes the existing political structure and does not intend to subvert it. This positive approach to the realities of power was best formulated in a statement by Bishop Albert Schönherr, the first president of the Federation of Evangelical Churches: "We don't want to be a church against socialism, nor a church alongside socialism, but a church within socialism."[33] Bishop Schönherr emphasized this programmatic outlook during his historical meeting with SED General Secretary Erich Honecker on March 6, 1978. Instead of blaming the church for this display of autonomy, the Honecker regime sought to foster cooperation, particularly during the late 1970s. The church is even officially authorized to "profess and evangelize," to build churches, and to broadcast religious services on radio and TV.

A new step in this cooperation was reached on the occasion of the five-hundredth anniversary of Martin Luther's birthday in 1983. The ceremonies were organized by a joint church-state commission chaired by Erich Honecker, an important propaganda action intended to portray Luther as a forerunner of the "progressive" East German state and part of the general attempt to consolidate an East German political and historical identity. The thrust of the Luther celebration was that everything "worthwhile and good" in German history had occurred on East German soil.[34]

Though less influential than it was in the early 1950s, the Evangelical Church still claims a membership of 8 million. Along with the much smaller Catholic Church, the East German Evangelical Church "represents the sole institutional structure in the GDR not subject to party control."[35] The church has offered independent pacifism more than symbolic support: It has acknowledged its legitimacy and thereby it has defended it against official slander and harassment. Unlike that in the USSR, Hungary, or Poland where autonomous peace movements have emerged out of civil-rights initiatives, the GDR case reveals an important potential role for religious institutions in the formation and development of unofficial groups. This is not to say that the East German pacifist, antinuclear movement is basically a religious one. We have to underline, however, its basic commitment to Christian values—particularly the dignity of the individual, the sacredness of human freedom, and the ethos of nonviolence. It is precisely this value system that collides with the official collectivist credo.

The church and the peace movement share worries about the brutal interference of the state in private affairs. For young East German pacifists, encouraged by members of the Evangelical clergy, the idea of turning "Swords into Plowshares" (*Schwerter zu Pflugscharen*) is more than a prophetic metaphor. It is the symbol of their decision to rebel against militarism, censorship, ideological manipulation, and police repression.[36]

From Religious Pacifism to
Independent Peace Activism

The independent peace movement in East Germany is first and foremost an effect of the widespread moral crisis that affects large strata of the East German youth, who are looking for stable values and are acutely dissatisfied with the government's revolutionary demagogy.[37] For these activists, peace and religious values are intimately intertwined. The semi-autonomous status of the Evangelical Church and the positive approach of the clergy to the peace initiatives from below have also favored the early 1980s coagulation of the independent peace movement. The interest of the Soviet Union and other Warsaw Pact countries in the development of the anti-nuclear movement in the West was another propitious circumstance: At a time when the Soviet bloc was engaged in a propaganda war against NATO's dual-track decision as indicative of Western militaristic psychosis, Erich Honecker could hardly deny his subjects the right to express concerns about the arms race and its impact on the future of both Germanies.

The independent peace activists rejected from the very outset the simplistic and reductionist definition of peace as the absence of war, giving it instead a comprehensive meaning. Together with the church, they emphasized the unity and coherence of all human values, including basic human rights. The independent peace movement in East Germany was also influenced by the huge antinuclear demonstrations in West Germany in the early 1980s, and by the nonviolent strategy for social change proposed by Solidarity in Poland before the declaration of martial law on December 13, 1981.[38]

In May 1981, members of the Evangelical Church in Dresden addressed a proposal to the *Volkskammer* (the East German Parliament) advocating a twenty-four-month "social service for peace" as an alternative to the mandatory eighteen-month military conscription.[39] Those undertaking such a service for peace were to be employed primarily in the following areas: residential care (children's homes, old people's homes, nursing homes); ancillary staff in the hospitals; social welfare; and environmental protection. The authors of the proposal expressed their concern about the continuous militarization of the East German society and suggested that instead of pursuing this dangerous course the government should think rather of the dramatic shortcomings in the social services, which the "social service for peace" could partially resolve. In August 1981, Saxon Bishop Johannes Hempel expressed the support of the church for this initiative: "We will obviously open our arms and speak openly with those whose motives originate in Evangelical beliefs."[40]

In November 1981, the government replied to the growing campaign for an alternative peace service through the authoritative voice of the GDR State Secretary for Church Affairs, Klaus Gysi: "The demand for a 'social peace service' cannot be justified either theologically or religiously. . . . Moreover, it is not the task of the church to change laws and the Constitution. In addition, there are people in the West who desire to see a confrontation between us. The current regulation with the construction soldier option is one of the most progressive in the world. There is no reason to deviate from it. We need everyone and cannot afford to abolish mandatory conscription."[41] According to Gysi, anybody who did not agree with the state's position showed a confrontational attitude. Werner Walde, a candidate member of the SED Politburo and party chief in the district of Cottbus, accused the initiative for alternative service of being directed against the "necessary military strength of socialism."[42] Instead of bowing to the SED's dictate, in September 1981 the Synod of the Evangelical Churches of the GDR adopted a resolution in support of the call for an alternative civil service. To counter the regime's criticism that they were playing a role in fomenting civic unrest, church leaders emphasized that the Evangelical Church is "neither a camouflaged government party nor a camouflaged opposition party."[43] The strategy of the church consisted of avoiding direct confrontation with the authorities without losing its powerful influence on the independent peace movement.

But the SED could not tolerate the epidemic of pacifism, and it raised ideological, "class-inspired" slogans in response: "Peace must be defended—peace must be armed" and "Make peace without NATO weapons." The FDJ (*Freie Deutsche Jugend*—Free German Youth), the communist youth organization, unleashed a campaign to propagate this "militant" slogan. Wearing the pacifist badge was forbidden, and repressive measures were enforced against young activists.

Independent peace initiatives intensified following the "Peace Week" (*Friedensdekade*) organized by the Protestant Churches in November 1981. The theme of the campaign was "Righteousness, Disarmament, Peace," and the "Swords into Plowshares" slogan was enthusiastically embraced by thousands of young people. This phrase was also the title of a statue donated by the Soviet Union to the United Nations in the late 1940s: A protest against official double-talk was thus inherent in the ironic decision to use an official propaganda symbol frequently manipulated to illustrate the Soviet bloc's commitment to the defense of peace. Initially, Soviet commentators described the "Swords into Plowshares" movement as a "reflection of their own attitudes."[44] But soon the real meaning of the badge carried by East German peace activists became clear: It was intended to draw attention to the striking conflict between professed and practiced values, between ideal symbols and actual behavior. Through this reference to the official peace rhetoric, the young activists were announcing their intention to remain within a legal framework. Clearly, the peace movement's strategy was to insert itself within those areas that were not totally pervaded by official ideology and where the individual was still relatively autonomous (independent discussion groups, spontaneous communication networks, church-sponsored workshops, and seminars, etc.). It attempted to regenerate the social fabric through appeals to such basic values as truth, trust, and solidarity. In the words of Hungarian writer George Konrád: "Antipolitics is the ethos of civil society, and civil society is the antithesis of military society. There are more-or-less militarized societies—societies under the sway of nation-states whose officials consider total war one of the possible moves in the game. Thus military society is the reality, civil society is a utopia."[45]

As mentioned, one of the major contributions to the development of a self-conscious, autonomous peace movement in the GDR was the publication of the "Berlin Appeal." In the first months of 1982, the Federation of the Evangelical Churches decided not to support the "Appeal," but to continue to oppose compulsory military conscription and training. Then in March the regime passed an expanded military training law, and in response the Catholic bishops, who had long refrained from criticizing the government, declared that "it is to be feared that this kind of (military) education will awaken the readiness to resolve conflicts by force and will thus weaken the next generation's attitude toward peace."[46]

An important meeting took place in April between the representatives of the Federation of Evangelical Churches (*Kirchenbund*) and the government's delegate Klaus Gysi. According to him, it was not the symbol "Swords into Plowshares" as such that had upset the authorities, but rather its impact on the readiness of the population to engage in military defense. He bluntly admitted that the symbol might weaken the GDR's defense capability (*Schwächung der Wehrbereitschaft.*)[47] Meanwhile, some bishops had been trying to convince radical pacifists that wearing the patch could be dangerous and that the church could not permanently protect them against police harassment. An incident during the Peace Forum in the Church of the Cross (*Kreuzkirche*) in Dresden in February 1982 had been indicative of these mounting tensions. When Bishop Hempel stated that the church could make use of the potential for political opposition only in extreme situations, "because God does not tolerate people saying prematurely that they are *in statu confessionis,*" a young participant's *cri de coeur* expressed the general feeling of frustration at such "appeasing" stances: "I am nineteen years old and nevertheless have nothing to lose. You talk and talk behind safe doors. Do you intend to keep putting us off until doomsday? What about the shining city on the hill?"[48] More than a temporary disagreement, this dissonance stems from the fact that the church has its agenda and so does the independent peace movement. Sometimes they overlap, sometimes they diverge.

More often than not, the church has expected the unofficial peace groups to demonstrate self-restraint and moderation, as explicitly stated in the response of the Protestant Church in Berlin-Brandenburg to the "Appeal": "The church leadership strongly advises against participating in the collection of signatures because this could generate misunderstandings and dangers not conducive to necessary impartial discussion." In turn, the well-known dissident physicist and philosopher Robert Havemann protested against the style and ideas of this statement: "One nearly gets a shock reading these sentences, which on top of everything else and for no apparent reason are written in language which in its coarseness and harshness is more than a formal break in style. However, I think these statements were formulated before all the parties concerned realized that it is impossible to deal in this way with the 'Berlin Appeal' without losing all credibility in the international arena of the peace movement."[49]

Without directly and organically joining the independent peace movement, the Evangelical Church has been an exceptional fulcrum for its development. For obvious reasons, the church hierarchy could not engage in direct confrontation with the government, and many peace activists have resented this "abstentionism" and felt betrayed by the clergy's failure to espouse all their demands. Those who had expected the church to champion the fight against militarism and human-rights abuses have thus been relatively and not entirely unfoundedly disappointed. In all fairness, however, such an evolution could hardly have been expected from religious institutions in a Communist country, for their mission is more comprehensive and enduring than merely to assume a leading role in a political battle. It was within the Evangelical Church that numerous Basic Communities and peace seminars were organized.[50] But it was difficult for the religious hierarchy to accept full identification with the independent peace movement. For its part, although the movement has benefited from the close association with church, it has evolved as an autonomous, grass-roots movement with its own philosophy, methods, goals, and organizational structure. It has become the most articulate and consistent channel of protest against militarism and repression within a society still governed by an unrepentant Stalinist party.

The East German Evangelical Church has, however, offered far more than mere Platonic support to the peace activists. Its moral and political assistance has been crucial for the survival of the movement during many difficult times. Its commitment to defending the persecuted has been a major asset for all those who disagree with the regime. But the religious leaders have to maintain a *modus vivendi* with the government and cannot transform the church into the headquarters of political protest. Their duties include not only protection for the dissidents and peace activists, but also support for the silent majority of the population. An open showdown with the government could lead to a crisis in state-church relations with dramatic consequences for the whole social climate in the GDR. In recent years, the authorities have emphasized the sharp distinction between peace activities taking place within the church and those that transcend these boundaries. The government's aim has been to channel independent activities back into church structures, but the divide between these two forms of political activism is often blurred. The tactic of the regime is to limit independent peace and human-rights campaigning to the limits of church-sponsored activities. This policy would allow the government to distinguish between "tolerable" and "intolerable" actions and force the church hierarchy to disassociate themselves from the most radical independent initiatives. Werner Fischer, one of the leaders of the independent group Initiative for Peace and Human Rights, has vividly described the predicament of the Evangelical Church caught between mounting activism from below and the regime's repressive attitude: "The church cannot but give in to that pressure. The relationship between the church and the state is a constant balancing act for the church leadership and they have to be prepared to say that they will tolerate and support certain activities but not others."[51]

There is, to be sure, a lot of truth in the statement that "the expectation that the churches would assume a leading role in the independent peace movement in the GDR, or at least grant it its sanction within their walls, has not been fulfilled."[52] But the church's political intentions should not be mistaken for more than they are: It does not aspire to become an actor in political confrontations or to set up a parallel power that would rival the government's authority. At the same time, activities organized and encouraged by the church have greatly contributed to civic mobilization. The peace education undertaken within the walls of the churches has paved the way for a new state of mind suspicious of the official militaristic ideology. After all, many of the independent peace activists started as religious pacifists.

In dealing with religious pacifism in the GDR, one must take into account the theological and historical traditions that have determined the Protestant approach to the notion of peace and to the peace movement. First, peace as a political, not eschatological, concept is a relatively new concern in Protestant theology. For a long time after 1945, the East German Evangelical Church resisted attempts to be integrated into the activities of the World Peace Council. Protestant philosophers do not accept the Marxist-Leninist definition of peace, according to which the international class struggle will culminate in the establishment of a universal Communist order; rather, they have developed their own philosophy of war and peace. The church's consistent opposition to the resurgence of militarism in East Germany should be considered the prelude to the genesis of the independent political-religious movement for peace and civil rights in the early 1980s. The Evangelical Church is a center for reflection and imaginative action on fundamental issues that inevitably lead to sensitive political topics, although this criticism of the government is disguised in the language of constructive dialogue. Such is the nature of the East German political equation: The state has shunned direct attacks on the church, and the church has reciprocated through what one might call *critical loyalty*. Bishop Kruse gave a crystal-clear formulation of this doctrine: "We have learned that it is right for a church not to feel to be above or beyond the social order in which it exists, that it should instead consciously accept this order as the place appropriated it by God for the testing of its faith and obedient discipleship, as its mission field and opportunity for service, and as the location for new, living experiences with the living God. . .not at a critical distance, but with critical—and that always means also constructive—participation."[53] In the same vein, following a crackdown on dissenters in January–February 1988, Manfred Stolpe, the president of the East Berlin church consistory, declared that the church does not conceive of its role as a shelter for an internal GDR opposition: "As a church we are independent and self-reliant. We are different from the social institutions in this country, the parties and mass-organizations, because we have other ties. In that respect we are different in our self-reliance from the normal functioning of the GDR society. I think, however, that society has accepted the existence of independent churches and that the churches act in accordance with their mission, carrying out certain tasks in society. That is what the church does, but not in conflict with the state. The church believes in its responsibility in the entirety." Referring to the need for a gradual opening of the East German political system, Stolpe expressed reservations about the wisdom of public demonstrations against repression: "Our country has been undergoing a slow and cautious change. . . . The process is continuing. It has to continue. In that process of change, controversy—the culture of controversy—is a very important element. In my view that process of change should not be strained by elements and moments that this society is still unable to cope with."[54]

Tensions and animosities have not been totally avoided in the relationship between religious personalities and independent activists. Young priests tend to be much more supportive of the independent peace initiatives than the established bishops. This does not mean however that the church has withdrawn support from the independent peace movement, but rather that the GDR churches do not consider that the current circumstances represent the extreme situation which would warrant their direct political involvement. Does it follow from this that the chances for an independent peace movement in the GDR are slim or that the peace movement represents a social actor that has no part in the basic agreement between the regime and the church?[55] The dynamics of the movement suggest a different view. While it is true that there is a *Realpolitik* compact between the church and the state under which the "rules of the game" for nongovernmental activities are confined to the church, this is not a binding agreement; the rise of the independent peace and human-rights movement may compel the church to reconsider both its social role and its political obligations. As a Christoph Semsdorf, a forty-nine-year-old Lutheran pastor, has recently put it: "As a pastor I am not interested in the problems of the country. I am interested in the problems of the people. There is a big difference."[56]

The development of independent peace activism was further catalyzed by the authorities' decision to enact the provisions of the March 1982 new Military Service Law. In an open letter to Erich Honecker, some 300 East German women vented their concerns about the introduction of the military service for women. The signatories of the document described army service for women as "not as an expression of their equal rights, but as inherently contrary to their nature as women." They protested against the obligation to defend a country whose population would be totally annihilated in a military conflagration. Moreover, they declared: "We are not willing to submit to this compulsory military service, and we demand that the possibility of refusal should be enshrined in the law. The right of refusal is necessary because our freedom of conscience is infringed by the promulgation of this law which extends the duty of military service to women."[57] Later, a number of signatories of this letter were harassed by security police officers. As for the reaction of the government, the late Army General Heinz Hoffmann, then Politburo member and defense minister, proclaimed the SED's refusal to accept any compromise with the independent peace initiatives: "The members of our army, our workers, and our women and children know that peace and socialism are inseparably linked. Our soldiers bear arms for peace, and the better command they have over their weapons, the better the peace is assured. As much as we would like to scrap our weapons, we know that one day socialism and peace will need both our plowshares *and* our swords."[58] This was an unequivocal repudiation of the main assumption of the independent peace movement: that peace is inextricably linked to civil rights and that no weapons, be they Eastern or Western, socialist or capitalist, can ensure the survival of mankind.

A Broader Agenda:
Peace and Human Rights

Following the March 1982 Dresden Forum, links between the independent peace activists and critical intellectuals intensified. The dissident counterculture exerted a profound intellectual and political influence on the emerging unofficial peace movement. Writers Stefan Heym, Stephan Hermlin, Christa Wolf, Jurek Becker, and Jürgen Fuchs were among the cultural personalities whose heterodox views most influenced the young peace activists.

Critical intellectuals and independent peace activists share the same anxiety about militaristic trends in the East German regime. They are equally obsessed with the specter of a nuclear Armageddon. Ideological stereotypes seem to them utterly inadequate to provide a sense of conscience and responsibility. Christa Wolf masterfully expresses this state of mind in her novel *Cassandra* when she writes: "To prevent wars, people must criticize, in their own country, the abuses that occur in their own country. The role taboos play in the preparation of war. The number of shameful secrets keeps growing incessantly, boundlessly. How meaningless all censorship taboos become, and how meaningless the conse-quences of overstepping them, when your life is in danger."[59] Her radical pacifism culminates in a call for unilateral disarmament for the Warsaw Pact: "I conclude that the sensible course may be the one for which there is absolutely no hope: unilateral disarmament. (I hesitate: in spite of the Reagan Administration? Yes, since I see no other way out: in spite of it!) By choosing this course, we place the other side under the moral pressure of the world public; we render superfluous the U.S.S.R.'s extortionary policy of arming itself to death; we renounce the atomic first-strike capability, and we devote all our efforts to the most effective defense measures. Assuming that this involves some risk, how much greater is the risk of further atomic arms, which every day increases the risk of atomic annihilation, by accident if nothing else?"[60]

"Armed peace" is rejected as an absurdity by both peace activists and critical intellectuals: "Twice in this century, war has arisen out of 'armed peace,' each war crueler than its predecessor. Brecht said exactly the same thing in the fifties. If we do not arm ourselves, we will have peace. If we arm ourselves, we will have war. I do not see how anyone could think differently about this."[61]

Contacts between the independent peace movement and the cultural opposi-tion deepened after the second Berlin meeting of writers in April 1983. On that occasion, poet Stephan Hermlin deplored the government's lack of understand-ing of the new movement: "We must first recognize that not everything that goes by the name of an independent peace movement in the socialist countries is concerned with peace; for the most part it is also concerned with quite different things. But there are many people, especially young people, who passionately want to make their own personal contribution to peace, but are regarded with suspicion. That is something I regret."[62]

Not surprisingly, the East German regime reacted nervously to the rise of the independent peace movement. In any communist dictatorship—and the GDR has never renounced some of the basic prerogatives of the totalitarian state, including the all-pervading presence of the political police—independent centers of initiative jeopardize the party's domination over society. The government arrested a group of young peace activists in Jena in January 1983 following spontaneous grass-roots demonstrations. Later, in the summer, the leaders of the group were expelled from the GDR, in accordance with a peculiar East German pattern of getting rid of dissidents and human-rights activists. But the origins of the affair went back to April 1981, when two Jena activists known for their pacifist penchants were interrogated for forty-eight hours by security police in the city of Gera. Only one of the two young pacifists was released; the other, Mathias Domaschk, hanged himself in prison. The victim's friends did their best to publicize the tragedy both in their country and in the West. At the same time, another young activist from Jena, Roland Jahn, publicly expressed his solidarity with Poland under martial law. When he was arrested by the security police, Jahn was adopted a prisoner of conscience by Amnesty International. On November 14, 1982, several dozen young pacifists organized a gathering in the central square of the city. They carried placards with the word *peace*, talked with the people on the street, then dispersed quietly. A text later elaborated in the base communities of the Evangelical Church expressed their opposition to mandatory military education. They demanded the right to carry pacifist badges and reject the idea of any military service for women. Of the demonstrators, some were Christian militants, others professed humanist atheistic convictions. Many were students from the Friedrich Schiller University, but there were also young workers from the big factories Zeiss, Jenapharm, and Schott. Some had experienced the war, but most were young and feared a nuclear apocalypse in the middle of Europe. Another demonstration was planned for December 24, 1982, but security police intervened and many activists were arrested.

In the summer of 1983, twenty young activists from Jena were expelled from the GDR. One of them was Roland Jahn, who continued in the Federal Republic his activities on behalf of the East German unofficial peace movement. According to Jahn, the question about the formal membership and organization of the movement misses the real point: the independent peace movement is first and foremost *an informal association of like-minded people:* "The movement is there in every person in the GDR. Among the young there are people who say, 'I can't accept things as they are anymore.' But it would only come to a mass movement of protest when things get a lot worse in a material sense."[63]

Understandably, East German independent pacifists are skeptical about official pledges of commitment to peace. When they criticize the government's militaristic record, they expose the regime's failure to live up to its promises. In its main aspirations and concerns, then, this is not only a political but also a cultural and moral movement. Bärbel Bohley, a leading activist of the group Women for Peace summed up the psychology of independent pacifism: "I have gotten used to not being afraid anymore. That is the precondition if one wants to work for peace here."[64]

The movement challenges the system's operational values in the name of a counterprinciple, peace. Its main aim is to promote grass-roots participation in independent initiatives and a new sense of awareness about the dangers generated by the competition between the two blocs. In an "Open Letter to the West

European Peace Movement," the dissident poet Jürgen Fuchs, who had been expelled from the GDR in 1977, wrote about the fate of East German pacifists and called for a new approach to the peace issue. In his view, as in that of most East European peace activists, peace should not be dealt with as an isolated issue. Peace without human rights was at best illusion, if not merely a form of capitulation. Governments who did not ensure internal peace could not be considered guarantors of international peace: "The matter is not to compel the peace movement 'to carry the burden of the issues dealing with human rights'! In the East, as well as in the West, the peace movement will succeed only if it will manage to dismantle the missiles, prevent the war, and open the doors of the prison cells!"[65]

The East German independent peace movement has persistently refused identification with any bloc ideology. While criticizing Western Cold War rhetoric, the peace activists have not concealed their opposition to the irrational ideology of the Communist leadership. An important document addressed by the East German independent peace movement to the European Nuclear Disarmament Conference held in Perugia in July 1984 illustrates this complex and often contradictory nature of the autonomous peace initiatives.

The authors of the memorandum defined the international, cross-frontier independent peace movement as the outcome of decentralized, grass-roots activities. They saw its main objective as emancipation, in the broadest sense: "It must therefore enjoy autonomy from the established political systems and must not be susceptible to being taken over by them. It must also enjoy autonomy from the two superpowers, and from those who represent their interests, and this in itself is a reason why the movement must transcend the two blocs."[66] The letter depicted the effects of continuous militarization of the social life in the GDR and informed Western anti-nuclear campaigners about the extraordinary pressure communist authorities exert on independent peace activists: "The population is to be disciplined by attempting to extend military forms of organization to every aspect of life (education of children, vocational training, civil defense exercises for working people) and by the doctrinaire, repressive behaviors of the organs of state (in particular the security apparatus and the judiciary) towards all citizens who publicly espouse opinions that deviate from the dogma, or even alternative projects."

After Brezhnev's death in November 1982, the East German leadership was confused by the mixed signals coming from Moscow. It seemed that détente had reached a dead end. Honecker's correct assumption was that the new Soviet leaders—first Yury Andropov, then Konstantin Chernenko—would encourage ideological orthodoxy and cement the political-military cohesion of the Warsaw Pact. Given the dogmatic cold wind blowing from Moscow, the campaign against independent peace activists intensified by the end of 1983. In December, graphic artist Bärbel Bohley and historian Ulrike Poppe, prominent members of the Women for Peace group, were arrested and charged under Article 99 of the GDR

Penal Code, which punishes "treasonable passing on of information" if that information is considered to subvert the interests of the GDR and is passed to "foreign organizations and their helpers." Women for Peace had a circle with over 100 participants at various times, and managed to collect more than 500 signatures for its appeal to stop drafting women. In January 1984, following twenty-two days of hunger strike and intense international campaign on their behalf, the two activists were released. They were too well known in the West, and the government could not afford to further aggravate their already problematic relations with Western peace movements. But on April 20, 1984, Sylvan Goethe, also an activist of an unofficial peace group, was sentenced to twenty months in jail for having circulated information abroad "harmful to the interests of the GDR."

The appearance and development of an unofficial peace movement made up of Christians and socialists has been a major challenge for SED's ideological and political monopoly. The party decided to strengthen its "educational" activities in order to prevent the propagation of pacifist views. The media were instructed to pillory the independent peace movement for playing into the hands of Western intelligence agencies. Pacifists became the target of relentless campaigns of persecution and intimidation.

In December 1984, the socialist pacifist Rolf Schälike was sentenced to seven years imprisonment for "incitement against the state" (Article 106) and "slander against the state" (Article 220). In reality, his "guilt" consisted of having opposed the deployment of both NATO and Soviet missiles on German soil.

Schälike's case evinces the regime's estrangement from people who once espoused its own ideology. The defendant had joined the independent peace movement primarily on moral grounds: born in Moscow of German exiled parents, Schälike was a child of the German Communist community. In the 1950s, his father was a prominent figure within the SED. In 1961, he graduated in nuclear physics from Moscow University and started a successful career at the Central Institute of Nuclear Research at Rossendorf (GDR). A "critical Marxist" in the Havemann vein, Schälike was expelled from the party for his "heretical" views and lost his job. After his March 1984 arrest, he continued even in prison to criticize censorship and repression in the GDR. His outburst of indignation in the Dresden courtroom before his December sentencing shows the ideological quandary of many East German dissenters confronted with a state apparatus that claims to defend the dictatorship of the working class: "I am and will remain a Marxist and will not accept the label of enemy of the state."[70]

Instead of deterring the pacifists, the official campaign convinced them that a broader agenda for their efforts was needed. In 1985, they decided to address the relation between peace and human-rights issues in a systematic way. A group of leading activists, including such veterans of the unofficial peace movement as Reiner Eppelmann, Ralf Hirsch, and Wolfgang Templin, launched a human-rights initiative. More than 300 people signed a letter addressed to Erich Honecker calling for the full implementation of the United Nations' Universal Declaration of Human Rights. The letter called for the demilitarization of public life and the creation of an alternative civil service for conscientious objectors. It also condemned travel restrictions and demanded freedom of expression and the abolition of censorship. The government preferred to simulate ignorance of this memorandum. But in July 1985 a new appeal sent to the official youth organization declared a major objective of the independent peace movement to be the revival of civil society: "Peaceful assembly and the founding of initiatives, organizations, associations, clubs, and political parties should not be dependent on official permission. The unrestricted work of independent groups would protect society from petrifying in an inflexible administrative order that inhibits creativity among its citizens."[71] Here we recognize the philosophy of the new evolutionism which has inspired the struggles of the Polish opposition and has become the common ideology of democratic activists in East-Central Europe.[72] Its major goal is to restore society in its own right and to check the power of the party-state apparatus by introducing legal guarantees for accountability and civic control.

The human-rights campaign became even more outspoken in September 1985, when activists released a new document critical of the travel restrictions imposed by the authorities: "It is unacceptable that we should receive our rights only as a favor granted to us, provided that we refrain from independent political activity. We demand the repeal of the prohibition against foreign travel that has been imposed on us. Only the implementation of human rights for all and a comprehensive expansion of the freedom of travel will help persuade people to remain willingly in this country, thereby reducing the number of emigrés."[73]

The radicalization of the independent peace movement created problems in relations with the church. In January 1986, the leadership of the Berlin-Brandenburg Protestant Church abandoned a project to organize a "human rights seminar." Disappointed with the clergy' attitude, a number of activists decided to found a new group called the Initiative for Peace and Human Rights which would function "throughout the GDR." At the same time, an appeal to the government of the GDR on the occasion of the UN Peace Year was signed by four prominent peace activists (Peter Grimm, Ralf Hirsch, Rainer Eppelmann, and Wolfgang Templin). Convinced that "only a state which is at peace with itself internally can work convincingly for global peace," the authors suggested ways to secure *internal peace* in the GDR. They called for an end to the humiliating restrictions on travel and asked the government to show more trust in its subjects. The appeal also touched on the delicate issue of the legal measures against dissident activities stipulated in the penal code: "Paragraphs 99 (treasonable disclosure of information), 106 (anti-state agitation), 107 (anti-constitutional association), and 218 (association in pursuit of illegal aims), and so forth, can be interpreted in such a way as to restrict basic human rights. The practice of juridical persecution for political activity is altogether questionable." The authors also asked for the revision of the laws that severely restricted freedom of assembly, public meeting, and association. Since democracy cannot exist without public participation, the appeal called for confidence-building measures that would allow the nomination of independent candidates for municipal and parliamentary elections. It also demanded that the regime legalize conscientious objection through the creation of an alternative civilian service independent of all military structures.[74] This growing pressure from below has borne fruit: Although conscientious objection has not been legalized, since 1986 no conscientious objector has been imprisoned in the GDR.

The Impact of Glasnost:
Pacifism and Political Activism

The recent insistence on the inextricable connection between peace and freedom clearly indicates a higher degree of radicalization of the East German independent peace movement. It is now obvious that some of its most articulate spokespersons have realized the need to transcend the self-limited peace agenda and tackle the issue of political change. This does not mean that East German pacifists have surrendered their original project, but rather that internal peace cannot be attained without a genuine dialogue between the rulers and citizens of different opinions. Political freedoms, particularly the rights to free expression and association, must be legally guaranteed.

This enhanced campaign for loosening political controls cannot be disassociated from what can be described as the glasnost effect. "Glasnost from below" has become a rallying slogan for most independent groups in the GDR. Whether Gorbachev intended it or not, his calls for openness and general restructuring have stirred independent political activism not only in the USSR, but also, and sometimes more forcefully, in East-Central Europe. Like their peers in Czechoslovakia, Hungary, and Poland, the East German human-rights and peace activists envision Soviet reformism as a chance for radical transformations in their country. The new elbow room created by Gorbachev's reforms permits an envisioning of political democratization as a realistic possibility. Many East European critical intellectuals consider that it is time to elaborate a strategy "based on independent associations, a 'parallel polis' influencing society through its activities and growing into a nationwide movement. . . . Such a strategy conceives the existing independent movement as the nucleus of a new society. It is not incompatible with reformism, least of all with the notion of reform from below. . . . Out of the ruins of the old unreformable bureaucratic 'transmission-belts' new organizations, institutions, and initiatives are born. Instead of repression and manipulation, they strive for the emancipation of society by creating the conditions necessary for the emancipation of each individual."[75]

In April 1986, a petition urging the authorities to engage in a dialogue with the society was made by twenty-one members of the independent peace movement to delegates to the Eleventh SED Congress. In its main orientation, the letter echoed the late Robert Havemann's philosophy of political reforms and individual rights. The signatories condemned the authoritarian-bureaucratic measures adopted by the party leadership to suffocate any criticism from below. They dealt extensively with the failure of the regime's economic, social, and cultural policies.

Exhilarated by Gorbachev's more flexible approach to intellectual matters, the authors of the document bemoaned the ideological constraints imposed on the body social: "Cultural needs are not determined by the people but are created and artificially manipulated by the Party according to pragmatic criteria. Cultural policy shaped by the Party is a channel for ideological infiltration of all areas of the arts and culture, thus hindering the release of artistic creativity." The absence of any genuine form of political participation, wrote the authors, has been one of the main causes of the infectious phenomena of resignation, consumerism, and apathy. The regime had consistently ignored basic societal needs, single-mindedly pursuing its own interests. Pre-military training had been imposed as a precondition for securing a place in higher education or vocational training. The militarization of the educational system had aggravated its already deplorable state: "There is an almost complete absence of education in democratic attitudes. The shortcomings in this field are alarming. Many people have difficulty in formulating their needs and demands, or even in recognizing them only partially. Instruction in the rights of the individual as well as in the means by which those rights can be enforced plays hardly any role in the education system."

With respect to peace issues, the authors expressed their appreciation for the numerous official initiatives to end the arms race. But they could not help questioning the relevance of such proposals as long as the GDR continued itself to engage in the arms race and pursue a militaristic orientation. They said that the government had rejected the dialogue with society on such meaningful demands as a ban on war toys; the abolition of military instruction at school; the abandonment of the practice of urging young people to serve longer in the army and of showing them preferential treatment in the allocation of college places if they did. The statement censured the authorities for their refusal to entertain the following proposals related to the military service: the rejection of call-up for women in the preparations for mobilization; a change in the military service law which would make it possible for reservists to renounce their military oath; and the use of construction soldiers exclusively in civilian service.

The authors deplored "another peculiar process—to be found also in the Western Hemisphere—in the relation between domestic and foreign policy: the greater the number of bi- and multilateral contacts at state level (which are to be welcomed), the more vigorously are politically important contacts below that level obstructed." In other words, they felt that the GDR government had monopolized contacts with the West and prevented independent cooperation at the grass-roots level; international cooperation between autonomous groups should be allowed in order to make citizens direct participants in a vitally important discussion.

The document advocated a strategy aimed at "the medium-range withdrawal of the GDR from the Warsaw Pact . . . to encourage the process of military disengagement. This applies also to the withdrawal from our territory of foreign troops together with their weapons of mass destruction. The long-overdue settlement of the questions relating to legal status arising from the still-existing rights of the victors of the Second World War would then also have to be achieved. If the complete sovereignty of the GDR is to be established, the question of the outstanding peace treaties with both German states can no longer remain a taboo subject." As a first step in this direction, the authors proposed a fair-minded discussion of the peace issues. A forum should be created to organize this national dialogue. The government-sponsored Peace Council could not play this role because of its too well known record of subservience to the authorities: "Its dependence on the foreign information department of the Central Committee of the SED means that its sole function is to be a mouthpiece and presenter of the peace policy of the state." An independent peace council should therefore be created which could enjoy the support of the several thousand members of the unofficial peace groups: "The peace and security policy of the GDR cannot simply be left to the party and government. Peace is a human right and thus each member of society must be able to discuss and help determine everything which affects this right." The conclusion was an open call for a "constructive dialogue" in which nobody would claim to retain the key to ultimate truths: "There are no ready-made solutions to the problems referred to so far. They are not insoluble, yet we can only overcome them in an open discussion in which many partners both have equal status and can participate creatively in the social process."[76]

This appeal illustrates the fact that the peace groups have to confront not only the repressive apparatus of the established dictatorships but also the reality of the Soviet domination in the region and their countries' subordination to the Kremlin's global strategy. Their political programs must thus include suggestions for internal democratization as well as proposals for the general reassessment of East-West relations. Independent pacifists in Eastern Europe refuse to separate these goals precisely because they understand the link between their regimes' domestic and foreign policies.

The political philosophy of independent pacifism inspired a joint statement signed by activists from Czechoslovakia and the GDR in November 1984. The long-term significance of this document should not be underestimated. It was indeed the first time since the end of World War II that Czechs, Slovaks, and Germans had signed a common platform. The fact that pacifism was the value that allowed these activists to discover a common language further adds to the importance of such social movements for political change in Eastern Europe. Moreover, the references to similar views held by activists in other Warsaw Pact countries indicated the beginning of a process of a genuine internationalization of East European dissent.

The appeal was timed for the first anniversary of the deployment of Soviet SS 21's and 22's in Eastern Europe, a measure that had aroused public revolt in those countries. It called for a missile-free Europe from the Atlantic to the Urals, the end of big-power politics in Europe, and the creation of a pluralistic society: "Those who think in terms of blocs and enemies render an honest dialogue impossible. Those who tolerate social inequality or even widen the gap are responsible for hunger and poverty. Those who deny the dignity of the individual human beings, who deny freedom of opinion, necessarily tend also to solve national and international problems by means of violence." The authors emphasized their conviction that a new approach to international relations should replace conventional dichotomies. In accordance with the views held by Polish, Soviet, and Hungarian independent peace movements, East German and Czechoslovak activists declared that nuclear armament is not the source of international tensions. Rather, in order to achieve real peace, human rights should be scrupulously observed: "Peace is indivisibly linked to the implementation and observance of all human rights. We want to live in an open society which respects its men and women. The road to such a society does not lead through military barracks, a polluted environment, missile launching ramps. . . ."[77]

The same themes were further developed in October 1986, when sixteen East German peace and human-rights activists signed the "Joint Declaration from Eastern Europe" commemorating the thirtieth anniversary of the Hungarian revolution. The document, signed by 123 dissidents from four Soviet-bloc countries—Czechoslovakia, East Germany, Hungary, and Poland—proclaimed the traditions and experiences of the Hungarian revolution of 1956 to be the common heritage and inspiration for their present efforts: "We proclaim our common determination to struggle for political democracy in our countries, for their independence, for pluralism founded on the principles of self-government, for the peaceful unification of a divided Europe and for its democratic integration, as well as for the rights of the minorities."[78]

The tremendous significance of the joint declaration—a real watershed in the development of dissident cross-frontier cooperation—was not missed by the East German authorities. They resorted to threats and abuse against the signatories from their country. The official propagandists clung to the description of the Hungarian revolution as a "fascist rebellion." An article published in the Berlin religious newspaper *Weissenseer Blätter* went so far as to say: "Anyone who, knowing what had happened there, identifies themselves with the revolt of the Hungarian Iron Cross, identifies themselves with something which can only be compared with the Black Shirts in Italy and the Brown Shirts in Germany." This was a blatant calumny, and the signatories filed a claim for libel against the author, a professor of theology at the Humboldt University in East Berlin.

Needless to say, the office of the Chief Public Prosecutor of the GDR refused to open action against the official propagandist. To add insult to injury, the office referred to Article 27 of the GDR Constitution, which guarantees the right to freedom of opinion. In an open letter to the public prosecutor, Gerd Poppe, one of the claimants, demolished the official version of the Hungarian revolution by showing its popular, anti-authoritarian nature. At the same time, he used his letter to express the political philosophy of the independent movements for peace and human rights: ". . . the use of force as a means of achieving political aims is rejected by the majority of East and West European peace and liberation movements today."[79]

For some time, in 1986 and 1987, it seemed that the government would avoid direct actions against the peace and human-rights movement. Following the Chernobyl disaster in the spring of 1986, the government permitted a limited popular discussion about nuclear energy. Independent peace activists and church leaders called for an overall reassessment of the country's nuclear-energy program. A petition signed by hundreds of East German citizens urged the authorities to renounce all use of nuclear energy by the year 1990.

Toward Radical Pacifism

Although there were many police actions directed against prominent dissidents during these years, the regime wanted to preserve its image of "repressive toler-ance." By the end of 1987, political developments in the Soviet Union and in other East European countries appeared to allow for a new impetus to the protest movement in the GDR.[80] At the same time, stronger contacts with West German alternative groups have generated increased self-confidence among East German peace and human-rights activists. The idea of a "third way," neither Marxist nor merely pro-Western, has become an appealing alternative to the frozen divisions imposed by the official rules of the game. As a result of this ongoing dialogue, West German alternative groups have started to voice more criticism of the GDR's bureaucratic-militaristic complex. They are now increasingly supportive of "East Germany's protest movement, which is demanding more freedom, *glas-nost* and a voice in how the country is run."[81]

In June 1986, activists associated with the Initiative for Peace and Human Rights (Initiative Friede und Menschenrechte—a group founded at the beginning of 1986) started to publish *Grenzfall*, a samizdat monthly bulletin on peace, ecology, and human-rights issues. The title is deliberately ambiguous: it means "borderline case" but also plays on the word *Grenze* (border). It is thus an allusion to the precarious status of the opposition and to the much-too-visible state border which has become part and parcel of East German political reality.[82] In the beginning of 1987, another samizdat political journal—*Umweltblätter* (Environ-mental Pages)—was launched. Its producers are members of the Ecology Center of the Church of Zion in East Berlin. Both publications cover the wide range of concerns and activities characteristic of the alternative social movements in the GDR. *Grenzfall* has reported not only on current East German political, social, and cultural issues but has also publicized the activities of unofficial peace and human-rights activists in other countries of the Soviet bloc. The journal reports about activities undertaken by independent activists and challenges the distorted versions disseminated through the official media. Some examples should illustrate the scope and goals of this thriving form of oppositional journalism:

From June 6 to 8, 1987, the East German police organized reprisals against hundreds of rock fans who had gathered at the Brandenburg Gate to hear Whitsuntide concerts on the Western side of the Berlin Wall. Brutally assaulted by plainclothes policemen, the young started to sing "The Internationale" and chanted "The Wall must go!" "Rosa Luxemburg!" and "Gorbachev!" Many East German activists pin their hopes on the Soviet leader's promises of liberalization; to the unconcealed dismay of the East German authorities, Gorbachev has become a symbol for the hopes for social regeneration and political change.

Understandably panic-stricken, the official media described the confrontation as "Western provocation." But in an article published in *Grenzfall*, peace and human-rights activists Wolfgang Templin and Peter Grimm spelled out the significance of what had started as a riot and then turned into a political demonstration: "It became clear how thin is the cover under which social conflicts in the GDR are concealed. The massive and brutal deployment of police and security forces produced not intimidation but rapid politicization. Naturally there were no political conceptions and programs behind the calls for Gorbachev, the singing of the Internationale, the demands for freedom and democracy and an end to the Wall. They indicate the pressure, particularly among the younger generation, for more free space and fundamental democratization." Even more important, Templin and Grimm pointed to the strategic lessons the independent peace movement should draw from the June clashes: "The East German peace movement and activist circles must ask themselves to what extent their persistence in self-contained modes of work, the writing of letters and petitions, and their self-isolation, is bypassing many conflicts and hopes. The June events will come to play a considerable role in the peace movement debate over independent activity, new points of departure, and new forms of action."[83]

Not everybody in the East German dissident community is convinced that Gorbachev deserves such unqualified support. For example, one contributor to *Grenzfall* found "somewhat inappropriate" the demonstrators' eagerness to identify themselves with Gorbachev's strategy of reforms from above. In his view, there is an enormous difference between chanting Rosa Luxemburg's name and the unfounded enthusiasm for the Soviet general secretary who remains the representative of the party bureaucracy: "The demonstrators' singing of the Internationale, even if horribly out of tune, but especially the chorus of calls for Rosa Luxemburg during the Stasi (security police) attack at the gate, seems to me more valid in this context than the name of Mikhail Gorbachev. The invocation of Rosa Luxemburg, outside the false appropriation of her person and the misuse and the distortion of her politics by the usual parades and state organizations, remains a wonderful gesture, an embittered statement of the real domestic politics of the regime and proof of the degeneration of its original goals. It clearly says: this state is a caricature of socialism and has nothing in common with the ideas and the struggle of revolutionary spirits like Rosa Luxemburg."[84]

Other riots occurred in the summer of 1987. On the occasion of the public celebrations commemorating the seven hundred and fiftieth anniversary of the founding of Berlin, the Protestant Church was for the first time allowed to organize its annual Church Festival (Kirchentag) in the East German capital city. As a result of conflicts with church authorities who wanted to exert increased control over the festival, the annual "Peace Workshop" in East Berlin was canceled and the whole Kirchentag agenda modified. The independent activists responded by convening their own Kirchentag von unten (Church Festival from Below—KvU). An article published in Umweltblätter described the tensions between the church hierarchy and the autonomous initiatives: The text criticized the church for "its increasingly repressive policy" toward peace and environmentalist groups in its parishes, and said that the alienation of the top church hierarchy from the independent activists "showed itself most clearly in the increasingly cynical treatment of the 'basis' groups, who were increasingly excluded as 'freeloaders' on the Church." There was a need to offer a platform to those basis groups who "stand in genuine Christian tradition and prefigure renewal in the Church. . . ."[85]

Slogans like "Glasnost in the state and in the church" or "The church from below for more Christianity, democracy, and human rights" capture the ethos of radical pacifism in the GDR. The "church from below" has expanded its popular roots—its membership has reached over one thousand—and even some prominent church figures have deplored the existing strains in the relations with the independent activists.

Radical pacifism advocates the democratization of the body politic and the transformation of society into a real partner to the government in the exercise of power. The times of police arbitrariness and centralized despotism are over. If the authorities want to be trusted, both internally and internationally, they must accept the dialogue with the independent groups who voice the major concerns of the population. Official pledges of peaceful intentions remain utterly hypocritical as long as the Communist regimes do not fulfill all their obligations assumed at the Helsinki Conference for Security and Cooperation in Europe. In November 1986, thirty East German citizens, most of them associated with the "Peace and Human Rights Initiative" joined hundreds of activists from other countries in signing a memorandum addressed to citizens, groups, and governments of all the CSCE states. The document insisted that in order to become real, détente must go beyond the governmental level and affect societies. The formula détente from below perfectly sums up their outlook: "We reject the use of military and paramilitary forces or secret activities to suppress social changes within a country as well as any interference by such forces or threats of such interference into the internal affairs of other countries. At the same time we strongly advocate trans-frontier solidarity, mutual support and cooperation between people and groups working for peace, civil liberties, trade union rights, social justice, women's emancipation, or ecological goals. . . . Mutual trust cannot be created solely by governments. It must be built up between citizens as well.[86]

Other issues discussed in the samizdat press are the status of political prisoners, the penal system, the restrictions on travel abroad, the continuous militarization of public life, and the persecution of conscientious objectors.

Communist ideology strongly opposes pacifism, for which it blames the weakening of the will to resist "imperialist aggression." Pacifist stances and attitudes may be socially acceptable in the West, but they do not fit at all into the prescribed behavior of the "socialist citizen." Conscientious objection is illegal in East Germany and the alternative service represented by construction units has not solved this problem. Those who serve as *Bausoldaten* (construction soldiers) are forced to work for the building of military facilities (airfields, barracks, etc.). Moreover, former construction soldiers suffer job discrimination. The "total conscientious objectors" (*Totalverweigerer*), those who refuse to serve both in military and construction units, are sentenced to prison terms from eighteen to twenty-six months. There are an estimated 200 per year, about half of whom are Jehovah's Witnesses.[87] Approximately forty conscientious objectors were jailed in September 1985, but were released a month later apparently as a result of church intervention. The status of total conscientious objectors has been intensely discussed by unofficial peace and human-rights groups. In opposition to the regime's inflexible attitude, both the church and the independent peace movement have long called for the establishment of a genuine "social service for peace."[88]

The status of conscientious objectors has thus remained a fundamental concern for independent activists. This may well become a new single issue to further catalyze the development of spontaneous initiatives in the Soviet-bloc countries. The announcement in January 1988 by the Polish government of its plan to introduce an alternative civilian service for conscientious objectors has certainly prompted East German activists to exert more pressure on their own authorities.[89] In fact, fifteen East German peace and human-rights activists signed the joint appeal on behalf of Soviet-bloc conscientious objectors published in March 1988. The appeal, sent to the Vienna follow-up of the Conference on Security and Cooperation in Europe, welcomed the January and March 1987 resolutions of the Council of Europe and the United Nations Human Rights Commission, which acknowledged conscientious objection to military service as a universal human right.[90] The publication of this joint appeal indicates a high degree of consensus between peace and human-rights groups in East-Central Europe. If this trend develops, it could eventually lead to "the formulation of a common political program between social forces in, for example, four front-line countries such as Czechoslovakia, Poland, East Germany, and Hungary."[91]

Pressure from below on behalf of the right to conscientious objection has forced the GDR government to soften its rigid attitude on this issue. For example, since 1986 no conscientious objector has been imprisoned in that country, but as Werner Fischer of the Initiative for Peace and Human Rights put it: ". . . that's not because the government has suddenly become nice and humanitarian. It's because it is aware of the protest that such a move would bring."[92]

A New Repressive Wave

Illusions about a readiness on the part of the regime to accept a dialogue with independent groups—and thus legitimize them—were soon dispelled. Jealous of their power privileges and prisoners of a monolithic mentality, the SED leaders have consistently rejected the calls for political democratization and structural changes. Tightening up the screws has always been the Stalinists' instinctive answer to social unrest, and the East German Communist elite is no exception. If there are some Gorbachevites in the SED Politburo, they certainly represent, for the time being, a silenced minority.

The new repressive wave started in November 1987, when the authorities organized a police raid on the Church of Zion in East Berlin, arrested two members of a peace and ecological group, and confiscated printing and mimeographing material. They also confiscated samizdat publications considered "hostile to the state." In response, protest vigils were organized until the two activists were released.

The raid against the Church of Zion was actually aimed at the producers of *Grenzfall*, the bulletin that had become the principal mouthpiece for critical attitudes and calls for political reform.[93] Without disavowing *Grenzfall*, Evangelical Church leaders reasserted the fact that their goals do not overlap with those of the political opposition. While admitting that the church's role in the GDR is also a "safety valve" for the oppressed and humiliated, Rev. Günter Krusche, general superintendant of the Evangelical Church of East Berlin, noted: "Our critics say, 'Jesus was here for everybody, but you throw them out.' We don't, but the church should stay the church. The task of the church is not the same as that of the political opposition."[94]

Before long, the authorities struck again; indeed, it can be safely assumed that the November 1987 crackdown was a general rehearsal for a wider, more radical anti-oppositional action. Disturbed by the confusing signals coming from the USSR—where thousands of independent groups, associations, and publications had come into being as a result of the current thaw[95]—and alarmed by potential disruptive developments in their own country, the hard-liners in the SED leadership decided to wage a determined campaign against all sources of political turmoil. This was an oblique indication of Erich Honecker's dissatisfaction with the effects of Gorbachev's policy of glasnost.[96]

The SED strategy seems to be one of more and more repression and pressure toward conformity. In accordance with this goal, during the first two months of 1988 the authorities organized the largest crackdown on dissidents in at least ten years.[97] According to information from church sources, from January until the middle of March 1988 more than 500 men and women were detained. In many cases, an application to emigrate to the FRG was sufficient reason for detention. More than 150 persons were sentenced to prison terms of between eighteen and twenty-four months in the wake of the outbreak of protests. Others were kept in prison awaiting trial, whereas those who had been released were required to report daily to the local police.[98] It is now absolutely clear that Erich Honecker and his comrades do not intend to indulge in any form of pluralism, even of the "socialist" variety represented by Karoly Grosz, Wojciech Jaruzelski, or Mikhail Gorbachev. The SED leaders seem united in their refusal even to consider the issue of internal democratization,[99] and appear to resent Soviet injunctions to break with the stagnation of Brezhnev's times.[100]

The detonator of this major repressive wave was the attempt by a group of human-rights and peace activists to stage a demonstration parallel to the official annual 17 January rally commemorating the death in 1919 of the founders of the German Communist Party, Rosa Luxemburg and Karl Liebknecht. Human-rights activists tried to unfold banners calling for the democratization of the political system. More than 100 persons were rounded up. The party newspaper *Neues Deutschland* accused the independent demonstrators of having intended to "maliciously disturb the mourning procession." A week later the security police deported to West Germany 54 of those arrested (in addition to members of their families) who had previously applied for emigration visas. On January 25, 6 leading dissidents were arrested. Eleven activists were eventually sentenced to prison terms ranging from six months to one year for illegal assembly. Seven of East Germany's most prominent dissidents, including the political folk singer Stefan Krawczyk, were placed under investigation for "treasonable ties with the West."[101]

What followed was a forceful demonstration of mass solidarity with those arrested. Night after night, in East Berlin and in some thirty towns throughout the GDR, people gathered in Protestant churches to voice their indignation. On many occasions, church personalities mentioned the need to liberalize the East German political system. Speaking in front of the youth gathered in East Berlin's Galilee Church, the Rev. Manfred Becker, head of the Berlin and Brandenburg Synod, spelled out the widespread discontent with Honecker's reluctance to emulate the Soviet trends: "Much hope in our country is linked with the name Gorbachev. . . . Glasnost and perestroyka belong on the agenda in our country, too."[102] On January 30, in a statement read to more than 2,000 people gathered in an East Berlin Church, the Evangelical Church leadership urged the government to release the imprisoned political activists. Several days later, on February 4, the East European Cultural Foundation, a London-based organization, issued the text of a petition protesting the persecution of East German peace and human-rights activists. Signed by 257 representatives of human-rights groups and private individuals from the Soviet Union and Eastern Europe, the statement further cemented the sense of international solidarity among anti-totalitarian activists. It is extremely important for these people to feel that their ideas and actions are widely publicized throughout the whole Soviet bloc, for they believe that international currents of public opinion—both from the East and the West— can eventually influence local rulers and force them to reconsider some of their more outrageous measures.

In fact, following the impressive popular reaction and massive international protests, all the dissidents were released during the first days of February. Some of them, including Krawczyk and his wife Freya Klier, were forced to emigrate. On February 3, in a statement to the West German press, Krawczyk revealed that they had not left the GDR voluntarily. According to him, the East German officials had not agreed to their request to be allowed to remain in the GDR. Instead, the authorities offered them the choice of emigrating or facing up to twelve years' imprisonment on charges of treason.[103] In addition, five members of the "Initiative for Peace and Human Rights" (Ralf Hirsch, Wolfgang and Regina Templin, Bärbel Bohley, and Werner Fischer), as well as human-rights activist Vera Wollenberger of the "Church from Below," left the GDR. They rejected the government's allegation that they would have left the GDR voluntarily. The government has thus resorted to the practice that it initiated in the 1970s: expelling the most outspoken members of the peace and human-rights movement and thereby eliminating a source of political turmoil.

An interesting episode during this massive clampdown on dissent was the government's decision to issue passports for two of the leading members of the "Initiative for Peace and Human Rights" (Bärbel Bohley and Werner Fischer) to go to England and allow them after six months to return to the GDR. According to Fischer, the authorities were intent upon seizing any pretext to accuse the two activists of having engaged in anti-GDR propaganda in the West and conse-quently to withdraw their passports. Fischer and Bohley were allowed to return to the GDR in August 1988, which is not only an indication of a new pattern of official handling of oppositional activities, but also a good sign of confusion on the part of the government. At any rate, as Fischer himself noticed: ". . .this is the first time in Eastern Europe that anyone has been let out of prison with a passport and the right to go the West and return home. The authorities made that offer because they were under pressure from various quarters. I believe that the authorities let us go with our passports in the hope that we would do something public in the West which would allow them to deprive us of our citizenship while being able to say: 'We did everything properly. They have brought this on themselves."[104]

The 1988 crackdown on protest movement activists was aptly described by Stefan Krawczyk and Freya Klier as a neo-Stalinist attempt to resist political change and safeguard a repressive dictatorship. In terms of economic relations, the SED leadership is increasingly Western oriented, but domestically, it seems to favor the extremely orthodox model symbolized by Nicolae Ceauşescu's Romania.[105] There is indeed much concern that the regime has become a citadel of intransigent Stalinism, ostentatiously opposed to the fresh wind of changes now blowing from the East. According to Manfred Stolpe, a leading Evangelical Church personality, the SED Politburo is divided between those who regret the bygone era of monolithic dictatorship and those who fear the grim prospect of following the disastrous Romanian course. An ominous indication of the latter possibility was the "fraternal greetings" sent to "esteemed comrade Nicolae Ceauşescu," together with the Karl Marx Order on the occasion of his seventieth birthday in January 1988. In a not surprising juxtaposition, the praises for the Romanian dictator were published on the front page of the same issue of the party daily *Neues Deutschland* which announced, on its second page, the arrest of Krawczyk and the other peace and civil-rights activists.[106]

By expelling Krawczyk and the other prominent activists, the SED scored only a temporary political victory. To be sure, the authorities managed to rid themselves of some of the most charismatic spokesmen for political change. On the other hand, the grass-roots human-rights and peace initiatives have intensified in the aftermath of the January arrests. Far from being ephemeral or marginal phenomena, they are rather the outcome of a long process of political radicalization of the East German youth. The youth revolt originates in a profound disaffection with the socialist model of civilization experimented with in the GDR. It is the expression of deeply ingrained feelings of malaise, hopelessness, and all-embracing pessimism. For many East German young activists, participation in the new social movements is the only opportunity to experience a genuine sense of identity and belonging. In a world where all the values seem shockingly empty, peace and human-rights activism provides the youth with the chance of doing something that is both useful and noble.

An effect of complex and contradictory social, political, and cultural processes, the independent peace and human-rights movement cannot be suppressed by decree. This movement indicates the search for innovative forms of political struggle and organization, strategically opposed to the bureaucratic logic of the system. Precisely because of its broad social appeal, the movement can gradually structure itself—as in Hungary or Poland—in the form of a *democratic opposition*. The pluralist virus cannot be combated with increased police forces.

In East Germany what started as a moral initiative for social demilitarization has now turned into a rapidly growing political movement. In spite of the unremitting police harassment, there are now about 200 independent groups active in the GDR, in and out of the church. According to activist Werner Fischer, each group has between 20 and 100 members, which amounts to a total membership between 40 and 100,000 people. Most of them are integrated in various social organizations where they can disseminate their views and which they can gradually influence. It is thus clear that these groups represent "an enormous critical potential."[107] The Evangelical Church has helped the young activists associated with the movement to develop both their independent stances toward the authorities and the feelings of mutual solidarity. Their goal is to transform the GDR into a more breathable and hospitable social space, where the individual does not feel helpless in his or her relations with the powers-that-be. In a letter to party leader Erich Honecker, graphic artist and peace activist Bärbel Bohley insisted on the need to bridge the abysmal gap between the rulers and the ruled, between "them" and "us": "This state does not belong only to you or to me, but to all of us. Like me, there are many people who feel lost [*heimatlos*] in this country. Like you, there are many who feel at home. But there are also those who have been forced into their corners. . .and who do not dare to express their wishes and views. I do not write you in the hope to have my personal situation changed. I would like you to contribute to change the social relations in the GDR in such a way that every person could publicly state his or her opinion, without being threatened in his or her existence."[108]

The January 1988 expulsions have convinced many people that joining the peace and human-rights groups and demonstrating with them could be the easiest—and fastest—way to emigrate. This situation helps the authorities in their effort to discredit the independent groups and accuse them of being nothing but a springboard for emigration. In September 1987, a group calling itself Civil Rights in the GDR was formed in East Berlin in order to defend and help those who wish to emigrate. Seventeen members of this group joined the January 17, 1988, parallel demonstration commemorating Rosa Luxemburg and Karl Liebknecht. On February 13, during a rally in Dresden commemorating the Allied bombing of the city, banners with unapproved slogans turned up on the fringe of the demonstration. The 300 demonstrators carried banners and chanted slogans demanding the dismantling of the Berlin Wall and the freedom to leave the GDR. In March, five artists were detained for several days in East Berlin for having decried in a letter to Erich Honecker the practice of deporting embarrassing critics of the regime. All the signatories of the letter had applied to emigrate a long time ago.[109]

It is clear that the issue of emigration has become a major concern for those peace and human-rights activists who want to continue their struggle in the GDR. Heated discussions have been reported between those whose main objective is to leave the GDR and those who want to remain and promote radical changes within the system. The regime's decision to forcibly deport Stefan Krawczyk, a most engaging symbol of the internal change strategy, dealt a forceful blow to the human-rights and peace movement. Those determined to remain and fight in the GDR felt perplexed and powerless learning of the emigration of the man who had epitomized the decision to stay and seek the improvement of domestic conditions, while potential emigrants saw in Krawczyk's deportation the possibility of a strategy. As for the church, although it has pressed for a more tolerant emigration policy, its leaders have avoided identifying themselves with those seeking visas to leave.

Prominent members of the independent peace movement have acknowledged the disconcerting impact of the January–February 1988 official onslaught on the dissidents. Ralf Hirsch, one of the leaders of the "Initiative for Peace and Human Rights" who has been expelled from the GDR, has bitterly pointed to the predicament of those who do not see their political activism as a rapid channel for emigration: ". . .one has to say that the demonstrators are mainly people who want to leave the GDR. They have now learned that if one takes part in a demonstration, one quickly gets out of the country. The people who want to change the GDR from within, who want to stay in this country, will have many difficulties."[110] In other words, they will have to work hard to restore their credibility. Hirsch expressed more than a personal mood when he disclosed his frustration with being forced to leave the GDR: "I am faced with the problem that I am here (in the FRG) and actually I wanted to stay in my country, to change something in the country where I lived. I do not feel well, at all. And, of course, I am sad. Now everything that I have been doing for years has been ruined."

But there are still many activists who continue their struggle in the GDR. The political agenda of the "Initiative for Peace and Human Rights" has become a dynamic factor in prompting the struggle for internal change. Recent developments have shown that this capital has not been lost as a result of the authorities' attempts to compromise the movement. In January 1989, an open letter was addressed to Erich Honecker by members of a group opposed to "the practice and principle of delimitation" (*Abgrenzung*) between the two German states. The authors took issue with the East German leader's statement according to which the Berlin Wall served the "well-interpreted interest of the GDR's population:" "Everybody knows that the wall is not directed against robbers from the outside but at those on the inside. Our country needs stability based on justice, and not stability based on fear. . . . we demand that a free, sincere, and public dialogue of all groups and forces in our society be permitted and opened up (*glasnost*). This would be the first and most important step to removing the reasons for maintaining the wall that are still effective today. The reasons are primarily internal not external ones. It is up to you to take and permit measures to overcome them. We, and our children, do not want to wait another 50 years."[111]

Also in January 1989, a group called the Initiative for the Democratic Renewal of Our Society distributed leaflets in Leipzip on the occasion of the seventieth anniversary of the assassination of Rosa Luxemburg and Karl Liebknecht. The authorities reacted by arresting eleven members of church, environmental, and peace groups in Leipzig.[112] The leaflet, symbolically titled "To Courageously Speak One's Mind," urged East German citizens to fight for the democratization of their society: "It is time to courageously and openly speak our minds and put an end to the paralyzing apathy and indifference. Let us advocate jointly the right to freedom of opinion, to freedom of association and assembly, to freedom of the press, and against the ban of the (Soviet) magazine *Sputnik* and of Soviet films."[113] At the beginning of 1989, the samizdat critical publication of *Grenzfall* of the Initiative for Peace and Human Rights appeared for the first time after a year. The new issue contained information about opposition groups in Eastern Europe, a conversation with two Estonian activists about perestroyka in Estonia, and data about GDR citizens who had been denied exit visas to visit other socialist countries.[114] In addition, a new samizdat magazine was launched in 1988 with the symbolic title *Gegendruck*, which means both counter-pressure and counter-publishing.

The Initiative for Peace and Human Rights was formed outside the church precisely because its members want to circumvent censorship exercised within the church on the one hand, and, on the other, because the activists try to define their own agenda in terms more radical than those of traditional religious pacifism. The group's attitude to the church, aptly described by activist Werner Fischer, indicates the growing secularization (autonomization from religious institutions) of radical pacifism in the GDR: "The 'Initiative for Peace and Human Rights' is not particularly interested in a relationship with the Church. We use the physical space which the Church provides but we regard ourselves as an independent group. The 'Initiative' works to maintain a good working relationship with the Church because of its important function in society."[115] The group's political aims transcend the original religious-pacifist set of goals. Their main purpose is to create a social climate based on internal peace: "Basic rights, such as freedom of opinion, of the press, and the right of assembly, which are guaranteed by the constitution, need to become reality. Laws, which do exist and some of which are not bad at all, can currently be applied just as the state organs wish."[116] A document prepared by the Initiative for Peace and Human Rights on the occasion of Human Rights Day (December 10, 1987) points out the organic connection between pacifism and social activism: ". . .peace is for us always a process of necessary social and political change. This change within society is not a threat to, but the precondition for a stable peace. We need a broad public opinion to emerge which can exercise effective control. The emergence of such a critical public opinion depends on the guarantee of human and civil rights."[117] Without discarding the need for a dialogue with the government, the movement sees democratization as a process of self-determined social emancipation which would abolish the current chasm between state and society: "Fundamental change in the sense of a non-violent policy geared to the preservation, or, rather, restoration of our natural environment and respect for human dignity is not to be expected from the 'all-powerful' perfect state. To achieve this, decentralization and self-organization of society, as well as self-management in all areas of life is required. If we wish to operate in such a context, we must learn to accept the pluralism which actually exists within society."[118]

Conclusion

The East German independent peace movement began as a form of nongovernmental critical activity primarily concerned with the growing militarization of the whole social life. As result of the qualified but consistent support offered by the Evangelical Church, the movement became increasingly popular and influential. Although on various occasions, radical activists have expressed disaffection with the clergy's reluctance to engage in direct confrontation with the authorities, many priests have not hesitated to join the independent movement and turn their churches into sanctuaries for persecuted activists. The "Church from Below" has thus appeared as a challenge to the "accommodationist" politics of religious authorities. One can expect this trend to develop in the future.

Religious pacifism is, however, only one current within the growing independent peace movement in the GDR. Other components of the unofficial peace movement include radical ecologists, democratic socialists, neo-Marxists, members of the rock counterculture, and so forth. They operate both within and outside the church. Their attitude toward the official Peace Council is extremely critical.

There is a large consensus among members of these groups about major goals and the most appropriate methods to achieve them. The independent peace and human-rights movement does not aim at overthrowing the existing social system: its intention is to democratize it. In other words, this is a spontaneous grassroots movement rather than an organized oppositional association.

In recent years, however, the East German independent groups have become increasingly critical of the existing social order. Some of their members wish to emigrate to the West, but most of them see their future in the GDR. Since they are all committed to the strategy of nonviolence, share the same long-term objectives, and frequently act in a coordinated way, these groups can be broadly described as a social movement.[119] But this is an informal, anti-authoritarian movement which programmatically refuses institutional freezing and/or co-optation. Its very appearance reveals deep-seated trends within East Germany society: Independent pacifism has become a major channel for the crystallization of pluralistic orientations. Since the mid-1980s, pacifist and human-rights initiatives have merged in the attempt to consolidate these burgeoning networks of autonomous political action. At the same time, Mikhail Gorbachev's policy of glasnost has encouraged the independent activists in their search for societal renewal. To the mounting protest movement, Erich Honecker's regime has reacted in its traditional repressive manner: raids, searches, beatings, arrests, interrogations, imprisonments, and expulsions. But instead of deterring them, this tactic has further radicalized the independent groups.

To conclude, East German peace and human-rights activism has profound social causes: discontent with the militaristic course of the regime, opposition to political and cultural repression, youth disaffection with officially propagated hackneyed dogmas, widespread attraction to a pluralistic order. It expresses the awakening of the civil society after the long and painful lethargy imposed by an unyielding authoritarian-bureaucratic regime. Taking advantage of the church's support and recruiting among the growing alternative subcultures, the movement will probably become the backbone of a Democratic Opposition interested in humanizing the social space and limiting the prerogatives of the powers-that-be.

NOTES

1.   See A. James McAdams, *East Germany and Detente: Building Authority after the Wall*, (New York: Cambridge University Press, 1985), pp. 9–63; J. F. Brown, *Eastern Europe and Communist Rule* (Durham, North Carolina: Duke University Press, 1988), pp. 230–63; Henry Ashby Turner, Jr., *The Two Germanies since 1945* (New Haven and London: Yale University Press, 1987), pp. 46–53 and 99–145. For a democratic-socialist critique of the East German system, see Franz Loeser, *Die unglaubwürdige Geselschaft: Quo vadis DDR?* (Koln: Bund Verlag, 1984).

2.   See Henry Krisch, "Official Nationalism," in Lyman H. Legters ed., *The German Democratic Republic* (Boulder, Co.: Westview, 1978), pp. 103–32.

3.   See Martin McCauley, "The German Democratic Republic: Internal and International," in George Schopflin, ed., *The Soviet Union and Eastern Europe* (New York and Oxford: Facts On File Publications, 1986), pp. 337–44; Jadwiga M. Staar, "Germany: German Democratic Republic," in Richard F. Staar, *Yearbook on International Communist Affairs, 1987* (Stanford: Hoover Institution Press, 1987), pp. 296–300.

4.   See the full text of Krenz's speech in FBIS, Eastern Europe, January 19, 1988.

5.   See Martin McCauley, *Marxism-Leninism in the German Democratic Republic* (New York: Harper and Row, 1979); David Childs, *The GDR: Moscow's German Ally* (London: George Allen & Unwin, 1988).

6.   This view has been reinforced by Alexander Dubček, the former Czechoslovak Communist leader, in a long interview with the Italian official Communist daily *L'Unita*. See FBIS, Eastern Europe, January 19, 1988, pp. 9–24.

7.   For a fascinating report on the preparations for the military coup in Poland, see "The Crushing of Solidarity," an interview with Col. Ryszard Kuklinski, *Orbis*, Vol. 32, No. 1, Winter 1988, pp. 7–31. The interview originally appeared in *Kultura* (a Polish-language journal published in Paris), No. 4/475, April 1987, pp. 3–57.

8.   See Gero Neugebauer, "The Military and Society in the GDR," in *Studies in the GDR Culture and Society 5* (Lanham, Mass. and London: University Press of America, 1985), p. 82.

9.   See Ian Jeffries and Manfried Melzer, eds., *The East German Economy*, (London: Croom Helm; New York: Methuen, 1988).

10.   See James McAdams, op. cit., p. 189.

11.   See *Der Spiegel*, September 1, 1986, quoted by B. V. Flow, "The Literary Avant-Garde Leaves the GDR," RFER, RAD Background Report/132, September 18, 1986.

12.   Ibidem; for the views of the East German cultural avant-garde, see Sascha Anderson and Elke Erb, eds., *Berührung Ist Nur eine Randerschein: Neue Deutsche Literatur aus der DDR* (Koln: Kiepenhauer & Wisch, 1985).

13.   See *Der Spiegel*, January 3, 1983, quoted by Pedro Ramet, "Disaffection and Dissent in East

Germany," *World Politics*, Vol. XXXVII, No. 1, October 1984, p. 93. According to Ramet, there are four basic sources of disaffection in the GDR today: the failure of resocialization, specific policy shortcomings, the contrast between Marxist promises and Communist policies, and the incipient erosion of the East German economy. (ibidem, p. 87). One should add the national variable and the emergence, in recent years, of a pluralistic-minded, post- (not necessarily anti-) Marxist opposition. In other words, disillusionment with Marxist revisionism has engendered a new political philosophy among activists who identify themselves with the anti-authoritarian left.

14.   Quoted in John Ardagh, *Germany and the Germans* (New York: Harper and Row, 1987), pp. 362–63.

15.   For the fate of Marxist revisionism and the dialectics of de-Stalinization in the USSR and Eastern Europe, see Vladimir Tismaneanu, *The Crisis of Marxist Ideology in Eastern Europe: The Poverty of Utopia* (London and New York: Routledge, 1988).

16.   See Robert Havemann, *Questions Answers Questions: From the Biography of a German Marxist* (Garden City, N.Y.: Doubleday, 1972), pp. 169–70; for biographical information on Havemann (1910–1982), see Robert A. Gorman, ed., *Biographical Dictionary of Neo-Marxism* (Westport, Conn.: Westwood Press, 1985), pp. 203–204. In November 1989, Havemann was posthumously rehabilitated and reinstated as a member of the East German Academy of Science.

17.   See Robert Havemann, *Ein deutscher Kommunist: Rückblicke und Perspektiven aus Isolation* (Hamburg: Rowohlt, 1978), pp. 98–103; excerpts from Havemann's book were published in Roger Woods, *Opposition in GDR under Honecker, 1971–85: An Introduction and Documentation*, with translations of the documents by Christopher Upward (New York: St. Martin's Press, 1986), pp. 165–69.

18.   See *Index on Censorship*, February 1973, quoted by Sharon L. Kegerreiss, "The Politics of Silence: Culture and Kulturpolitik in the GDR," *RFER*, RAD Background Report/212, October 2, 1979, p. 5.

19.   Biermann had anticipated this measure when he wrote in the "Minstrel's Maiden Speech": "Those who once stood before machine guns with steadfast courage now fear my guitar," ibidem. For a perceptive analysis of East German dissent in the 1970s, see Werner Volkmer, "East Germany: Dissenting Views during the Last decade," in Rudolf L. Tökés, ed., *Opposition in Eastern Europe* (Baltimore and London: Johns Hopkins University Press, 1979), pp. 113–141.

20.   See Karl Wilhelm Fricke, *Opposition und Widerstand in der DDR* (Koln: Verlag Wissenschaft und Politik, 1984), pp. 175–89.

21.   Ibidem, p. 7.

22.   See *Neues Deutschland*, June 24, 1979.

23.   See *Neues Deutschland*, December 30, 1988. For the current tensions in Soviet–East German relations, including the unprecedented ban on the Soviet press digest *Sputnik*, see "Where Sputnik can't land," *The Economist*, November 26, 1988, p. 52; Barbara Donovan, "East Germany Bans Soviet Journal," *RFER*, RAD Background Report/233 (Eastern Europe), November 23, 1988; Henri de Bresson, "Berlin-Est pris de vitesse par l'évolution de l'URSS," *Le Monde* (Paris), December 25 and 26, 1988. In December 1988, Erich Honecker criticized Moscow for tolerating the revision of Soviet history by "bourgeois types gone wild." See Serge Schmemann, "2 Germanies' Political Divide Is Being Blurred by Glasnost," *New York Times*, December 18, 1988. For the implications of the "mutual dependence" between East Berlin and Moscow and the meaning of the Honecker's autonomist course, see A. James McAdams, "The New Logic in Soviet-GDR Relations," *Problems of Communism*, Vol. XXXVII, No. 5, September–October 1988, pp. 47–60.

24.   For the SED's methods to combat opposition, see Michael J. Sodaro, "Limits to Dissent in the GDR: Fragmentation, Cooptation, and Repression," in Jane Leftwich Curry, *Dissent in Eastern Europe* (New York: Praeger, 1983), pp. 83–116.

25. See Ronald D. Asmus, "Is There a Peace Movement in the GDR?" *Orbis*, Summer 1983, p. 311.

26. Woods, ibidem, p. 195.

27. Ibidem, p. 196.

28. Ibidem.

29. "The Berlin Appeal was the first independent peace manifesto in the 1980s to popularize the organic connection between freedom of expression and calls for removal of weapons and peace activity."—see *From Below: Independent Peace and Environmental Movements in Eastern Europe and the USSR. A Helsinki Watch Report* (October 1987), p. 29. The theme of the "democratic peace" has been extensively developed in the political thought of the Charter 77 in Czechoslovakia. See Václav Havel et al., *The Power of the Powerless: Citizens against the state in central-eastern Europe* (Armonk, N.Y.: M.E. Sharpe, 1985), and Václav Havel, "An Anatomy of Reticence," *Crosscurrents: A Yearbook of Central European Culture* (Ann Arbor: University of Michigan), no. 5, pp. 1–23.

30. See Peter Maser, "The Protestant Churches and the Independent peace Movement in the GDR," in *Studies in the GDR Culture and Society*, op. cit., p. 47.

31. Ibidem; Joyce Marie Mushaben, "Swords to Plowshares: The Church, The State, and the East German Peace Movement," *Studies in Comparative Communism*, Vol. XVII, No. 2, Summer 1984, pp. 123–35.

32. Quoted in B. Welling Hall, "The Church and the Independent Peace Movement in Eastern Europe," *Journal of Peace Research*, Vol. 23, no. 2, 1986, p. 200.

33. See Ronald D. Asmus, op. cit. p. 322; Albert Schönherr, *Horizont und Mitte* (Munich: Christian Kaiser Verlag, 1979).

34. See George B. von der Lippe, "Ich weiss jetzt, wer ich bin': The Figure of Martin Luther as Presented in the Literature of the GDR," in *Studies in GDR Culture and Society*, op. cit., pp. 339–55; Robert F. Goeckel, "The Luther Anniversary in the GDR," *World Politics*, Vol. XXXVII, October 1984, pp. 112–33.

35. See Asmus, op. cit., p. 306.

36. See "Die Aktualität des Pazifismus. Ein Diskussionspapier für die Gemeinden (November 1981)," in Wolfgang Büscher, Peter Wensierski und Klaus Wolschner, eds., *Friedensbewegung in der DDR, Texte 1978–1982* (Hattingen: Edition Transit, 1982), pp. 245–63.

37. See Wolfgang Büscher and Peter Wensierski, *Null Bock auf DDR: Aussteigerjugend im anderen Deutschland* (Hamburg: Rowohlt Verlag, 1984) especially the chapter dealing with the relations between the Church and the peace movement, pp. 133–64.

38. See "Poetisches Prinzip Aufrichtigkeit: Eine polnisch-deutsche Diskussion im Herbst 1981," in Jürgen Fuchs, *Einmischung in eigene Angelegenheiten: Gegen Krieg und verlogenen Frieden* (Hamburg: Rowohlt Verlag, 1984), pp. 53–79—a fascinating discussion between Jürgen Fuchs, an East German poet and human rights activist, and two Polish intellectuals.

39. See W. Büscher et al., *Friedensbewegung in der DDR*, pp. 169–71.

40. Quoted by Asmus, "Is There a Peace Movement in the GDR?," *Orbis*, p. 308.

41. See Karl Wilhelm Fricke, *Opposition und Widerstand in der DDR*, (Koln: Verlag Wissenschaft und Politik, 1984), pp. 194–95; Woods, Opposition in the GDR, pp. 36–7.

42. See Fricke, ibidem, p. 195.

43. See Asmus, p. 324.

44. See B. Welling Hall, "The Church and the Independent Peace Movement in Eastern Europe," *Journal of Peace Research*, p. 202.

45. See George Konrád, *Antipolitics* (San Diego: Harcourt Brace Jovanovich, 1984), p. 92.

46. See Welling Hall, p. 203.

47. See Maser, "The Protestant Churches and the Peace Movement in the GDR," *Studies in GDR Culture and Society,* op. cit., p. 40.

48. Ibidem.

49. See Büscher et al, *Friedensbewegung in der DDR,* pp. 284–8.

50. See Pedro Ramet, *Cross and Commissar: The Politics of Religion in Eastern Europe and the USSR* (Bloomington and Indianapolis: Indiana University Press, 1987), pp. 80–96.

51. See "Hidden opposition of the GDR" (an interview with Werner Fischer), *East European Reporter,* Vol. 3, No. 3, Autumn 1988, p. 66. According to Fischer, the government would not tolerate actions which take place outside church property in public. Moreover, the regime keeps for itself the right to decide which activities organized on church premises are church-related and consequently generate tensions between the religious hierarchy and the independent groups.

52. See Maser, "The Protestant Churches," p. 41.

53. See Büscher et al, *Friedensbewegung,* p. 233.

54. See "Wir brauchen die Kultur der Meinungstreit," an interview with the president of the East Berlin church consistory president Manfred Stolpe, *Der Spiegel,* February 15, 1988, pp. 23–7.

55. See Maser, p. 49.

56. See Thomas F. O'Boyle, "Winds of Change Coming From Moscow Stir Hopes for Liberty in East Germany," *The Wall Street Journal,* February 19, 1988.

57. See "Open Letter to Erich Honecker," in Woods, *Opposition in the GDR,* pp. 197–9.

58. See *Neues Deutschland,* March 27–28, 1982; Asmus, p. 315.

59. See Christa Wolf, *Cassandra: A Novel and Four Essays* (New York: Farrar, Straus and Giroux, 1984), p. 258.

60. Ibidem, pp. 229–30.

61. Ibidem, p. 268.

62. For Hermlin's speech, see Woods, *Opposition in the GDR,* pp. 200–201. More recently, Hermlin called for the democratization of political and social life in the GDR, but he blamed those activists who use leftist slogans and references to Rosa Luxemburg and Mikhail Gorbachev only to cover their desire to emigrate to the West. See "Wir brauchen vor allem Glasnost" (an interview with Stephan Hermlin), *Der Spiegel,* No. 6, February 6, 1989, pp. 69–80.

63. See James M. Markham, "In Militaristic East Germany, the Pacifists Mobilize," *The New York Times,* November 28, 1983.

64. Quoted by Elizabeth Pond, "East Germany's Unique Peace Movement Faces Harder Times," *Christian Science Monitor,* January 5, 1984.

65. See Jürgen Fuchs, "Lettre ouverte au movement pour la paix d'Europe occidentale," *L'Alternative* (Paris), No. 21, March–April 1983, pp. 28–9.

66. See "On Questions of the Autonomy and 'Ideological Independence' of the Peace Movement in East and West," in Woods, op. cit., p. 204.

67. Ibidem, pp. 205–206.

68. See *From Below,* p. 32.

69. Ibidem.

70. See Karl Wilhelm Fricke, "Marxist, Pazifist, aber Staatsfeind," *Deutsche Tagespost,* February

13, 1985; "Pacifist Marxist But Enemy of the State," *L'Unita,* January 11, 1985; "Wenn aus Lesen und Diskutieren staatsfeindliche Hetze wird," *Frankfurter Allgemeine Zeitung,* December 8, 1984.

71.   See A. Wynton Jackson, *Introduction* to "GDR: Appeal on the occasion of UN Peace Year," *East European Reporter,* Vol. 2, No. 1, Spring 1986, pp. 60–61.

72.   "The new evolutionism aims at gradual and slow change. But this does not mean that the movement for change will always be peaceful—that it will not require sacrifices and casualties. . . .the democratic opposition must be constantly and incessantly visible in public life, must create political facts by organizing mass actions, must formulate alternative programs. Everything else is an illusion."—See Adam Michnik, *Letters From Prison and Other Essays* (Berkeley: University of California Press, 1986), pp. 145–47; for an assessment of this political strategy, see, Jane Leftwich Curry, "Polish Dissent and Establishment Criticism," in Jane L. Curry, ed., *Dissent in Eastern Europe,* op. cit., pp. 153–72; for the views of the Hungarian Democratic Opposition on the peaceful democratization of the existing regime, see "The Social Contract: Prerequisites for Resolving the Social Crisis," *Beszélö* (Budapest), special issue, 1987.

73.   See *East European Reporter,* Spring, 1986, art. cit.

74.   See "Appeal to the Government of the GDR (January 24, 1986)," *East European Reporter,* Vol. 2, No. 1, Spring 1986, p. 62.

75.   See Petr Uhl, "A Czechoslovakian Perspective," *New Politics, Vol. 1, No. 4, (New Series), Winter 1988, p. 109.*

76.   *See "Invitation to Dialogue: GDR Citizens Petition SED Party Congress" (A report by Susan Buckingham), East European Reporter,* Vol. 2, No. 2, 1986, p. 44–47; *GDR Peace News* (A newsletter published by the GDR Working Group of END), Summer 1986, No. 3.

77.   See *The Independent* (London), November 23, 1984; *Die Presse* (Vienna), November 24, 1984; *Le Monde* (Paris), November 28, 1984. Among the East German signatories of this statement were Katja Havemann, Robert Havemann's widow, as well as religious pacifists and activists of the "Woman for Peace" group. On the Czechoslovak side, the document was signed by Václav Havel, Patr Uhl, Jaroslav Sabata, and other Charter 77 activists.

78.   See *Le Monde,* (Paris), October 2, 1986. For a general assessment of the concerted actions of East-Central European dissident and critical intellectuals, see Vladimir Tismaneanu, "Dissent in the Gorbachev Era," *Orbis,* Summer 1987, pp. 234–43.

79.   See Gerd Poppe's "Open Letter to the Public Prosecutor," (with a foreword by Roland Jahn), *East European Reporter,* Vol. No. 4, 1987, pp. 53–54.

80.   For the intensification of dissident activities in the glasnost era, see Michael Waller, *Peace, Power, and Protest: Eastern Europe in the Gorbachev Era* (London: The Centre for Security and Conflict Studies, 1988).

81.   See Patricia Clough, "Germany's Divided Young Discover Unity in Dissent," *The Independent* (London), February 16, 1988.

82.   See *From Below,* p. 36.

83.   See Peter Grimm and Wolfgang Templin, "The Internationale at the Brandenburg Gate," in A. Winton Jackson, "The New Samizdat," *Across Frontiers,* Vol. 4, No. 1, Winter 1988, p. 16.

84.   See "The General demand for Freedom Through the Calls for Gorbachev and Rosa Luxemburg at the Brandenburg Gate," *Across Frontiers,* ibidem, pp. 16–17.

85.   See "Church Festival from Below—the Prehistory," *Across Frontiers,* ibidem, p. 17.

86.   See "Giving Real Life to the Helsinki Accords: A memorandum to citizens, groups and governments of all CSCE countries," published by European Network for East-West Dialogue, Berlin, November 1986; see also Vladimir Tismaneanu, "Dissent in the Gorbachev Era," *Orbis,* pp. 238–40.

87. See *From Below*, pp. 38–40; Barbara Donovan, "Conscientious Objection in Eastern Europe," *Radio Free Europe Research, RAD Background Report/9*, January 26, 1988.

88. See Edgar Lamm, "Höchste, heilige oder heiligste Pflicht," *Deutsche Tagespost/Katholische Zeitung für Deutschland*, January 15, 1987.

89. For the new Polish approach to conscientious objection, see Martin Sieff, "Growing Pacifist Movement Gains Concessions in Poland," *The Washington Times*, March 30, 1988.

90. See John Tagliabue, "In East Bloc, an Expanding Network of Dissenters," *The New York Times*, March 22, 1988.

91. See "A Dream of East-West Accord: An Interview with Jan Kavan," *Sojourners* (Washington, D.C.), Vol. 16, No. 9, October 1987, p. 17.

92. See "Hidden Opposition in the GDR," *East European Reporter, Vol. 3, No. 3*, Autumn 1988, p. 68.

93. *Grenzfall* appeared monthly in 1986–87 with a run of about 1,000.

94. See Henry Kamm, "In East Berlin, Dissenters Resist a Crackdown," *The New York Times*, November 30, 1987.

95. See Vera Tolz, " 'Informal Groups' in the U.S.S.R.," *Radio Liberty Research, RL 220/87*, June 11, 1987; Moshe Lewin, *The Gorbachev Phenomenon: A Historical Interpretation* (Berkeley: University of California Press, 1988), pp. 73–82; for the official response to this unprecedented upsurge of unofficial social activism, see the editorial "Democracy and Initiative: Social Activity in the Service of Perestroyka," *Pravda*, December 27, 1987; Julia Wishnevsky, "Conflict Between State and 'Memorial' Society," Radio Liberty, *Report on the USSR*, January 20, 1989, pp. 8–9.

96. See "You Can't Just Sit Around Waiting" (An interview with an anonymous East German oppositionist), *Uncaptive Minds* (New York), Vol. 2, No. 1, January–February 1989, pp. 46–48.

97. See Barbara Donovan, "Crackdown on Dissidents in the GDR," *Radio Free Europe Research, RAD Background Report/22*, February 17, 1988.

98. See DPA dispatch, FBIS, Eastern Europe, April 1, 1988.

99. An unmistakable signal of the SED's elite displeasure with the current de-Stalinization in the Soviet Union was the harsh attacks on the Soviet anti-Stalinist film *Repentance*, in the pages of the official party newspaper *Neues Deutschland* and the FDJ paper *Junge Welt*. See Barbara Donovan "Criticism in the GDR of the Soviet Film *Repentance*," *RFE Research, RAD Background Report/215*, November 9, 1987. The East German leaders have reasons to fear that Gorbachev's reformist drive could inspire similar attempts in their own country.

100. See E. Kautsky, "Gorbachev and the GDR," *RFE Research, BR/83*, December 16, 1986; Barbara Donovan, "The GDR's Attitude toward the Soviet 'Reforms'," *RFE Research, BR/23*, February 20, 1987.

101. See Barbara Donovan, "Crackdown on Dissidents. . .".

102. See John Tagliabue, "East Germany Faces Unrest Among Youth," *The New York Times*, February 4, 1988.

103. Ten years ago, the East German regime used the same type of slanderous accusation of "contacts with Western secret services" against social critic Rudolf Bahro, who was condemned to a prison term of 8 years for having written a critical analysis of "really existing socialism." Bahro was released from jail under a general amnesty and then forced into exile into the FRG where he has become a prominent member of the Green Party. On many occasions, Bahro has advocated a rapprochement between West and East German alternative movements on the basis of an anti-bloc alliance that would abolish the conflict East–West: "When you look at the opposition in Hungary in 1956, in Czechoslovakia in 1968 and now in Poland, and compare that with what exists in the

GDR, you will see that this non-antagonistic eco-pacifist movement, which is not simply seeking a confrontation with Honecker, is much more a German than an Eastern-bloc opposition. The identity of this youthful, deeply-rooted opposition in both German states demonstrates that, beyond the Federal Republic and the GDR, there is still Germany." See Rudolf Bahro, *From Red to Green: Interviews with New Left Review* (London: Verso and New Left Books, 1984), p. 194. In fact, radical pacifism in East Germany with its anti-totalitarian thrust has taken a path increasingly convergent with the strategy of other East–Central European opposition movements.

104. See "Hidden Opposition in the GDR," *EER*, op. cit., p. 66.

105. For insightful views on the new dogmatic freeze in East Germany, see "Ein schwerer Rückfall in die fünfziger Jahre" (a discussion with the GDR protesters Freya Klier and Stefan Krawczyk), *Der Spiegel*, No. 6, February 8, 1988, pp. 27–32; see also Susan Buckingham, "The Freedom to Think Differently: A Report on the Latest Crackdowns on GDR Independents," *East European Reporter*, No. 3, Vol. 2, March 1988, pp. 55–57.

106. For an extensive analysis of the youth rebellion in the GDR and its implications for the political culture in that country, see "Lass ihre Politik scheitern," *Der Spiegel*, no. 5, February 1, 1988, pp. 18–27. The Karl Marx Order was personally delivered to Ceauşescu by Erich Honecker during the Romanian leader's visit to East Berlin in November 1988. Perhaps not accidentally, the ceremony coincided with the one year anniversary of the mass riots in Romania's second most important city, Brasov. East German dissidents who had planned to protest Ceauşescu's repressive policy were kept under house arrest during the Romanian president's stay in the East German capital.

107. See "Hidden Opposition in the GDR," *EER*, op. cit., p. 68.

108. Ibidem, p. 20.

109. See FBIS, Eastern Europe, March 2, 1988, p. 21, and March 7, 1988, p. 25.

110. An interview with Ralf Hirsch in *Profil* (Vienna), February 22, 1988, translated in FBIS, Eastern Europe, February 23, 1988, p. 20.

111. See *Frankfurter Rundschau* (Frankfurt/Main), January 28, 1989.

112. The police also searched several apartments and seized numerous books, documents and personal effects such as diaries. This operation prevented a planned independent demonstration scheduled to coincide with an official ceremony commemorating Rosa Luxemburg's and Karl Liebknecht's murder. See "Police Operations Yield Arrests," (AFP in English), FBIS, Eastern Europe, January 17, 1989, p. 21.

113. See *Frankfurter Rundschau*, January 16, 1989. For the official commemoration, see *Neues Deutschland*, January 16, 1989.

114. See "Human Rights Publication Reappears After a Year," (DPA in German), FBIS, Eastern Europe, January 26, 1989, p. 17.

115. See "Hidden Opposition in the GDR," *EER*, op. cit., p. 65.

116. Ibidem. Hirsch's political biography is emblematic for the ordeal of independent pacifists in East Germany: "Once I was imprisoned for 2 years on charges of subversion; I had distributed fliers against military service. But arrests for between 24 and 48 hours—well, there were at least 50 in the past 10 years. For years I was taken from my apartment or arrested off the street almost every Friday morning."

117. See "Thoughts of the Initiative for Peace and Human Rights on the Occasion of Human Rights Day, 10 December 1987, in the Gethsemane Church," *East European Reporter*, Vol. 3, No. 2, March 1988, p. 59.

118. Ibidem.

119. For the discussion of the peace movement as an "integrative concept" (*Sammelbegriff*) see Eberhard Kuhrt, *Wider die Militärisierung der Gesellschaft: Friedensbewegung und Kirche in der DDR* (Melle: Verlag Ernst Knoth, 1984), pp. 12–14.

Epilogue

The independent peace movements have not changed the nature of contemporary communism. But this has not been their objective. What they have tried to obtain, and to a large extent have accomplished, has been an opening of the public space for a free discussion on issues that directly affect all citizens' destinies. They have questioned the authorities' pretense that only governments have the right to fight for peace. Having attacked the hypocrisy of state bureaucracies who proclaim peace as their most cherished goal and in the meantime force people to live under fear and repression, they have dispelled the propaganda smokescreen meant to cover the communist regimes' increasing militarization. In this respect, the autonomous peace movements have greatly contributed to the restoration of civil society as a new actor of the political game within post- totalitarian regimes.

The theory of the civil society as formulated by such activists like Adam Michnik, Václav Havel, János Kis, Miklós Haraszti, and George Konrád is relevant both for its analytical potential—it explains the changes going on in the communist world—and for its predictive power. As a theory it challenges long-held assumptions about the nonreformability of communist totalitarian regimes. It shows that small islands of autonomy can eventually torpedo the continuum of state-controlled heteronomy. It argues that the transition is possible from a totalitarian dictatorship to first an authoritarian and further to a pluralist order. It is thus an antidote to the historical despair captured in George Orwell's frightening image of the boot placed forever over a human mouth. These skeptical assumptions were first undermined by the revolutionary events in Hungary in 1956. Later, during Brezhnev's times of "stagnation," it seemed that no historical breakthrough was possible in East-Central Europe because of Big Brother's threatening shadow. The Prague Spring was crushed by Warsaw Pact tanks in 1968 because Czechoslovak reformers dared to promise their citizens a "socialism with a human face." Now, with Gorbachev in the Kremlin, the

181

humanization of socialism has been heralded as the official objective of Big Brother himself. Do we witness the demise of the most important deterrent against true change in the Soviet Bloc?

Many peace and human-rights activists in the Soviet Union and East-Central Europe would argue that the Gorbachev factor is uniquely important in permitting the current emancipation. And they are perhaps right. Whatever his personal motivations, the Soviet general secretary has come to embody the democratic hopes of many in post-Stalinist Europe. We probably deal with the birth of a political myth, but as we know it from Georges Sorel, such myths have their own impact on the course of events. The grass-roots initiatives have overstepped the officially drawn boundaries of the permissible. In other words, thanks to this extraordinary conjunction of objective and subjective circumstances, what is official and what is unofficial in the communist world have ceased to be frozen antipodes. Gorbachev was acclaimed in Prague and East Berlin, and Polish intellectuals expected him to understand their plight. Mircea Dinescu, a dissident Romanian poet went so far as to call Gorbachev "the Messiah of socialism with a human face." In the meantime, communist leaders in the Warsaw Pact countries do not know how to react to the rise of the new movements. Nervous and confused, they try to seek refuge in the realm of hard-line rhetoric, but most of them realize that the writing is on the wall.

Civil society has been a major vehicle to recreate the conditions of a normal social life. It has been within its emerging nuclei that citizens have learned the rules of democratic dialogue and the virtues of the common endeavor to recreate a genuine body politic. For its theorists and practitioners, civil society is not a disruptive undertaking. On the contrary, its major aim is to construct and reshape the broken bonds of human solidarity, to rehabilitate the notion that human beings have the right to hold their rulers accountable for acts supposedly carried out on their nation's behalf.

Its spontaneous origin notwithstanding, civil society is institutional pluralism *in statu nascendi.* It includes autonomous unions, the independent professional associations, independent religious institutions, human-rights, ecological, and pacifist movements, as well as other groups committed to rescuing the individual from the all-embracing official ideology (the Jazz Section in Czechoslovakia, the Orange Alternative group in Poland, etc.) In their initial stage, most of these initiatives are characterized by their informality and opposition to bureaucratic solidification.

Sociologists link the return of civil society to the growing interest in the marketization of the bankrupt communist economies. Historically, as Daniel Bell has recently put it, civil society has been the counterpart of liberalism understood as a pluralist system where individuals organize themselves outside the orbit of statal domination. The more authoritarian and centralized the system, the fewer the prospects for the existence and flourishing of a civil society. It is important to understand that civil society is an *idea,* a political "archetype," that has become part of the story in East-Central Europe. The opposition self-consciously invokes this concept and proudly emphasizes its originality.

For Americans, civil society is both easy and difficult to grasp. On the one hand, as Alexis de Tocqueville pointed out, American civil society—made up of voluntary associations of free individuals—is very well developed and the American state is relatively weak. On the other hand, Americans take their civil society so much for granted that they have not felt the need to discuss it within a theoretical framework.

But a closer look at "civil society" as it is articulated by East Europeans would help us understand better what has gone on in the Soviet bloc. Civil society in East-Central Europe has a history of struggle, temporary defeats, partial and total recoveries, hesitations and expectations, that explain both the victory of Solidarity in Poland and the spectacular breakdown of communism in Hungary. This configuration of loosely structured networks of social cooperation and communication has long defied the totalitarian controls over human affairs. It is not that the communists wished to yield power—and as of the moment these lines are written, the question of political power in Poland and Hungary remains unresolved—but rather that their impotence was caused by the growth of alternative actors, i.e., the Polish and Hungarian societies.

To be sure, Gorbachev's policies of glasnost and perestroika have catalyzed these changes in East-Central Europe. But the ongoing Soviet reformation is not only—and not even primarily—the consequence of some benign intentions on the part of an enlightened group within the *Nomenklatura,* but rather the response of a beleaguered and disenchanted Soviet elite to a systemic crisis bordering on the catastrophic. At the same time, it is an attempt to cope with the pressures exerted by social groups and movements for whom the old Stalinist model appears as a historical failure. For more than two decades, the Soviet society has more or less visibly secreted phenomena we tend to associate with the term civil society: alternative subcultures, informal associations, in short the beginnings of a culture of critical discourse. No doubt, these phenomena were held in check during Brezhnev's era, but the extraordinary proliferation of civic activism in recent years, the mushrooming of thousands of informal groups and associations, would have been unthinkable in the absence of a pre-existent civil society. One can say that the rise of civil society is in direct proportion to the weakening of the party-state monopoly on ideology and power. The same is true about countries in Central Europe, where totalitarianism has never totally annihilated the wellsprings of civic autonomy. For instance, regardless of ceaseless attempts to create an atomized social order totally subordinated to the Communist parties' dictates, Poles and Hungarians, and to a lesser extent, Czechs, Slovaks, East Germans, Romanians, and Bulgarians, have sought and partially managed to create centers of grass-roots activism that escaped and opposed the official prescriptions and constraints. The protection of the Catholic and Protestant churches was highly instrumental in this respect, since even under mature Stalinism these institutions could not be totally regimented and silenced. In spite of endless harassments and harsh repression, these groups have created exemplary communities of like-minded individuals. They established forms of cooperation based on solidarity and dignity rather than on fear and coercion.

Within the post-Stalinist order, civil society is the human region where individuals can rediscover and practice long-denied values of universal morality and truth. For many years, these efforts to reconstruct politics in the figure of "anti-politics" were decried by those adept at *Realpolitik* as utterly quixotic. But now, with the benefit of hindsight, we can realize the profound resilience of their efforts. Václav Havel's call for an "anti-political politics" expressed this new strategy based on the restoration of civic dignity to individuals long subjected to totalitarian methods of manipulation and debasement: "Yes, anti-political politics is possible. Politics 'from below.' Politics of the people, not of the apparatus. Politics growing from the heart, not from a thesis. It is no accident that this hopeful experience has to be lived just here, on this grim battlement. In conditions of humdrum "everydayness", we have to descend to the very bottom of a well before we can see the stars."*

What can be said about the ruling elites? As part of the official society, they are not impervious to the signals of civil society. They are not a perfectly cohesive bloc, committed to mere survival in power. Like Poland, East Germany has a number of satellite parties who can one day rebel against the communist dictatorship and consider a dialogue with the opposition. They may even become the mouthpieces for civil society. The most reform minded among the ruling elites recognize the historical defeat of Stalinism. In the words of Imre Pozsgay, a communist who became a prominent leader of Hungary's recently formed Socialist Party, this version of socialism must be jettisoned. According to him, Stalinism has created an authority-oriented, paternalistic system in which citizens are kept at the most infantile level and continuously humiliated: "The omniscient and omnipotent ruling group requires no legitimacy; its theories and omniscience contain everything the people need. It is this view, and its inclination to degeneracy, terror, and violence, that must be cleared away. . ." To be sure, Pozsgay is still a *rara avis* among East European communists. But his formulation of the crisis of Stalinism is indicative of a state of mind that has already infected those members of the power elites who have understood that terror (preventive or punitive) is incompatible with civic participation. The capitulation of Stalinism has gone hand in hand with the return of the civil society.

---

*See Václav Havel, "Anti-Political Politics," in John Keane, ed., *Civil Society and State* (London and New York: Verso, 1988), p. 398.

Index

185

Contributors

Miklós Haraszti, a leading Hungarian social critic and human-rights activist, is the author of two books: *A Worker in a Worker's State* and *The Velvet Prison: Artists under State Socialism*. He is one of the leaders of the Alliance of Free Democrats, one of Hungary's major opposition parties.

Milan Hauner is an associate scholar at the Foreign Policy Research Institute. He recently finished *The Soviet Invasion of Afghanistan and Russian Patterns of Imperialism* for the Philadelphia Papers Series.

Eduard Kuznetsov, a former Soviet dissident, spent more than fifteen years in jail and was sentenced to death; author of *Prison Diaries* and *Russian Novel*. He now works with Radio Liberty in Munich.

Christopher Lazarski, a Polish historian with special interest in Soviet and East Europe history, lives in the United States and is now completing work on his doctorate at Georgetown University.

Vladimir Tismaneanu, a resident scholar at the Foreign Policy Research Institute and a lecturer in political science at the University of Pennsylvania, is the author of *The Crisis of Marxist Ideology in Eastern Europe: The Poverty of Utopia*. He is an editor of *East European Reporter* and a contributing editor to *ORBIS*.

www.ingramcontent.com/pod-product-compliance
Ingram Content Group UK Ltd.
Pitfield, Milton Keynes, MK11 3LW, UK
UKHW020352010325
455677UK00021B/408